The Secularization Debate

The Secularization Debate

EDITED BY WILLIAM H. SWATOS, JR.
AND DANIEL V. A. OLSON

Copublished with the
Association for the Sociology of Religion

ROWMAN & LITTLEFIELD PUBLISHERS, INC.
Lanham • Boulder • New York • Oxford

ROWMAN & LITTLEFIELD PUBLISHERS, INC.

Published in the United States of America
by Rowman & Littlefield Publishers, Inc.
4720 Boston Way, Lanham, Maryland 20706
http://www.rowmanlittlefield.com

12 Hid's Copse Road
Cumnor Hill, Oxford OX2 9JJ, England

British Library Cataloguing in Publication Information Available

Library of Congress Cataloging-in-Publication Data

The secularization debate / edited by William H. Swatos, Jr. and Daniel V. A. Olson.
    p. cm.
    Includes bibliographical references.
    ISBN 0-7425-0761-0 (pbk. : alk. paper)
    1. Secularization (Theology) 2. Religion and sociology. I. Swatos, William H. II.
Olson, Daniel V. A., 1953–

BT83.7 .S63 2000
306.6—dc21

                                     00-036921

Printed in the United States of America

♾™ The paper used in this publication meets the minimum requirements of American
National Standard for Information Sciences—Permanence of Paper for Printed Library
Materials, ANSI/NISO Z39.48–1992.

Contents

Preface

This book has its origin in a suggestion by Rod Stark to Karel Dobbelaere that the two come together in some forum to "discuss" their alternate views on secularization. Karel subsequently proposed to me that we devote a session at the 1997 meetings of the Religious Research Association and Society for the Scientific Study of Religion to such an encounter — but augmented by the contributions of a few other scholars. And so it was, largely thanks to some last minute endeavors of Jim Wellman, the RRA program chair.

Seeing the potential for further dissemination of this important exchange, I encouraged Joe Tamney, the editor of *Sociology of Religion*, the official journal of the Association for the Sociology of Religion, to sit in on the session, and he was excited about the possibility of its publication in that journal. Augmented by an essay from Yves Lambert, who was invited to participate in the original panel but could not attend, and by an opening statement in the authorship of which Kevin Christiano was good enough to join me, "The Secularization Debate" became volume 60, number 3 of *Sociology of Religion* (September 1999). In that process, Dan Olson served as outside reader and offered significant suggestions toward the final product, thus it is appropriate that although reviewers remain anonymous at the journal level, his contribution should be recognized here as co-editor of the book version, in which Peter Cooper of Rowman & Littlefield has helped us to bring the essays to a wider audience. Whether or not the result is what either Stark or Dobbelaere intended in his suggestions at the outset, the volume offers a balanced and creative set of approaches to the perduring questions of understanding religion and religious change in and through our time.

WHS, Jr.
Holiday, Florida

1

Secularization Theory:
The Course of a Concept

William H. Swatos, Jr.
Executive Office, Association for the Sociology of Religion

Kevin J. Christiano
University of Notre Dame

This chapter provides an introduction to the secularization debate as it presents itself at the turn of the twenty-first century. After a conceptual survey from the mid-1960s to the present, we focus on the empirical and historical elements that undergird the claims of secularization theory and those of its principal critics. Secularization theory is placed in relationship both to the Religion of Reason of the Enlightenment and developments in European religious historiography during the nineteenth century. The underlying conflict to be resolved with respect to "secularization" is whether the term can be used in a relatively value-neutral analytic way or whether it inherently carries unsubstantiated value presuppositions.

In 1967 the *Journal for the Scientific Study of Religion* published a collection of essays on church-sect theory that some people at the time interpreted as intending an obituary for the church-sect concept. If so, it must instead be taken as evidence for the resurrection of the dead, for at least a decade of both debate and research, use and abuse, of the church-sect framework occurred before a gradual consensus arrived in the 1980s, wherein sociologists of religion in the United States achieved a level of comfort in talking about sectarian religion and mainline denominations, spared prolegomena wherein we defend our use of these concepts. In that process, though, something else happened as well; namely, the concept of "cult" increasingly became dropped from use in the sociology of religion as already too emotionally loaded to carry scientific freight (see Richardson 1993). Like the concept "race" in ethnic studies, we at least put "cult" in scarequotes. We can talk about anticultism, like racism, but to term a group a cult is sociological bad manners: it biases analyses from the start.

Like church-sect and so many other seminal concepts in the sociology of religion, the term *secularization* was given to us by Max Weber (1930), but ever so lightly, and was picked up by his sometime associate Ernst Troeltsch (1958).

It did not appear significantly in American sociology, however, until the late 1950s. In spite of a cautionary article by Larry Shiner as early as 1967 about the muddled meanings that had come to be attached to the term, hence his suggestion that "we drop the word entirely" (see also Martin 1965), nevertheless by the early 1970s, secularization was the reigning dogma in the field.[1]

Twenty years would pass between Shiner's expression of reservations about secularization "theory" and the next major assault on the thesis. In between, Bryan Wilson, Peter Berger, Thomas Luckmann, and Karel Dobbelaere would become the principal proponents of the concept. Not insignificantly, Wilson, Luckmann, and Dobbelaere are Europeans, and Berger is a European emigré to the United States. All were products of a European Christian intellectual heritage and educational system that, we might now say, romanticized the religious past of their nations.

It was in his 1986 presidential address to the Southern Sociological Society that Jeffrey Hadden (1987: 588) presented a clear, comprehensive, and trenchant analysis of the weakness of secularization theory in both in its genesis and its predicted outcomes. The core of his argument is that in and from its genesis secularization constituted a "*doctrine* more than a theory" based on "presuppositions that . . . represent a taken-for-granted *ideology*" of social scientists "rather than a systematic set of interrelated propositions." Over time in social scientific circles (which continued to widen in their influence), "*the idea of secularization became sacralized*," that is, a belief system accepted "on faith." Even more than a statement about the present, the ideology of secularization relies on beliefs about the past. (This flank of Hadden's assault, as a matter of fact, was presaged in a series of pieces by Roland Robertson beginning in 1971.)

The second thrust of Hadden's attack is a fourfold challenge: (1) Secularization theory is internally weak in its logical structure — "a hodgepodge of loosely employed ideas" — first so revealed, indeed, by Shiner in 1967; (2) such secularization *theory* as does exist is unsupported by data after more than twenty years of research, a point also made by Glasner (1977) in his critique of secularization theory as a "myth" a decade earlier;[2] (3) New Religious Movements (NRMs) have appeared and persisted in the most supposedly secularized societies — indeed, Stark and Bainbridge (1985) have shown that the lower the level of practice or saturation on the part of traditional religion in modern societies, the higher the likelihood of NRM activity;[3] and finally, (4) religion

---

[1] The course of the Shiner article is an interesting case of what Robert Merton (1968) has called the "Matthew effect" in the sciences: Shiner continued no publishing program in this area, and although his article is frequently cited in passing, it apparently had no effect on stemming the tide of secularization theory.

[2] Similarly Peter Berger wrote in 1992 of the sociological prediction of secularization "theory": "By the late 1970s it had been falsified with a vengeance. As it turned out, the theory never had much empirical substance to begin with" (p. 15). The Glasner book also suffers from the Matthew effect.

[3] An alternative view, proposed by Wilson (e.g., 1985) *inter alia*, sees the rise of NRMs as a "proof" of

has emerged as a vital force in the world political order (cf., Hadden and Shupe 1989). Hadden concludes this thrust with a series of forecasts of the place of religion in society and in sociology for the next fifty years, concluding that we should "return once more to the past to see the future. Max Weber's search for clues about the place of religion in human society took him deeply into the study of the world's major religions. The future will take us back to where Weber began" (Hadden 1987: 598, 609 *et passim*).

To what extent does the debate over secularization theory, represented in the articles of this issue, reflect some of the same concerns that ran through church-sect theory three decades ago? In other words, is "secularization" an analytic tool or a value judgment? Karel Dobbelaere refers to a "descriptive concept" that denotes "the particularization in the religious subsystem of the general process of functional differentiation on the macro level." And Rodney Stark, otherwise contending with Dobbelaere, agrees that "[i]f this were all that secularization means, there would be nothing to argue about." What Stark argues, however, is that the concept carries much more freight than this and in so doing makes assertions about people's religiousness that are not so.[4] Although Stark and his colleagues once used such phrases as "limits to secularization" or secularization as a "self-limiting process" (in, e.g., Stark and Bainbridge 1985, 1987), he now wishes to bury the term.[5]

BACKGROUND

The word "secularization" itself comes from the Latin *sæculum*, which could be taken to mean both an age (or era) but also, at least by the fourth and fifth centuries, "the world," probably as an extension of the idea of a "spirit of an age." By this date, too, the word had already developed an ambiguous meaning. It could be used to mean something like unending time (the phrases "world without end" or "forever and ever" that still often appear at the end of formal Christian prayers are translations of the Latin *in sæcula sæculorum*), or the world "out there" (for example, monastic priests, who were "enclosed" and under a formal "rule of life," were distinguished from "secular" clergy, meaning the parish clergy who served the people "out in the world"), but it was also used to mean a life or life-style that is at odds with God (thus people would enter monastic life to flee "the world"). Later the term would come to be used to distinguish

---

secularization; Berger (1996-1997: 9) now terms this idea "the last-gasp thesis," and judges it to be "singularly unpersuasive."

[4] Curiously, Stark remains one of those sociologists of religion who continues to try to use "cult" as an analytic concept, though "*in pianissimo*" as compared to his earlier work.

[5] The secularization debate, also like church-sect "theory" in its heyday, continues to burgeon even as we write, and is by no means restricted to the articles in this volume (recent examples include Bruce 1992; Sommerville 1994, 1998; Yamane 1997, 1998; Laermans *et al.* 1998).

between civil and ecclesiastical law, lands, and possessions. In the nineteenth century, furthermore, the term was adopted formally by the British freethinker G.J. Holyoake, who founded the Secular Society as a group committed to a just world order and moral program of individual action that would address human problems without the use of supernatural explanations. Thus, the term already had an ambiguous, but increasingly negative, use by the time it was adapted into social science (see Shiner 1967).

To the extent that one may ever speak legitimately of a single integrating focus in a body of work as extensive as Max Weber's corpus, it must be said to be that of *rationalität*, or *the processes of the rationalization of action*, the specific form of *social change* that enabled "the modern world" to come into being. Weber was interested in how it was that methods of rational calculation had come to dominate virtually the entirety of modern life. He referred to this as the "spirit of capitalism." His studies convinced him that from the sixteenth century forward a process had been occurring in Western civilization as a result of which one after another sphere of life had become subject to the belief that explanations for events could be found within this-worldly experience and the application of human reason; as Shiner (1967: 216) puts it, the world was "a self-contained causal nexus." The consequence of this worldview was that explanations referring to forces outside of this world were constantly being laid aside. The flip side of rationalization Weber termed *Entzauberung* — a word usually translated *disenchantment*, though perhaps more accurately rendered de-magi-fication or de-myster-ization. Disenchantment did not simply mean that people did not believe in the old mysteries of religion, but rather that the concept of mystery or "the mysterious" itself was devalued. Mystery was seen not as something to be entered into but something to be conquered by human reason, ingenuity, and the products of technology. Weber gave the name secularization to this double-sided rationalization-disenchantment process in religion. Secularization was both the process and the result of the process; however, it is also the case that the term occurs only rarely in Weber's writing.

It is not clear that Weber himself considered secularization to be a specific domain of the sociology of religion. In his essay "Science as a vocation" (1946: 139), *intellectualization* is used as a virtual synonym. In some respects then, it seems that secularization ought to be more properly considered an aspect of the sociology of knowledge, hence to deal with questions of *epistemology*, the ways people "know" or the conditions upon which we receive "knowledge" of "the ways the world works" (see Glock 1988). Weber's claim is that appeals to divine authority have lost credibility relative to the past as providing sure knowledge for social action, and that practical economic considerations (as contrasted to a heavenly bank account) have come to play an increasing role in measuring the worth of knowledge. At most, "the religious point of view" will be treated as one among many competing claims to authority. Priests, ministers, rabbis, and mullahs are less sought for solving world problems than economists, physicists, and political scientists, while psychologists, social workers, and medical doctors are the societally recognized experts at the individual or microsocial level. Mark Chaves (1994), for example, explicates secularization along these lines in referring to it as a declining scope of religious authority.

Olivier Tschannen (1991) has provided a graphic summary of the "exemplary infrastructure" or "primitive cognitive apparatus" that may be derived from the efforts of various secularization theorists. In the boldest terms, as Shiner points out however, secularization theory's claims mean the "decline of religion," that is, religion's "previously accepted symbols, doctrines, and institutions lose their prestige and influence. The culmination of secularization would be a religionless society." In this issue Rodney Stark most fully accepts this definition as paradigmatic of secularization " theory," and it is this one with which he takes issue. All of the propositions advanced by Shiner as well as the map of Tschannen share a common presupposition: namely, that there has been an enormously significant *change* in the ways in which society and religion have interacted in the past from the ways they do now. With this there is no argument among our contributors.

At the purely descriptive level, secularization may be said to refer to the process of the separation of state and church in Europe, which was much more complex than it was in the United States. Tschannen's application of his map to specific secularization theorists shows that the one element they have in common is that of institutional *differentiation*. According to Ralf Dahrendorf (1959), for example, the entire European social system was characterized by a state of *superimposition* wherein one institutional system overlay another, and each had a hand in the other. Church, state, education, health and welfare, the law, and the like were so intertwined that sundering them caused a significant shock to all sectors of the system, from which religion was not immune. The United States, by contrast, was characterized by relative pluralism from its earliest years (cf., Butler 1990; Christiano 1987: 49-60; Conser and Twiss 1997; Finke *et al.* 1996; Finke and Stark 1988). Church and state were constitutionally separated, and free market, *laissez-faire* economics circumscribed the role of the state as far as other institutional sectors of the social system were concerned. Nevertheless, even in the United States there grew to be a view that "religion" was in decline.

Two important observations before we discuss the thesis and the evidence further: The first is that *secularization*, secularity, or the secular *is always relative to* some definition of *religion* or the religious. As Edward Bailey puts it, "[S]ecular is really quite easy to define! Its meaning keeps changing yet remains consistent. It always means, simply, the opposite of 'religious' — whatever that means" (1998: 18). This suggests not only that the "definition of religion question" is not an arcane philosophical debate, but it also shows how premises can influence evidence and outcomes, hence why it is important to examine premises carefully. The second observation is that the "truth" of secularization claims depends on *historical* evidence. If we say, "people are less religious now than they were a hundred years ago," we have not only invoked some presumed definition of religion, but we have also said that we know how religious people were a hundred years ago. Yves Lambert makes this point clearly in setting contemporary survey data in context, but it somewhat bedevils Dobbelaere's argument that NRMs in effect validate the secularization thesis because they are responses to secularization, while at the same time he does not see the pillarization process in Europe as emerging in the same way in an earlier epoch.

THE ARGUMENTS

There is no question that in most of the Western world there has been at least sufficient separation of church and state, the primary locus of differentiation, that people are capable both of living their lives apart from direct "interference" on the part of religion and that people may choose among various religions without suffering civil disabilities. If only this is what is meant by secularization, then there is no debate over "the secularization thesis." But if this is all that secularization meant, there would also have been far less excitement about the topic. It would not have been so much something to investigate as simply to state as a factual condition (or as not existing in other parts of the world). Indeed, on this basis we could develop a fairly simple classification system of those societies that had or had not been legally "secularized." (In fact the term is used in this uncontroversial way to describe institutions that once were controlled by a religious organization and now are not; thus a school or hospital may be said to have been "secularized in 1983," meaning that in that year it went from being under the formal ownership of a religious organization to control by an independent board of trustees or a for-profit corporation.)

There is also no doubt that the separation of church and state has consequences for religious organizations and for the lives of individual citizens (see Finke 1990; Finke and Stark 1992). At the organizational level, for example, a previously established religion may lose tax support, as happened in colonial Virginia; on the other hand, as also happened in colonial Virginia, other religious organizations gain free access to the religious "market" — that is, other religions get to operate on an equal basis. Whether or not this means the "decline" of religion, therefore, becomes an empirical question. Individuals no longer may be required to pay taxes to support religion, and they may also be required to conform to certain state norms (such as registering names of children at birth rather than waiting to name a baby in a religious ritual like baptism or circumcision). These may open or close religious options and freedoms, as people can choose to support or reject religious alternatives.

The principal thrust in secularization theory has, however, been stronger than simply church-state issues or the scope of religious authority. It has been a claim that, in the face of scientific rationality, religion's influence on all aspects of life — from personal habits to social institutions — is in dramatic decline.

Regardless of the sociostructural level of the argument, the underlying assumption was that "people" have become or are becoming "less religious." Many social theorists (e.g., Wallace 1966) doubted that modernity could combine religious traditions with the overpowering impersonal features of our time: scientific research, humanistic education, high-technology multinational capitalism, bureaucratic organizational life, and so on. Reacting on the basis of a functional definition of religion, religion appeared to these theorists denuded of almost all the functions it had previously appeared to perform. In this view, religion harked back to some prior level of human evolution and was now uselessly appended to the modern cultural repertoire. People today are awed by human achievements, not divine forces; societies of the future would be constructed around these, not antiquity's notion of "the sacred."

This view was evoked in some forms of empirical research as well. In the 1920s, for example, the Institute of Social and Religious Research sent Robert and Helen Lynd to the American midwest to study the life of a "typical" community. They went to Lynd's home state of Indiana and settled on Muncie, a town sufficiently unexceptional to allow them to attach to it the pseudonym, *Middletown*. Robert Lynd returned to Muncie again in 1935 to see how typical "Middle America" was surviving the Depression. *Middletown in transition* was the product of this research. Both of these books included assessments of Muncie's religious organizations, but neither yielded positive outlooks. In the first book, the Lynds concluded that "religious life as represented by the churches is less pervasive than a generation ago" (1929: 407; but note that neither they nor anyone else had done research on the community's religious life a generation previously). In the Depression-era assessment, religious life seemed to have declined further: people attending church were older and appeared more passive, as if reflecting the economic downturn. Although the religious institutions continued to provide "the reassurance so urgently needed" in the face of "the perplexities of a too-perplexing world," these organizations were facing a future of continued displacement (1937: 315).

In the 1970s, however, the National Science Foundation funded a re-study of Middletown: "Middletown III." If religious organizations were on the skids already in the mid-1930s, what would be their state fifty years out from the original study? The results came as a surprise to the proponents of the "decline of religion" thesis. This project plotted 15 time series of religion data for Muncie between 1924 and 1978. Among the 15 trend lines, only two pointed downward (which would indicate a secularization effect). Three more showed no trend, while the remaining 10 (67 percent of the total) displayed an upward curve, showing *greater religiosity* in Middletown in the 1970s than the 1920s (Caplow 1982; Caplow *et al.* 1983: 34-35, 294-97).

National survey data from the late 1940s to the present support this finding. In *Religious change in America*, Andrew Greeley reported that in every Gallup Poll that has asked whether or not the respondent believes in God, more than

90 percent say they do. Three fourths believe in the possibility of life after death and in the messianic divinity of Jesus of Nazareth. Around 70 percent, with only the slightest deviation, think that "people who have led good lives" receive some reward in the hereafter, while over 50 percent also believe in hell. Ninety percent of Americans pray to God, and about two-thirds claim membership in a religious congregation; neither of these percentages has changed significantly in fifty years. About 40 percent of Americans claim to attend religious services each week, and this fraction has altered little over the last thirty years (Greeley 1989: 13-15, 20-43, 58).[6]

Roger Finke and Rodney Stark's *The churching of America* (1992) has provided a wealth of historical data to undergird these observations across two centuries. They mine early records, for example, to estimate that only 17 percent of Americans claimed religious membership at the time of the Revolution, and that in spite of the revivalism of the Great Awakening of the early nineteenth century, by 1850, only 34 percent claimed membership. While this represents a 100 percent increase over the span, it is also only half the religious organizational membership that we find in the United States today.

Americans in a vast majority, according to survey data, do not appear to have abandoned secularization theory's dying religion, nor to have fulfilled the Lynds' predictions. "The replacement of religious superstition by enlightened science predicted since the time of Voltaire may at last be taking place," Greeley noted tongue-in-cheek in the late 1960s, when secularization theory was all the rage. "It may well be; though it should be remembered that the prediction has generally been wrong every time it has been made" (1969: 6; cf., Greeley 1995; Stark and Iannaccone 1994). Now, thirty years after Greeley's generous concession, it seems more true than ever that the predicted demise of religion is probably wrong, certainly premature. Virtually no empirical research supports the prediction of a societal slide from a peak of sacrality into a valley of secularity; indeed, the issues of conceptual confusion raised thirty years ago by Shiner now seem all the more urgent for social scientific theory development.

It was Sigmund Freud who referred to religion as "the future of an illusion," but to the contrary, Rodney Stark and William Sims Bainbridge in *The future of religion: Secularization, revival, and cult formation* (1985: 1) claim "the vision of a religionless future is but illusion." Contrary to the unilinear theories of religious decline, Stark and Bainbridge there adopt a more cyclical approach reminiscent of the general theory of sociocultural development of Pitirim Sorokin (1937-1941). As inevitable change takes place in social systems, religions that responded to the needs and conditions in conceptual forms suited to one historical epoch become less effective in addressing core problems of human experience. Death is one such example. The problem does not go away. The death rate is the

---

[6] Recently, the credibility of American reports of high weekly church attendance has been called into question (see Hadaway *et al.* 1993; but cf., Caplow 1998; Woodberry 1998).

same: one per person. Hence, the need for a solution remains.

Two things happen: on the one hand, movements arise from within existing religious organizations that attempt to restate with even greater certitude the same answers the tradition has always provided; on the other hand, however, new movements also arise from outside the existing traditions, offering new answers to the same questions. Because the existential questions are perennial and their solutions lie beyond rational determination, religious answers will always have a place in human experience. Hence religion as a whole is revived, and secularization is "self-limited." In fact, harking back to Sorokin, one might say that secularization is a healthy part of a cycle of religious growth and development. "The transcendent may no longer be coterminous with all human activity" (if ever it was), as Greeley (1969: 169) observes, "but the 'really real' will still persist where the core problems of interpretability are faced."

THE "RELIGION" OF SECULARIZATION

Max Weber's decision at the outset of his sociology of religion not to define "religion" is well known. So, too, is the definition of Émile Durkheim (1915), preeminently as it was refabricated at the hands of Talcott Parsons and his school of functionalism. Central to the Parsonian thrust was the integrationist or solidarity theme within the Durkheimian formulation; that is, that religion *unites all who adhere to it into a single moral community*. Religion was the glue of society, the source of social solidarity. So strongly believed was this proposition among social scientists that, in cases where it was manifestly clear that what participants in the action system termed "religion" did not integrate the social system, some sociologists nevertheless proceeded undaunted to search out the "real" religion of society — its latent source of solidarity — and proclaim this as sacred rite and ceremony. This approach enjoyed great success in the sociology of religion when applied in monopolistic settings (for example, the Marxist regimes of the Soviet Union or Chairman Mao's China), but encountered problems with pluralism (wherein, for instance, Babe Ruth's bat was proclaimed the "sacred object" of the United States' "national religion" [of baseball]).

What is wrong with this approach to religion? There are, first, a number of problems inherent in Durkheim's work itself. W.G. Runciman has summarized three of these, the most telling of which is that Durkheim's "explanation" of religious beliefs in a this-worldly terminus (society) does not actually "explain" them at all (except to explain them away): "Why, after all," Runciman (1970: 98) asks, "is the worship of society any more readily explicable than the worship of gods?" Intimately connected with this "explanation," however, is Durkheim's search for the source of social solidarity, and behind this is his *presumption* of solidarity. Although Durkheim is generally cited for "abolishing the role of individual judgment and subjective meaningfulness of social reality in his theory" (Sahay 1976: 167), in the concept of solidarity he reintroduces two types (mechanical and organic solidarity) of sociological "sticky stuff" (the glue that holds society together), that are *not* in fact structural but psychoemotional, though collective rather than individual. As Calvin Redekop (1967: 149) has observed, "the integrating power in society of religion" is *not* a social fact, but a largely unsubstantiated social-anthropological *belief* stemming from Durkheimian sources. This belief underlies the "religion" of secularization; that is, contemporary secularization theory is based on the view that religion is defined by this integrative function. Not only is the notion of solidarity as definitive of society now suspect (see Beyer 1989), but even if we do accept some concept of solidarity into our theoretical arsenal, there is no reason to presume an integrated wholeness that certainly is now difficult to see — and may well have never existed.

Compounding these problems within Durkheim's theory is the problem of the translation of the title of Durkheim's central text in the sociology of religion into English as *The elementary forms of the religious life.*[7] The difficulty is with the French word *élémentaire*, a word that has a double connotation in French, but in English must be rendered as either "elementary" or "elemental." Joseph Ward Swain, the translator, chose the former. In so doing he gave a particularly *evolutionary* twist to Durkheim's work that was in the original, but was also balanced there by "elemental." This sense was the far more crucial contribution of Durkheim's research — namely, a study of "what pertains to or is one of the constituent parts or basic components . . . of humanity's religious life." Admittedly, Durkheim "did not wrestle with the fact that modern 'primitives' have just as many years of history behind them as do the rest of us to-day," but the use of "the *elementary* forms of religious life, in the sense of an early stage of development," was not the central thrust of Durkheim's work. The choice of "elementary" over "elemental" reflects "the far from insignificant fact that the translation was made at a phase in Western cultural evolution when sophisticated secular intellectuals tended to hold that chronologically early and in its wake present-day tribal religious life was closer, or more manageably close, to the truth about religion generically than our more developed forms" (Smith 1984: 28-29). In short, "elementary" was more consistent with the Great Transformation's incipient *doctrine of secularization* than was elemental. Rather than a paradigm study *of* religion, *The elementary forms* became a doctrinaire statement *about* religion.

That this is more than a semantic exercise may be seen quite clearly when we turn to Talcott Parsons's work as the major interpretive treatment on Durkheim in Western sociology for over a quarter of a century, for Parsons increasingly employed an evolutionary approach in his work over the years (e.g.,

---

[7] The recent retranslation of Durkheim's text by Karen Fields under the title *The elementary forms of religious life* (Durkheim 1995) may help resolve this problem slightly for a future generation of scholars, but the historical problematic noted here is not altered thereby.

1977). Where did Parsons begin his evolutionary scheme but with Durkheim's (and others') descriptions of the Australian aborigines — a *contemporary* people? As his work develops, he adds other contemporary accounts of "contemporary peoples, distributed over the earth's surface . . . rearranged to form a general *historical sequence* of societal evolution," while admitting that he is "able to say little about the detailed sequence of events in the course of which primitive societies begin their differentiation into more stratified societies" (Vidich and Lyman 1984: 78; cf., Kuper 1988). The point, however, that is easily lost in such an analysis is that it is for all practical purposes a *completely ahistorical* analysis. The Parsonian evolutionary scheme is *not* based upon a study of religious history but on the more-or-less contemporary religious lives of peoples throughout the world whose evolutionary "stage" has been determined by some *a priori* definition of development. "Secularization" feeds into this evolutionary structure as a "modern" entailment of universal developmental tendencies — although Parsons himself saw secularization far more positively than many subsequent secularization theorists.

Hadden quotes C. Wright Mills's (1959: 32-33) succinct critical summary of Parsons's theory: "Once the world was filled with the sacred — in thought, practice, and institutional form. After the Reformation and the Renaissance, the forces of modernization swept across the globe and secularization, a corollary historical process, loosened the dominance of the sacred. In due course, the sacred shall disappear altogether except, possibly, in the private realm." Although this statement implies historical description, *it is in fact based on almost no historical evidence.* Rather than systematic studies of the *past*, it draws from commonsense generalizations about history related to systematic studies of the *present.*

THE MYTH OF THE AGE OF FAITH

The underlying religious myth of secularization theory, as Stark notes, is that "in the past" people were significantly more religious than they are today. That is, that sometime, someplace in the past there was a solidary Age of Faith in which "the world was filled with the sacred." (People who accept this myth usually believe that the Age of Faith gave way to the Age of Reason.) Europeans and Euro-Americans often point to the Medieval era. Yet Dutch historian Peter Raedts maintains that there is a growing consensus that both the Catholic Middle Ages and the Age of Reformation are nineteenth-century creations. "A new era for Christianity in Europe began when after 1800 the churches gradually lost the support of the state and had to organize themselves. And it was not until then that the new mass media and the schooling of all the population made the christianization of everyone a reality" (Ruyter 1996: 7). In short, the Age of Faith myth reflects a particular educational process that did not begin to occur until about two hundred years ago. What happened in that process was that precisely as a serious attempt was made to "Christianize" the entire population, a counter attempt at resistance also emerged. The "Age of Faith," if it ever existed, did so for at most a few decades of the nineteenth century.

If we think only a little about the Medieval period, for example, we run into the contradictions of the putative Age of Faith. In this era, the monastic communities throughout Europe are adduced as evidence for this designation. Leaving aside for a moment the question of how "really religious" the motivations of those who entered these monastic communities actually were (or even whether or not people entered of their own free will), consider the paradox: monastic life is understood to be other-worldly asceticism, that is *withdrawal* from the *world*. If the Medieval world was so full of the sacred, why did people want to withdraw from it in such numbers? A better history, more attentive to popular religiosity (and lack thereof), would suggest that this was a "secular" world (as the term itself implies), not particularly any more or less "religious" than any other "world," and that this world — which more and more as it drew toward the Renaissance came to display what Agnes Heller (1981) has termed "practical atheism" (that is, less and less concern about the supernatural in day-to-day affairs) — slowly penetrated even the monastic foundations until it was hard in many cases to distinguish between the two. At this point the Reformation constituted a renewed demand for sacrality in all relationships — which was then itself undermined in due time, allowing Max Weber at the turn of the twentieth century to write *The Protestant ethic and the spirit of capitalism*, and Peter Berger (1967: 129) to say more concisely that "Christianity has been its own gravedigger."

Not clear either within the secularization account is the derivation of much scientific, medical, and agricultural history from the monasteries. The great geneticist Mendel, for example, was a monk, and some of the earliest experiments with electricity were conducted by the abbot and monks of the monastery of Nolet. Whence this interest, if these foundations were so unworldly? Monasteries also preserved not only "sacred" but secular texts as well. John Paterson (1982: 26) writes in his history of St. Brigid's Cathedral foundation at Kildare that "a scriptorium for the production of written books seems to have become active" as early as the seventh century, and "this would suggest that the monastery had become involved in secular affairs." Prior to the heavy hand of the Christian *reconquista* in Spain, Jews, Arabs, and Christians collaborated in the capital of Toledo translating important scientific texts from the ancient east. The monasteries were the essential repositories for the texts of Aristotle and other ancient Greek philosopher-scientists — so much so that the historical novelist Umberto Eco could frame his *The name of the rose* (1983) convincingly in such a setting.

PLURALISM

What can we say of secularization now? We can say that over time our epistemologies have changed, that our ideas of "the ways the world works" have changed, and that these have entailed corresponding shifts of emphasis in global explanatory structures or bases upon which we attribute credibility or truth. The Medieval worldview, the Renaissance, the Enlightenment, Romanticism, and the era of modern science represent such alternative epistemologies. When we consider the relatively short history of the scientific worldview, it is not surprising that its epistemology has not fully jelled; furthermore, the phenomenon of globalization creates a contestation among religious episte-mologies themselves that, though it has analogs in the past, is unprecedented in its scope today. Perhaps because he is now an American, it is Peter Berger (1992, 1996-1997, 1997) who, of the leading lights of secularization theory, has come fully to repudiate it.

The theory of secularization as a self-limiting process as proposed by Stark and Bainbridge, however, can help us to understand some of the important social dynamics that lie behind religious developments in our own day. In many respects, secularization theory was an attempt to account for how *pluralism* was reshaping the religious map — both geographically and cognitively; that is, there is a world religious ferment of contesting epistemologies that, though it is probably more immediately apparent to the average citizen of the West than to the average Middle Easterner, is in fact going on without limit around the globe. Contemporary pluralism means that far more religious worldviews are in imme-diate competition with each other than has ever been the case in the past. Whereas the United States could once settle on a shared "Judeo-Christian" ethic (see Silk 1984), its religious map now must accommodate Muslims and Buddhists in increasing numbers.

Furthermore, the nature of pluralism is multiplicative. Each "new" religion (or newly imported religion) spawns more new religions, and as some secular-ization theorists rightly noted, ever-increasing pluralism does undermine the element of absolute certainty that has been claimed by at least some religions, though new religions will simultaneously continue to arise making precisely this claim. That is, the more one becomes aware of more and more religions competing in a marketplace-like setting, the harder it becomes to assert that any one religion contains all truth and that others must be all wrong. While it is certainly possible to make "better" and "worse" type comparisons, all-or-nothing rigidity simply does not hold up.

In some respects, historically Islamic nations may be more sensitive to this than some of the liberal democracies of the West. As a result, these nations intentionally prohibit the "free commerce" of religion that has become a hallmark of Western democracy. Accounts of the Ayatollah Khomeini's program for Iran, for example, make it quite clear that he saw the Western presence, particularly exemplified by Americans, as a threat to the integrity of Islam. As a matter of fact, Pope Pius X attempted to sketch a similar program at the end of the nineteenth century when he issued a ruling, the apostolic letter *Testem benevolentiæ* (1899), that specifically condemned "Americanism." Because the Pope at that time lacked the political-economic resources at the disposal of the Ayatollah in the 1980s, however, his ruling could not have the dramatic impact that the actions of the Ayatollah had. Nevertheless, part of the prejudice that was directed against Roman Catholics in the United States for a considerable number of years must be seen in light of this document. Each case, like Communist ideology in the Soviet regimes, is an attempted monopoly of thought control — or the social condition of *monopolism*, the antithesis of pluralism.

Religious (or, more broadly, ideological) pluralism clearly creates a market-place of ideas wherein absolute claims for ultimacy are always at some degree of risk (see Borhek and Curtis 1975). This gives rise to a model of religious competition or marketplace, and in a double sense. Not only is there competition among religions themselves, but there is also the freedom on the part of buyers (people) to pick and chose among the ideological wares that different religions proffer. This has been referred to as "religion à la carte" and the result as *bricolage* (e.g., Luckmann 1967; Bibby 1987). The outcome of increased competition is clearly shifting market shares. However, Finke and Stark (1988) have shown that the reality of increasing religious competition in American cities was not a decrease in religious mobilization but an increase. Stark (1992) has also shown that this increase extended to rural areas, but that these changes were often unreported as newer, "marginal" churches were not counted in religious censuses. European religious activity follows this pattern least well, perhaps because the state-church tradition there has created a mind-set to which any and all religion is simply a less desirable "good" than it is elsewhere, due to its having been taken for granted for so long, hence so closely identified with a taken-for-granted culture. With certain notable exceptions, European religious participation has been historically low; yet curiously, for example, European immigrants to the United States generally acted quickly to recreate the church of their homeland, and along with their immediate descendants were *much more* religious (or at least organizationally active) than was the custom in their countries of origin.

That people are more likely to want their religion à la carte does not necessarily mean that they are "less religious." The metaphor is helpful: first, people who order meals à la carte often actually spend more than they would have if they bought a *prix fixé* meal. Of course, choosing à la carte does mean that people do not simply take whatever is dished out to them. However, it should not be assumed that as a result they will eat irresponsibly — three desserts and no veggies. People may just as often use the carte to choose wisely, passing over rich sauces and heavy starches. Certainly it is true, as Chaves has noted, that the authority of religious officers is reduced in this process; on the other hand, it must be remembered that religious officers are nothing but lay folk who have become "hyped" on the religious message. The quality of motivation that leads to becoming a religious officer may change, but in fact this may again result in more rather than less: consider the surplus of (male and female, married and single, straight and gay) priests in the Episcopal church, where being a bishop has been likened to shepherding a herd of cats, compared to the shortage of (celibate male) priests in the Roman Catholic church where hierarchical clerical authority is still maximized. Episcopal church membership has shrunk while its number of clergy has grown, whereas Roman Catholic membership has grown while its number of clergy has shrunk.

The numbers of options among which people may choose (or the degree of pluralism) obviously increases with globalization and with the advance of alternative knowledge paradigms. However, again, it is not the case that pluralism did not exist in the past. One may read, on the one hand, the *Confessions* of Augustine of Hippo in North Africa during the fifth century, and find that he tried out several belief systems before settling on Christianity. Indeed, the Roman world into which Christianity came was filled with competing ideological systems, wherein part of the putative uniqueness of Christianity was its claim to exclusivity. Studies by Nielsen (1990a, 1990b) of both the early Christian era and of the Inquisition show how much people were willing to suffer for persisting in holding alternative beliefs from the dominant tradition — first, Christianity versus the imperial cult; later, heterodox Christian beliefs versus the consolidated official church. Rodney Stark makes a similar point in the chapter on martyrdom in his *The rise of Christianity* (1996: 163-89).

With respect to the secularization thesis, then, two aspects of pluralism must be taken into consideration. On the one hand, there is a substantial body of evidence that pluralism of belief — including disbelief — has been an option throughout history that is simply intensified by globalization. On the other hand, pluralism forces us to make a distinction between secularization and what might be called "de-Christianization": that is, new religious movements may emerge or other world traditions may gain dominance over Christianity in the West.[8] Although we do not think this is likely to happen, it is sociologically important to understand that, if people cease to believe that Jesus Christ is God and instead believe that Saytha Sai Baba is God, no secularization has occurred. If Muslims in the United States outnumber Episcopalians (or even active members of the Church of England in England!), no secularization has occurred. *Religious change* of course has occurred, and this will have consequences for the societies in which it takes place. Rodney Stark suggests that we focus our work

---

[8] Recently, the literature on the question of pluralism's effects on religion has mushroomed (cf., Christiano 1987: 118-49; Finke *et al.* 1996; Olson 1998; and Finke and Stark 1998, which contains a fairly thorough bibliography of work on the topic to date).

on religious change without the conceptual baggage of "secularization," whereas Karel Dobbelaere and others urge that there is something especially significant about religious change that sufficiently differentiates it from other forms of institutional change as to necessitate a unique conceptual framework.

An underlying assumption of secularization theory that pluralism thus challenges is the idea that "religion" is something fixed. Instead, sociologists of religion need to recognize the tentativeness and fragility of religious structures of meaning. Religious concepts easily lend themselves to reification. As ideational systems, religions are always in interaction with material culture, social structure, other cultural systems, and individual personalities. The theological bias of secularization theory within the sociology of religion has underwritten conceptions of "religion" as essentially fixed, rather than essentially variable. *Sociologically*, however, there is far more reason to conceive religion as variable — indeed, whereas among social institutions religion deals uniquely with a nonempirical, "uncontrollable" referent, religion is *infinitely* variable in a way that other action orientations are not. As Anthony Blasi has written (1990: 151): "The sociologist of religion needs to see this tentativeness, the casuist nature of much religious conduct, as a reality rather than attempt to explain the activity away as an unreflective outcome of predisposing factors and environmental influences." Only ecclesiological presuppositions and prejudices warrant the notion of religious fixity; thus analyses in the sociology of religion need to be attentive to change as *inherent* in religion, just as change is in other institutional spheres and cultural dimensions, precisely because religion is a sociocultural institution.

IMPLICIT RELIGION, SECULARIZATION, AND THE SACRED

To speak of "implicit religion" is to acknowledge that in the pluralistic culture of high-technology multinational capitalism (which some call postmodernity) the historical religions are less likely to carry the level of isomorphism between individual experience and larger cultural context that has been the case in the past, but simultaneously to recognize that the spiritual seeks coherence over time — objectifying thereby the subjective disposition toward ultimacy into an ultimate, or at least a potential ultimate, that becomes sacred. This sacred *always* reflects human experience precisely because it arises from human experience, and human experience is *always* and *everywhere*, to the extent that it is *human* experience, social. Hence the sacred *always* reflects the social, yet it is not the worship of the social, but rather the feeble simultaneous seeking-grasping of a transformation of present social relations that we can imagine, yet not realize.

In taking this approach, it seems to us that we are standing within "new paradigm" rather than "old paradigm" sociology of religion; that is, that our understanding of spirituality-religion-sacredness finds its root in the limitless dissatisfaction that is a species characteristic of *homo sapiens*. In other words, humans are never satisfied, or at least enough humans are never satisfied as to create social formations to increase satisfaction for themselves and others. We keep thinking we can do better. Religion is the institution of doing better *par excellence*. Sacred is the best you can get.

What has come to be called "secularization" is the process by which societies in the experience of "modernization" have created competing institutions for doing better. Pluralism is not only competition among multiple historic religious traditions, but it is also competition between historical religious approaches to doing better and other systems of doing better. People who say they "believe in education," for example, are making an implicitly religious statement, just as much as people who say they "believe in Christianity;" and — as Edward Bailey (1998: 18) points out — there are two "religious" concepts in each of these statements that need to be unpacked. People who "believe in" education or science may have lessened the apparent remoteness of their sacred, placing comparatively more control over outcomes at the human level, but note that their language is often similar. They "have faith" in our schools or in their doctors. They hope for a brighter future and so on. Peace, justice, even postage-stamp love emanate from these competing systems of ultimacy: "Ultimately" science or education will solve all our problems.

Rather than speak here of secularization, however, we should really recognize these expressions as manifestations of the "new religion" of Reason that emerged in the Enlightenment, which at least in its early forms identified rationality with Divinity — albeit the *deus absconditus* of Deism — and found in the pursuit of knowledge a spiritual quest. Max Weber in fact alluded to this in his remark about Robespierre as the apotheosis of "the charismatic of glorification of 'Reason'" (1978: 1209), and both Sartre (1955: 185-239) and Löwith (1949: 33-51) also pointed to it in their critiques of "dialectical materialism" — namely that the dialectic is a spiritual hope which must be accepted on faith, hence it contradicts the premises of materialism. Postmodernity, so called, is nothing more than the disenchantment of that sacrality the Enlightenment gave to Reason. It is the secularization of secularism (cf., Marsden 1994).

That we see a so-called "return to the sacred" or a resacralization or the rise of a new spirituality today suggests that these institutionalized alternatives that are the heirs of the Church of Reason are themselves not fulfilling the quest dynamic to which we have pointed within the human psyche. But, if one "believes in" the new paradigm, that dynamic will not go away, hence new sacred vistas will emerge and old sacred vistas will be revisited, but in a way that is relatively consistent with the sociocultural conditions imposed by high-technology multinational capitalism. This is not to say, however, that religion *reflects* (or is a "mere reflection of") sociocultural formations, but rather, that at its spiritual core in activating the sacred, the religio-social complex always seeks to overcome *specific* sociocultural formations (see Swatos and Gissurarson 1996: 233-37; Reeves 1990: 172-73).

REFERENCES

Bailey, E. 1998. "Implicit religion": What might that be? *Implicit Religion* 1: 9-22.
Berger, P. L. 1967. *The sacred canopy*. Garden City, NY: Doubleday.
————. 1992. Sociology: A disinvitation? *Society* 30(Nov.): 12-18.
————. 1996-1997. Secularism in retreat. *National Interest* 46(Winter): 3-12.
————. 1997. Epistemological modesty. *Christian Century* 114: 972-78.
Beyer, P. 1989. Globalism and inclusion. In *Religious politics in global and comparative perspective*, edited by W. H. Swatos, Jr., 39-53. New York: Greenwood Press.
Bibby, R. W. 1987. *Fragmented gods*. Toronto: Irwin.
Blasi, A. J. 1990. Problematic of the sociologists and people under study in the sociology of religion. *Ultimate Reality and Meaning* 13: 145-56.
Borhek, J. T., and R. F. Curtis. 1975. *A sociology of belief*. New York: Wiley.
Bruce, S., ed. 1992. *Religion and modernization*. Oxford: Oxford University Press.
Butler, J. 1990. *Awash in a sea of faith*. Cambridge, MA: Harvard University Press.
Caplow, T. 1982. Religion in Middletown. *Public Interest* 68(Summer): 78-87.
————. 1998. The case of the phantom Episcopalians. *American Sociological Review* 63: 112-13.
Caplow, T., H. M. Bahr, and B. A. Chadwick. 1983. *All faithful people*. Minneapolis: University of Minnesota Press.
Chaves, M. 1994. Secularization as declining religious authority. *Social Forces* 72: 749-74.
Christiano, K. J. 1987. *Religious diversity and social change*. Cambridge: Cambridge University Press.
Conser, W. H., and S. B. Twiss, eds. 1997. *Religious diversity and American religious history*. Athens: University of Georgia Press.
Dahrendorf, R. 1959. *Class and class conflict in industrial society*. Palo Alto, CA: Stanford University Press.
Durkheim, É. 1915[1912]. *The elementary forms of the religious life*. New York: Free Press.
————. 1995[1912]. *The elementary forms of religious life*. New York: Free Press.
Eco, U. 1983. *The name of the rose*. San Diego, CA: Harcourt Brace Jovanovich.
Finke, R. 1990. Religious deregulation. *Journal of Church and State* 32: 609-26.
Finke, R., and R. Stark. 1988. Religious economies and sacred canopies. *American Sociological Review* 53: 41-49.
————. 1992. *The churching of America*. New Brunswick, NJ: Rutgers University Press.
————. 1998. Reply to Olson. *American Sociological Review* 61: 761-66.
Finke, R., A. M. Guest, and R. Stark. 1996. Mobilizing local religious markets. *American Sociological Review* 61: 203-18.
Glasner, P. 1977. *The sociology of secularisation*. London: Routledge.
Glock, C. Y. 1988. The ways the world works. *Sociological Analysis* 49: 93-103.
Greeley, A. M. 1969. *Religion in the year 2000*. New York: Sheed and Ward.
————. 1989. *Religious change in America*. Cambridge, MA: Harvard University Press.
————. 1995. The persistence of religion. *Cross Currents* 45(Spring): 24-41.
Hadaway, C. K., P. L. Marler, and M. Chaves 1993. What the polls don't show. *American Sociological Review* 58: 741-52.
Hadden, J. K. 1987. Toward desacralizing secularization theory. *Social Forces* 65: 587-611.
Hadden, J. K., and A. D. Shupe, eds. 1989. *Secularization and fundamentalism reconsidered*. New York: Paragon House.

Heller, A. 1981. *Renaissance man*. New York: Schocken.

Kuper, A. 1988. *The invention of primitive society*. Boston, MA: Routledge.

Laermans, R., et al., eds. 1998. *Secularization and social integration*. Leuven: Leuven University Press.

Löwith, K. 1949. *Meaning in history*. Chicago, IL: University of Chicago Press.

Luckmann, T. 1967. *The invisible religion*. New York: Macmillan.

Lynd, R., and H. Lynd. 1929. *Middletown*. New York: Harcourt Brace.

———. 1937. *Middletown in transition*. New York: Harcourt Brace.

Marsden. G. 1994. *The soul of the American university*. New York: Oxford University Press.

Martin, D. 1965. Towards eliminating the concept of secularisation. In *Penguin survey of the social sciences*, edited by J. Gould, 169-82. Baltimore, MD: Penguin.

Merton, R. K. 1968. *Social theory and social structure*. New York: Free Press.

Mills, C. W. 1959. *The sociological imagination*. New York: Oxford University Press.

Nielsen, D. A. 1990a. The inquisition, rationalization, and sociocultural change in medieval Europe. In *Time, place, and circumstance*, edited by W. H. Swatos, Jr., 107-22. New York: Greenwood Press.

———. 1990b. Max Weber and the sociology of early Christianity. In *Time, place, and circumstance*, edited by W. H. Swatos, Jr., 87-105. New York: Greenwood Press.

Olson, D. V. A. 1998. Religious pluralism in contemporary U.S. counties. *American Sociological Review* 63: 759-61.

Parsons, T. 1977. *The evolution of societies*. Englewood Cliffs, NJ: Prentice-Hall.

Paterson, J. 1982. *Kildare*. Kildare: No publisher given.

Redekop, C. 1967. Toward an understanding of religion and social solidarity. *Sociological Analysis* 27: 149-61.

Reeves, E. B. 1990. *The hidden government*. Salt Lake City: University of Utah Press.

Richardson, J. T. 1993. Definitions of cult. *Review of Religious Research* 34: 348-56.

Robertson, R. 1971. Sociologists and secularization. *Sociology* 5: 297-312.

———. 1974. Religion and sociological factors in the analysis of secularization. In *Changing perspectives in the scientific study of religion*, edited by A. W. Eister, 41-60. New York: Wiley.

———. 1978. Biases in the analysis of secularization. In *Meaning and change*, edited by R. Robertson, 258-76. New York: NYU Press.

Runciman, W. G. 1970. *Sociology in its place*. Cambridge: Cambridge University Press.

Ruyter, W. de. 1996. Dark, backward, and barbarous. *Leiden Institute for the Study of Religions Newsletter* 1: 3-8.

Sahay, A. 1976. The concepts of morality and religion. *Sociological Analysis and Theory* 6: 167-85.

Sartre, J. P. 1955. *Literary and philosophical essays*. New York: Criterion.

Shiner, L. 1967. The concept of secularization in empirical research. *Journal for the Scientific Study of Religion* 6: 207-20.

Silk, M. 1984. Notes on the Judeo-Christian tradition in America. *American Quarterly* 36: 65-85.

Smith, W. C. 1984. On mistranslated book titles. *Religious Studies* 20: 27-42.

Sommerville, C. J. 1994. The secularisation puzzle. *History Today* 44 (Oct.): 14-19.

———. 1998. Secular society/religious population. *Journal for the Scientific Study of Religion* 37: 249-53.

Sorokin, P. A. 1937-1941. *Social and cultural dynamics*. New York: American.

Stark, R. 1992. The reliability of historical United States census data on religion. *Sociological Analysis* 53: 91-95.

———. 1996. *The rise of Christianity*. Princeton, NJ: Princeton University Press.

Stark, R., and W. S. Bainbridge. 1985. *The future of religion*. Berkeley: University of California Press.

———. 1987. *A theory of religion*. Bern: Lang.

Stark, R., and L. Iannaccone. 1994. A supply-side reinterpretation of the "secularization" of

Europe. *Journal for the Scientific Study of Religion* 33: 230-52.

Swatos, W. H., Jr., and L. R. Gissurarson. 1996. *Icelandic Spiritualism*. New Brunswick, NJ: Transaction.

Troeltsch, E. 1958[1912]. *Protestantism and progress*. Boston, MA: Beacon Press.

Tschannen, O. 1991. The secularization paradigm. *Journal for the Scientific Study of Religion* 30: 395-415.

Vidich, A. J., and S. M. Lyman. 1984. *American sociology*. New Haven, CT: Yale University Press.

Wallace, A. F. C. 1966. *Religion*. New York: Random House.

Weber, M. 1930[1904/5]. *The Protestant ethic and the spirit of capitalism*. New York: Scribner.

———. 1946[1919]. Science as a vocation. In *From Max Weber*, edited by C. W. Mills and H. H. Gerth, 129-56. New York: Oxford University Press.

———. 1978[1922]. *Economy and society*. Berkeley: University of California Press.

Wilson, B. 1985. Secularization. In *The sacred in a secular age*, edited by P. E. Hammond, 1-20. Berkeley: University of California Press.

Woodberry, R. D. 1998. When surveys lie and people tell the truth. *American Sociological Review* 63: 119-22.

Yamane, D. 1997. Secularization on trial. *Journal for the Scientific Study of Religion* 36: 109-22.

———. 1998. A sociologist comments on Sommerville. *Journal for the Scientific Study of Religion* 37: 254-56.

2

Toward an Integrated Perspective of the Processes Related to the Descriptive Concept of Secularization

Karel Dobbelaere

University of Leuven

Taking into account the analytical distinction between system levels, this chapter proposes an integrated perspective of the different processes related to secularization. Several levels of analysis are discussed: the macro, meso, and micro levels, and the interconnectedness between them. Secularization is seen here as the particularization in the religious subsystem of the general process of functional differentiation on the macro level. The purpose is to propose a more integrated theoretical view of secularization and related processes rather than a paradigm, and to stimulate international comparative research.

Secularization is at first sight a controversial *concept* because of its distinct use in different disciplines, e.g., philosophy, social sciences, and theology (Lübbe 1975). Even in the social sciences, various levels of analysis of the religious situation result in different definitions and divergent evaluations of the situation. If the founding fathers rarely used the term, nonetheless concepts and views related to theories of secularization were already present, e.g., generalization and differentiation (Durkheim 1964). Weber used the term (1920: 212) — but to typify the way in which, in the United States, membership in distinguished clubs and fraternal societies replaced membership of sects, in guaranteeing moral rectitude and credit worthiness. Later generations of sociologists continued to employ the term, but attached different meanings to it (Shiner 1967). Not until the 1960s were several *theories* of secularization developed, most prominently by Berger, Luckmann, and Wilson. These theories subsequently led to discussions concerning their reliability and validity (e.g., Hammond 1985; Hadden 1987; Lechner 1991). In similar vein, others have suggested an alternative, i.e., rational choice theory, to explain the religious situation in the United States which they considered to be radically different from that of Europe, where secularization theory emerged. Subsequently, they have applied their theory to explain both high and low rates of religious involvement in different countries (c.f., Stark and Bainbridge 1987). Finally, some sociologists have systematically analyzed the existing theories, since some discussions failed to scrutinize the ideas, levels of analysis, and arguments of those being criticized. Tschannen has suggested treating secularization theories as a paradigm (1992), and I have stressed the need to differentiate between levels of analysis: the macro or societal level, the meso or subsystem level, and the micro or individual level (1981), suggesting convergences and divergences between existing theories (1984).

Here, I offer the different "exemplars" which Tschannen distinguishes in the secularization paradigm, and I refer to authors who have written extensively about each exemplar, without suggesting, however, that these authors were the only ones to do so.[1] Some exemplars are re-named, and one is added. I order the exemplars according to the levels of analysis: institutional differentiation or segmentation (Luckmann 1967), autonomization (Berger 1967; Wilson 1969), rationalization (Berger 1967; Wilson 1982), societalization (Wilson 1976), disenchantment of the world (Weber 1920; Berger 1967), privatization (Berger 1967; Luckmann 1967), and generalization (Bellah 1967; Parsons 1967) are located on the societal level; pluralization (Martin 1978), relativization (Berger 1967), and this-worldliness (Luckmann 1990) are situated on the meso-level; and, finally, individualization (Bellah *et al.* 1985), bricolage (Luckmann 1979), unbelief (Berger 1967), and decline of church religiosity (Martin 1978) are located on the micro-level.

According to Tschannen, three exemplars are central to the secularization paradigm: differentiation, rationalization, and this-worldliness. The other exemplars are related to these. I start with the analytic distinction between system levels. Beginning with the macro level, it seems possible, using Luhmann's conceptual distinction between three types of differentiation — segmentary, social, and functional differentiations (1982: 262-265) to come to a better integrated perspective of the processes related to secularization. The so-called exemplars of Tschannen's paradigmatic solution are discussed by level of analysis.[2] Their functional relations are described, while distinguishing between processes and consequences. Special attention is given to the relationships between system levels.

THE SOCIETAL SYSTEM

Since modern societies are primarily *differentiated* along *functional* lines, subsystems developed different functional domains (economy, polity, science,

---

[1] Exemplars or shared examples are central elements of a paradigm (Tschannen 1992: 20-21, 26; see also Kuhn 1970: 174-210).

[2] To mark them, they are italicized in the text.

family). Each subsystem's communication is based on its own medium (money, power, truth, love), and each has developed its own values (success, separation of powers, reliability and validity, primacy of love), and norms. Regarding religion, they claim autonomy and reject religiously prescribed rules, i.e., the *autonomization* of the subsystems — e.g., the emancipation of education from ecclesiastical authority, the separation of church and state, the rejection of church prescriptions about birth control and abortion, the decline of religious content in literature and arts, and the development of science as an autonomous secular perspective.

Diagnosing the loss of religion's influence in the so-called secular world, members of the religious subsystem were the first to talk about secularization. In this context Luhmann speaks about secularization in the sense of a specifically religious conception of society as the environment of the religious system (1977: 225-232). Churches, most importantly the Roman Catholic church, reacted with a counteroffensive, stimulating among other things the organization of Catholic Action in the first part of this century and, in more recent years, calling for a second evangelization of Europe. At the end of the last century, adapting to the modern world, a process of pillarization was also instituted to protect believers from the secular world. A Protestant and a Catholic pillar emerged in the Netherlands, and Catholic pillars were gradually established in Austria, Belgium, Germany, Italy, and Switzerland. Pillars are organizational complexes that are religiously or ideologically legitimized, striving toward autarky or self-sufficiency.[3] The more services a pillar renders, the more self-sufficient it is (Coleman 1979; Dobbelaere 1988).[4] Pillarization is a form of segmental differentiation in a functionally differentiated society, which promotes social exclusiveness and an in-group mentality.

Consequently, secularization is *not* a causal concept, it describes the consequences of functional differentiation for the religious subsystem and expresses the interpretation of this experience by the religious staff. The sociological explanation of secularization starts with the process of functional differentiation. Secularization is situated on the *societal level* and should be seen as resulting from the processes of functional differentiation and the autonomization of the societal subsystems. In fact, secularization is only the particularization of the general

---

[3] In Belgium and the Netherlands, socialist pillars were also erected to emancipate the lower classes.

[4] In Belgium, the Catholic pillar is the most self-sufficient — it provides almost all possible services from the cradle to the grave. Catholic institutions embrace the majority of schools (from kindergarten to university), hospitals, old people's homes, youth movements, cultural associations, sport clubs, newspapers, magazines, book clubs, and libraries. The Catholic pillar also has a health insurance fund, a trade union, and banks. These organizational complexes make up the corporate channel, and according to Rokkan (1977), we may speak only of an institutionalized pillar if this corporate channel is interlocked with a political channel, in our example, the Christian People's Party. Indeed, it is the political party that represents the corporate channel in the political arena and ensures that no legislation is adopted that is to its detriment. It also seeks to promote legislative actions that favor the corporate channel.

process of functional differentiation in the religious subsystem. If secularization is only that, why should we then keep the term? I concur fully with Chaves's argument: because it refers to a specific social conflict, to wit, a religiously based resistence to functional differentiation (1997: 443). Additionally, modern societies may have different levels of secularization even if functionally highly differentiated in other sectors.

With Wilson, I state forcefully that secularization "maintains no more than that religion ceases to be significant in the working of the social system" (1982: 150). This says nothing about the religious consciousness of individuals, although it may affect it. We may then define secularization as a process by which the overarching and transcendent religious system of old is being reduced in a modern functionally differentiated society to a subsystem alongside other subsystems, losing in this process its overarching claims over the other subsystems. As a result, the *societal* significance of religion is greatly diminished. This conception of the process of secularization allowed Chaves to state that it refers to the declining scope of religious authority on the societal level (1994: 754). And distinguishing the same levels of analysis as I do, Chaves calls it *societal* secularization, to differentiate it from respectively *organizational* (meso level) and *individual* (micro level) secularization (1997: 445-447).

Declining religious authority allowed the development of *functional rationality*. The economy lost its religious ethos (Weber 1920: 163-206). Consequently, the political subsystem had also to rationalize, and little room was left for traditional and charismatic authority. Political authority became rational. Economic production and distribution developed large-scale economic organizations, and modern states extended their administration. These structures needed more and more people trained in science and rational techniques. Consequently, in education, a scientific approach to the world and the teaching of technical knowledge increasingly replaced a religious-literary formation. The development of scientifically based techniques had their impact also on the life-world: domestic tasks became increasingly mechanized, and even the most intimate, sexual relationships and their "consequences" were considered to be calculable and controllable. Not only could one better control the consequences, but in modern "handbooks" the sexual act itself was also presented as "technically improvable." The consequences of these developments were *the disenchantment of the world* and the *societalization* of the subsystem.

First, the disenchantment of the world: Indeed, the world is increasingly considered to be calculable and man-made, the result of controlled planning. Such a world has engendered not only new roles, but also new, basically rational and critical, attitudes and a new cognition. According to Acquaviva (1979), this new cognition has eliminated pre-logical, and thus religious, concepts and has been objectified in a new language that has changed the image of reality. The media, using this new language, have radicalized this development and made it a social phenomenon. This suggests a possible impact of the social system on the micro level, i.e., the consciousness of the individual; people have internalized this new language and may have lost to a certain degree the vision of a sacred reality.

Second, subsystems were also societalized or became more *gesellschaftlich*. The organized world is "based on impersonal roles, relationships, the coordination of skills, and essentially formal and contractual patterns of behaviour, in which personal virtue, as distinguished from role obligations, is of small consequence" (Wilson 1982: 155). In such systems, Wilson goes on, control is no longer based on morals and religion, it has become impersonal, a matter of routine techniques and unknown officials — legal, technical, mechanized, computerized, and electronic. Thus, religion has lost one of its important latent functions; as long as control was interpersonal, it was based on religiously-based mores and substantive values. In Wilson's view, there is another argument why "secularization is a concomitant of societalization": since religion offers redemption, which is personal, total, an "indivisible ultimate" unsusceptible to rational techniques or "cost-efficiency criteria," it has to be offered in a "community" (Wilson 1976).

Berger and Luckmann stressed another consequence of the process of functional differentiation and the autonomization of the secular spheres, i.e., *the privatization of religion*. According to Luckmann (1967: 94-106), the validity of religious norms became restricted to its "proper" sphere, i.e., that of private life, and Berger (1967: 133) stressed the "functionality" of this "for the maintenance of the highly rationalized order of modern economic and political institutions," i.e., the public sphere. This dichotomy, private-public, carries with it at least two shortcomings (Dobbelaere 1981: 79-84). It suggests that secularization was limited to the "public" sphere which is incorrect: family life was also secularized. Second, it is the adoption in sociological discourse of ideological concepts used by liberals and socialists in the nineteenth century to legitimate functional differentiation and the autonomization of "secular" institutions: "Religion is a private matter." Later, these concepts were used by workers to defend their political, religious, or family options against possible sanctions and eventual dismissal by the management of Christian organizations, e.g., schools or hospitals, if they failed to behave according to ecclesiastical rules in matters of family life, politics, or religion. They defended their "private" options, their "private" life, in what managers of ecclesiastical organizations called the "public" sphere, since, according to them, the private options were publicly known.

Clearly, the dichotomy "private-public" is not a structural aspect of society, but rather a legitimizing conceptualization of the world, an ideological pair used in conflicts by participants.[5] Sociologists might, of course, study the use of this

---

[5] It is not a societal subsystem with institutionalized complementary roles (professionals versus a public), such as for example occurs in the economy (producers and consumers), the educational system (teachers and students), the polity (politicians and voters), and the judicial system (magistrates and lawyers versus clients).

dichotomy in social discourse and conflicts, but it is not a sociological conceptualization. In sociological theory this ideological pair should be replaced by Habermas's conceptual dichotomy: system versus life-world (1982: 229-293), used in a purely descriptive sense. It is in the systemic interactions that societal-ization occurs: relationships became basically secondary, segmented, utilitarian, and formal. By contrast, in the life-world — the family, groups of friends, and social networks — interactions may still be more or less communal. Primary relations are the binding forces of such groups: relationships are total, trustful, considerate, sympathetic, and personal (see also Wilson 1976, 1982). The trend toward societalization is very clear in the distribution and the banking sector — e.g., the replacement of neighborhood stores by large department stores where the interactions between shopper and seller are limited to a money exchange for goods, and in the banking sector where the tellers are replaced by money distri-butors which function electronically at the command of customers using bank cards and a personal code. Beyond the life-world, interactions became societal-ized. We ask below whether this has had an impact on the religiosity of individuals.

RELATIONSHIP BETWEEN THE MACRO AND MESO LEVELS

Pluralization, or the segmentary differentiation of the subsystem religion, was only possible, according to Parsons (1967), once the Christian ethic was institu-tionalized in the so-called secular world, in other words, once the Christian ethic became *generalized*. Consequently, pluralization may not be considered an indicator of secularization, quite the contrary (for a critique see Lechner 1991: 1109-1110). However, the relationship is not unidirectional, since a growing pluralization will augment the necessity of generalization. Indeed, together with Bellah (1976), Parsons stressed the need for a civil religion which, to legitimize the system, overarches conventional religions. One may also consider the need for secular laws overarching divergent religiously inspired mores. Martin suggests that when religion adapts to every status group "through every variety of pullulating sectarianism," then there is a need to preserve the unity of the nation "by a national myth which represents a common denominator of all faiths: one nation under God" (1978: 36). Indeed, civil religion generalizes the different notions of God present in the various denominations: the God of Jews, Catholics, Unitarians, Calvinists, and so forth. The national myth sacralizes its prophets, martyrs, and historical places: it has its ritualistic expressions and may also use biblical archetypes (Bellah 1967: 18). Such myths, such legitimations are not always religious: civil religion is one possibility, there are also secular myths, like the French myth based on *laïcité*, which legitimizes the French state, its schools, and laws.

What explains the emergence of a "religious" rather than a "secular" myth, or vice versa? And more generally, what explains how such a myth — religious or secular — emerges? Fenn suggests that this is possible only when a society conceives itself as a "nation," as a "really 'real'" — typical examples are the United States, Japan, and France. On the other hand, the myth is rather seen as a cultural "fiction," according to Fenn, to the extent that a society sees itself as an arena for conflicting and cooperative activities of various classes, groups, corporations, and organizations (1978: 41-53). Another issue for inquiry is how and to what extent in certain countries a conventional religion may function as a civil religion in a religiously pluralistic society, e.g., Anglicanism in England, Lutheranism in the Scandinavian countries, and Calvinism in the Netherlands? What degree of pluralism is incongruent with a church fulfilling the role of civil religion?

THE MESO LEVEL

On the meso level, pluralization has resulted in a religious market, where different religions either compete for the souls of the people or make agreements not to proselytize, as the Anglican church has agreed with the Catholic church in Belgium. Religious pluralism and competition augments the *relativity* of their respective religious messages, or in Berger's terms "it relativizes their religious contents," their religious message is "de-objectivated," and more generally, "the pluralistic situation . . . *ipso facto* plunges religion into a crisis of credibility" (1967: 150-151). We return to this when discussing the micro level, below.

The emergence of New Religious Movements (NRMs) is related to the process of secularization. The "Christian collective consciousness" of the West was disintegrating. Pluralism had undermined its "objectivity," and the slowly perceived useless character of Christian religions on the societal level accompanied by a loss of status and power, allowed exotic religions to improve their position on the religious market. Some, such as the Unification church, the Family, or ISKCON wanted to resacralize the world and its institutions by bringing God back in, e.g., the family, the economy, even the polity. Wallis designates them "world-rejecting new religions." However, the vast majority are of another type, they are "world-affirming" (1984). The world-affirming NRMs offer their members esoteric means of attaining immediate and automatic success, recovery, heightened spiritual powers, assertiveness, and a clearer mind. Mahikari provides an "omitama" or amulet; TM, a personal mantra; Scientology, auditing and the E-meter; Human Potential movements offer therapies, encounter groups, or alternative health and spiritual centers; Soka Gakkai promotes chanting of an invocation before a mandala; while Elan Vital offers the Knowledge revealed by Maharaji or one of his appointed instructors.

Luckmann suggests that the level of transcendence in many new religions was lowered: religions became "*this worldly*" or *mundane* (1990). The historical religions are examples of "great transcendences," referring to something other than everyday reality, notwithstanding the fact that they were also involved in "this worldly" or mundane affairs: however, the reference was always transcendental, e.g., the incantations. To the contrary, many new religions, especially the world-affirming religions appear to reach *only* the level of "intermediate transcendences." They bridge time and space, promote intersubjective communion, but remain at the immanent level of everyday reality. Consequently, some, e.g., TM, claim to be spiritual rather than religious movements. If one employed a substantive definition of religion, referring to transcendent beliefs and practices, the supernatural or the sacred, many NRMs would not be considered as religions. They would not qualify as religions even according to some functional definitions. Luhmann, for example, might consider some of them not to be religion, since they do not relate "to the problem of simultaneity of indefiniteness and certainty" (1977: 46), the typical function of religion. Indeed, these world-affirming religions are not concerned with the problems of *simultaneity* of transcendence and immanence since they focus only on the immanent, on everyday life. Stark and Bainbridge (1987) miss the point when they criticize secularization theory referring to these changes on the meso level. Moreover, their argument, that the newly emerging "spiritual movements" prove that secularization is a self-limiting process, backfires since these so-called new religious movements are "religious" adaptations to a secularized world.

This mundane orientation of religion is not new. Berger and Luckmann have suggested that the higher attendances in American churches compared to the European might be explained by the mundane orientation of religion in America. Luckmann (1967: 36-37) called it internal secularization: "a radical inner change in American church religion . . . today the secular ideas of the American Dream pervade church religion." In asserting that American churches were "becoming highly secularized themselves" (Berger 1967: 108), these authors sought to reconcile data at the level of the individual which conflicted with secularization theories. However, they missed the point: church attendance is not a valid indicator of the process of secularization, which is a societal process. This does not imply that people's religious consciousness and their behavioral practices may not be influenced by the societal situation, but that the explanation of individual behavior may not be reduced to a simple direct effect of the secularization process on the societal level: the motivational structure on the micro level is more complex.

THE MICRO LEVEL

These arguments bring us to the individual or micro level and the exemplars: *individualization, unbelief, bricolage,* and *decline in church religiosity*, i.e., the *unchurching* of individuals and the lower *church involvement* of members.

The individualization of religion has been related to its becoming part of the "private sphere." The church is the local congregation, but a *"chosen community,"* "a loving community in which individuals can experience the joy of belonging," consequently "the ultimate meaning of the church is an expressive-individualistic one," and love is shared within the community not with the world at large (Bellah *et al.* 1985: 219-237). The local church is considered to be part of the life-world; however, if one follows Bellah's arguments, the local church must be a chosen, loving community. Choice is possible only in a pluralistic situation, which is the case in the United States, but not in major parts of Europe, and certainly not in the so-called Catholic countries like Austria, Belgium, France, Italy, Portugal, and Spain, where the choice is practically limited to a dominant religion and an a- or anti-religious option. In olden times, the Catholic church had been part of the life-world. Most people continued to live where they were born; migration to other communities was exceptional; the local church was part of a community that lived, worked, and prayed together. The embedding of the Church in the life-world — in fact the Church performed each Sunday and on the holy days the *corrobori* for the local community — and the sacralization of its structure (Kaufmann 1979) — people used to call the pope "our holy father," referred to the Church as "our holy mother," and called the Church "a community" — concealed to a large extent the organizational structure of the Church.

After World War II, the traditional communal structure was largely destroyed, and the Church appeared more and more to the public as an organization with a strong hierarchical structure, as an authoritarian institution. In this context and as a reaction, the Church fathers started, in the Second Vatican Council, to discuss the Church as "the people of God." In the mind of some bishops, many priests and lay people, this notion had to legitimize theologically changes in the structure of the Church: collegiality, ecumenism, religious freedom, decentralization, equality, and democracy. The geographically defined parish should also give way to a parish of one's choice, and people reacted in this way, but on important religious occasions they were reminded that the ancient parish structure had not changed. In fact, after the Vatican II, many dedicated themselves enthusiastically to bringing about the changes they were hoping for. The disillusionment came within a decade. By interdicting most of the proposed changes, the hierarchical power structure of the Church appeared in its full nakedness (Dobbelaere and Voyé 1991: 215-218). The Catholic church was more and more seen as an organizational structure belonging to the religious subsystem, differentiated from the life-world, and certainly not as the manifestation of expressive individualism. It appeared more and more as a service station to which people turned on certain occasions. This functional approach reflects more fully a utilitarian rather than an expressive individualism. Furthermore, Bellah and associates suggest that "the ultimate meaning of the Church is an expressive-individualistic one." However, in a study of European Catholics — using the data from the European Values Studies — Voyé and I have found a negative association between different dimensions of religiosity and expressive individualism (Dobbelaere and Voyé 1996: 226) — operationalized in the qualities of independence and imagination, which are basic to the "freedom to express oneself" (Bellah *et al* 1985: 34). These results were confirmed in an analysis of all the data of the European Values Studies and data collected in the United States and Canada with the same questionnaire (Dobbelaere 1995b: 14-21). Utilitarian individualism promotes an image of churches as "service stations," and expressive individualism is negatively associated with religiosity, which was also confirmed by Waege's study in Flanders (1997: 333-334).

How did individualization come about? First, although the social system and the subsystems are still "an objective reality," a given, functional differentiation can only "work" if the independence of the subsystem is maintained. However, this independence cannot be enforced on the micro level, i.e., the level of individual motives, where interferences may occur, e.g., people voting according to their religious beliefs, or choosing a type and level of education in conformity with their religion. Luhmann suggests that a structural equivalent of enforcement is found in the "individualization of decisions" which may produce a statistical neutralization of these individually motivated choices, that is to say, that they may cancel each other out (1977: 233-242; Beyer 1990: 374-376). Functional differentiation has stimulated individualization of choices, and this has had its impact on the life-world. It was made possible by the de-traditionalization of the life-world: ascriptive roles were becoming less pressing; cars allowed people to escape the control of family and neighborhood; traditions were relativized; TV carried conflicting visions, messages, ideas, and values into the living room; women were liberated from their ascriptive, biological roles by the pill; and the educational level rose. The "golden sixties" amounted to an economic boom, offering people more freedom, more choices, less constraint; and church members claimed the same freedom in religious and ethical matters. The rejection of the encyclical on birth control by an overwhelming majority of Catholics — i.e., criticism of an imposing "infallible" religious authority, and the rejection of its rules and legitimations — was symptomatic, as were the Underground Church in America and the National Pastoral Council in the Netherlands. The Underground Church was a place where Protestants and Catholics met to discuss theology and ethics, and to celebrate the *Agape* with bread and wine. Church authorities opposed the uncontrolled ecumenical rapprochement between Protestants and Catholics, and the use of bread and wine which was a direct reference to the Eucharistic meal. In the Netherlands, the Pastoral Council (1966-70) was set up by the bishops themselves who wanted to involve priests and laity in a consultation to implement the changes necessary in the light of Vatican II. A new climate was created. Reflection on belief, taking into account subjective experiences, replaced an objectified belief, reified in formulas, and dictated from the top down. According to the resolutions of the Pastoral Council, Church authorities should invite rather than impose and should recognize the maturity of believers even in questions of church policy. These resolutions were to be implemented by consulation, but the Vatican opposed the continuation of the Council in its existing form. A reaction ensued, new conservative bishops were nominated, the incumbent bishops were publicly disqualified, and the authority of the hierarchy was restored. A national council subverting the authority of individual bishops was unacceptable to Rome (see Coleman 1979; Laeyendecker 1992: 105-106). In fact, all attempts at renewal were an expression of a new understanding of Descartes's *Cogito ergo sum*. It was now to be understood as *I* think and *I* choose, not only my networks, my friends, my dress patterns, but also the beliefs, norms, and practices which express my religious feelings.

The loss of church authority, a more pluralistic religious market, and the growing individualization have led to a religious *bricolage*, an individual patchwork or recomposition. The religious menu of the churches was not accepted, rather a "religion à la carte" was individually constructed. Referring to postmodernity, Voyé suggests that individual religiosity is characterized by the "end of Great Narratives," a "mixing of codes" and a certain "re-enchantment of the World." "The mixing of codes . . . is reflected in the religious field in a three-fold manner: references and practices blending the institutional and the popular; occasional borrowings from scientific discourses as well as from religious ones; and inspiration sought in diverse religions, notably, oriental religions" (1995: 199-204, esp. 201). In olden times, the churches were able to impose their doctrines, at least publicly. What people thought we may only guess, but they would never publicly proclaim a religion à la carte. Now bricolage is publicly accepted, notwithstanding the official opposition of the churches. Also new is the mixing of inspirations of diverse religions, notably oriental religions, e.g., according to the European Values Studies about 20 percent mix Christian beliefs with a belief in some form of reincarnation.

The foregoing arguments make clear that the religious situation at the individual level cannot be explained exclusively by the secularization of the social system: other factors — individualization of decisions, de-traditionalization, mobility, and utilitarian and expressive individualism — were at work. Consequently, the religiousness of individuals is *not* a valid indicator in evaluating the process of secularization. But, did secularization also have an impact on the micro level? Or, in Chaves's terms, did societal secularization produce individual secularization?

Secularization indicates that since religious institutions have lost authority and relevance in society and its subsystems, then, as a consequence of the declining impact of the buttressing organizations, the religious collective consciousness, in the Durkheimian sense, must be changing. That the religious consciousness is becoming less specific may be deduced from the changing collective consciousness of the more than century-old Catholic pillars: their general values are less imperative than the former precise churchly norms. Recent research has demonstrated that the core philosophy no longer consists of the strict religious rules of this church, but rather refers to so-called typical values of the gospel such as social justice, a humane approach toward clients and patients, well-being, solidarity between social classes with special attention to marginal people, and *Gemeinschaftlichkeit*. These are values which have a universal appeal, and which are not specifically Christian. However, by backing them up with a religious source they acquire a sacred aura, which is occasionally solemnized with religious rituals. This new "sacred canopy" is still symbolized by a "C," referring more and more to Christian, that is evangelical, instead of to Catholic, the latter being considered to have a more restricted appeal and to be more confining. This "sociocultural Christianity" functions now as the collective consciousness of the segmented Catholic world of olden days (Dobbelaere 1988: 83-90; Dobbelaere and Voyé 1990: S6-S8; Laermans 1992: 204-214). The mixing of the codes also suggests that specific beliefs have been replaced by more general notions — e.g., a general belief in a hereafter has replaced the specific Christian notions of heaven, hell, and purgatory — leaving a greater place for individual variation, which is expressed in the prevailing bricolage of beliefs and practices. As Durkheim already noted:

> [I]f practices and formulae, when they are precise, determine thought and movements with a necessity analogous to that of reflexes, these general principles, on the contrary, can pass into facts only with the aid of intelligence. But, once reflection is awakened, it is not easy to restrain it. When it takes hold, it develops spontaneously beyond the limits assigned to it. One begins by putting articles of faith beyond discussion; then discussion extends to them. One wishes an explanation of them; one asks their reasons for existing, and, as they submit to this search, they lose a part of their force. . . . Because it becomes more rational, the collective conscience becomes less imperative, and for this very reason, it wields less restraint over the free development of individual varieties" (1969: 290-291).

This means that secularization is one of the preconditions for rational choice, and that the individal may now engage in more mixing of codes, and develop unorthodox beliefs and various degrees of belief and unbelief.

Empirical research records a growing unbelief and a decline in the belief in the Christian notion of "God as a person" (see Halman and de Moor 1993; Dobbelaere and Jagodzinski 1995: 210-214). To explain this I have related it to changes on the societal level, referring to functional rationality and societalization in the steps of sociologists and anthropologists who have shown that people develop a concept of personified supernatural beings directly from the model which their society provides (Dobbelaere 1995a: 177-181). Functional rationality promoted an attitude in people that either they themselves or specialists could solve their problems, as they took command of their physical, social, and psychological worlds, which removed God more and more from those worlds and stimulated unbelief. However, if for some people the notion of God lingers on, God is more and more conceived of as a general power and not as "a person," a spirit, "something" vague and general, a "higher power" and not as a "personal God." How could God be thought of as a "personal God" if, outside the life-world, people experience fewer and fewer "personal relationships," the systemic interactions being based on impersonal roles. If they can no longer believe in "God as a person," they drop out of Christian rituals, since these are centered on a relationship with "God as a person." Consequently, the number of unchurched people grows, and the involvement in the churches of church members diminishes. These consequences have been clearly established (Jagodzinski and Dobbelaere 1995: 87-96).

In order to explain the degree of unchurching and of a declining involvement in the churches, Jagodzinski and I have referred to secularization, seen as *one* of the explanatory factors (Jagodzinski and Dobbelaere 1993, 1995). With the help of a regression analysis the relation was examined between, on the one hand, the level of church involvement in European countries — based on interview data gathered by the European Values Studies in 1981 and 1990 — and, on the other hand, the GDP per capita in standard purchasing power units, as an indirect indicator of the degree of economic rationalization. Warning that the regression analysis should be taken as a parsimonious description of the relationship and not as a statistical test, we concluded that the comparison between countries provided evidence in favor of the secularization thesis (Jagodzinski and Dobbelaere 1995: 96-101). Halman also tested the impact of secularization on individuals; however, his approach was different. He calculated the degree of correlation between, on the one hand, the religious values of the persons, and, on the other hand, their political and moral values and those related to the life-world, in reference to the level of structural modernization in ten European countries, Canada, and the United States. The data used were assembled with the questionnaire of the European Values Study. In general, in the more modern countries, the political and moral values, and those related to the life-world of individuals were the most independent of their religious values (Halman 1991: 258-59). These two approaches are in fact short cuts to a valid testing of individual secularization.

To test validly the impact of societal secularization on individuals we need first to establish on the societal level that modern societies which have a high degree of functional differentiation and functional rationality also have a high degree of secularization, i.e., the particularizaton of the general process upon the religious subsystem. Indeed, it is conceivable that in some countries functional differentiation of the religious subsystem from the secular subsystems may be less developed than the functional differentiation between the secular subsystems themselves. This means that we need international comparisons between countries to establish that. Then we should check if higher levels of secularization on the societal level produce higher degrees of compartmentalization between the individual's religious values and his other values, to wit, whether there is a higher degree of segregation on the level of individuals' consciences between their religious values and their political, economic, familial, scientific, and other values in countries with a higher degree of secularization. Finally, one should be able to establish a relationship between the value-compartmentalization on the level of the individual's conciousness and the beliefs and religious practices of the individual: the theory would expect that the more pronounced the compartmentalization, the less religious people are. Halman related structural modernization directly to compartmentalization, and Jagodzinski and Dobbelaere related functional rationality directly to religious beliefs and practices.

Age has also been used as a proxy variable to measure the impact of degrees of secularization on the religious beliefs, attitudes, and behavior of individuals, since older cohorts have lived in a less secularized world than the younger ones. All studies have established that the older cohorts are more religious, whatever the religious dimension under study. Controlling for expressive and utilitarian individualism, cultural changes such as postmaterialism and cultural progressiveness, level of education, and sex, we found that age had the strongest direct and indirect effect on all latent religious traits (Dobbelaere and Voyé 1996: 226; Dobbelaere 1995b: 18-20). Once this was established, the next question was: did age express a life-cycle effect, period effects, or generational differences? On the basis of a broader data set than the European Values Studies, Jagodzinski and I came to the conclusion that the differences between cohorts should be attributed to generational and period effects, the latter having a greater impact on the younger than the older generations. We checked three models of generational changes against our data. The *standard model*, which suggests that changes are largely restricted to the "formative" years: once beliefs, values, and norms are internalized and behavior routinized, change is less likely to occur. If secularization gradually undermines traditional religion, each new cohort should be less religious than older ones. Consequently, at the aggregate level, religiosity should gradually decline, since older cohorts are replaced by younger ones. The standard model of generational change may also be related to Inglehart's idea of formative influence (1990). This model should produce a watershed between post-war and older cohorts and not a gradual decline of religiosity. For that reason we called it the *watershed model*.

We suggested a different model, the *contagion model* of religious change. Secularization may gradually undermine the basic beliefs of traditional religion, but this does not immediately become manifest in behavioral change. Specific events are necessary before these internal doubts turn into overt protest and exit. For example, criticism from theologians and public debates in the media about church documents and policies, or public discussions of synodal or conciliar resolutions, make it apparent that religious beliefs and the religious understanding of ethics and church authority are already very much undermined. A convergence of one's *public* behavior and *personal* disbelief follows, which promotes both exit from the churches and a decline in church involvement of those staying (for an example see Dobbelaere 1988: 98-99). Jagodzinski and I expected that the younger cohorts would react more rapidly to these specific events since they do not have to give up ingrained habits. Older cohorts might always remain at higher levels of church involvement, partly because they are less affected by the process of secularization, and partly because some of them are unwilling to change their religious beliefs. However, in general, we expected a change in all cohorts within fairly short time periods. To be sure, this model also postulates a generational change because, after the periods of rapid decay, all cohorts are much less religious than before. However, change in our model is not restricted to the formative years nor is it produced by post-war affluence.

On the basis of data about Protestants and Catholics from Belgium, Denmark, France, Great Britain, Italy, the Netherlands, Norway, and West Germany, we demonstrated that the contagion model best fits the data (Jagodzinski and Dobbelaere 1995: 105-114). The criticism of churchly traditions and the public discussion accompanying it have "contagiously" undermined the religious behavior of all generations, but particularly of the younger generations (see Chaves 1991, for linking cohort effects to family structure). However, this major trend does not exclude some small life-cycle effects: parents, especially mothers, returning for a short period to church on Sundays during the period that their children undergo one or two years of cathechism prior to confirmation, or some people in their old age returning to higher levels of church involvement (see also Stolzenberg et al. 1995).

SECULARIZATION: A MECHANICAL, STRAIGHTFORWARD, EVOLUTIONARY PROCESS?

Most authors indicate national and regional variations in degrees of functional differentiation, as well as varations among social institutions (Wilson 1969: 75-95). They sometimes refer to it implicitly by stating that "political, religious, and economic institutions became increasingly specialized" (Luckmann 1967: 95), thereby suggesting a differential evolution. Berger quite explicitly speaks about "cultural lags" when comparing institutional spheres and nations (1967: 128-130). Martin tries to explain more systematically these differences and the impact of secularization on the conciousness and behavior of individuals. If — using Chaves's labels — societal, organizational, and individual secularizations tend to occur, other things being equal, Martin quickly adds, "[b]ut things are not equal — ever — and . . . they are most conspiciously not equal with respect to the particular (and general linguistic) complex within which they operate" (1978: 3). His analysis of the impact of the sociocultural complex focuses primarily on a categorization of countries taking into account whether the "frame" of the society is established through conflict against external or against internal oppressors (respectively Poland and France, for example), or whether or not there is a monopoly of religion or some degree of religious pluralism, but also on the size of religious minorities, their territorial dispersion, and the nature of their exclusion from elites. His study is not limited to the effect of the social location of a religion, it also incorporates the inherent character of different religions: pluralistic and democratic versus organic, e.g., Protestant denominations versus the Catholic church (1978: 15-58). His points add weight to our argument that religiosity of the individuals is not a valid indicator of societal secularization, since sociocultural factors, apart from degrees of secularization, may have a positive or negative impact on the religiosity of individuals.

Neither is the relationship between the macro and the micro level one-sided, since the processes discussed are manifestly or latently set in motion by people. Consequently, we may expect that growing unbelief and distancing from the denominations might lead to increasing secularization on the societal level, even were the religious hard core and some fundamentalist groups to do everything possible to prevent this by sacralizing critical issues, such as life as a God-given gift, in the euthanasia debate. The effect of a sacralizing counter-weight in a New England city was studied by Demerath and Williams. They concluded: "In our view, there is no question that secularization is the more dominant tendency. . . . However, there is also evidence of sacralization." The sacralizing counterweight within the community's political arena was provided by minority movements, which were "more likely to share a basic ecumenism rather than a zealous religious particularism," they "took up specific issues in a kind of single-interest politics," were rather "*ad hoc* movements" and, conse-quently, "smaller, more flexible" but also "less enduring" than the "established church structures," which served "as staunch bulwarks of the mainstream and the status quo."[6] In fact, none of the conventional churches, synagogues, or other religious organizations were involved as major protagonists in the different issues; the Catholic religious and clergy of various faiths were "acting more on their own initiative than as formal representatives of their basic communities," and, in one of the issues "several of these clergy found themselves at odds with home congregations over their tactics and belligerent behavior." Indeed, they "are far more likely than their secular opponents to take on the shrill tone and extreme tactics of the true believer." The "resources mobilized" for effective action in taking the issues to the public, were "cultural" rather than "structural," to wit "sacred cultural images and arguments which had retained some currency even in a secularizing religious economy" and "moral fundamentals" (Demerath and Williams 1992: 201-205). There is more to be said about this interesting study, which I use here only to point out the dialectical and discordant process of secularization in which people are manifestly or latently involved.

CONCLUSION

The religiosity of individuals cannot be explained exclusively by the secular-ization of the social system; other factors like the individualization of decisions,

---

[6] Three instances in which religion played a critical role were: homelessness, black neighborhood development, abortion and sex education.

detraditionalization, mobilty, and expressive and utilitarian individualism are also at work. Consequently, the decline of religious beliefs and practices may not be considered as a valid proxy variable for the secularization of the social system. However, this does not imply that the secularization of the social system does not have an influence on the religiosity of individuals: several hypotheses were presented to link the macro and micro level. Reference was made to Acquaviva's hypothesis that modernization engendered a new type of cognition, which, under the influence of the media, became a social phenomenon eliminating pre-logical, and thus religious, notions. It was further suggested that the loss of church authority undermined the "objectivity" of the Christian collective consciousness of the West promoting a "mixing of religious codes." Still another connection was made between the macro and the micro level. Functional rationality removed God from the physical, social, and psychological worlds, thus stimulating unbelief and unchurching. If the notion of God lingered on in some people, the process of societalization changed their conception of God: the typical Christian conception of God as a person changed into a general abstract power or spirit, lowering their involvement in Christian churches. It was also shown that the direction of the causal relationships is not unidirectional but rather dialectical, e.g., between generalization on the macro level, and pluralism on the meso level, but also between secularization and individual religiosity: growing unbelief may produce a manifest process of secularization on the macro level.

The analysis of secularization theories, distinguishing levels of analysis and reordering the concepts employed, has made it possible to link processes and consequences, to suggest relationships between different levels of analysis, and to reformulate general theoretical propositions. This facilitates the deduction of hypotheses to be tested in empirical research. Many of these hypotheses and relations can be tested only on the basis of comparative international research, and such research is rare in the sociology of religion. However, good monographs also give valuable insights into the processes of secularization and sacralization. A theoretical framework, rather than a paradigm, and international comparative research should help us to construct a more valid theory of secularization.

REFERENCES

Acquaviva, S. S. 1979. *The decline of the sacred in industrial society.* Oxford: Blackwell.

Bellah, R. N. 1967. Civil religion in America. *Daedalus* 96: 1-21.

Bellah, R. N., R. Madsen, W. M. Sullivan, A. Swidler, and S. M. Tipton. 1985. *Habits of the heart: Individualism and commitment in American life.* Berkeley: University of California Press.

Berger, P. L. 1967. *The sacred canopy: Elements of a sociological theory of religion.* Garden City, NY: Doubleday.

Beyer, P. F. 1990. Privatization and the global influence of religion in global society. In *Global culture: Nationalism, globalization, and modernity*, edited by M. Featerstone. 373-95. London: Sage.

Chaves, M. 1991. Family structure and Protestant church attendance: The sociological basis of cohort and age effects. *Journal for the Scientific Study of Religion* 30:501-14.

———. 1994. Secularization as declining religious authority. *Social Forces* 72: 749-74.

———. 1997. Secularization: A Luhmannian reflection. *Soziale Systeme* 3: 439-49.

Coleman, J. A. 1979. *The evolution of Dutch Catholicism, 1958-1974*. Berkeley: University of California Press.

Demerath III, N. J., and R. H. Williams. 1992. Secularization in a community context: Tensions of religion and politics in a New England city. *Journal for the Scientific Study of Religion* 31: 189-206.

Dobbelaere, K. 1981. Secularization: A multi-dimensional concept. *Current Sociology* 29: 1-213.

———. 1984. Secularization theories and sociological paradigms: Convergences and divergences. *Social Compass* 31: 199-219.

———. 1988. Secularization, pillarization, religious involvement, and religious change in the low countries. In *World Catholicism in transition*, edited by T. M. Gannon, 80-115. New York: Macmillan.

———. 1995a. The surviving dominant Catholic church in Belgium: A consequence of its popular religious practices? In *The post-war generation and establishment religion: Cross-cultural perspectives*, edited by W. C. Roof, J. W. Carroll, and D. A. Roozen, 171-90. Boulder, CO: Westview Press.

———. 1995b. Religion in Europe and North America. In *Values in Western societies*, edited by R. de Moor, 1-29. Tilburg: Tilburg University Press.

Dobbelaere, K., and L. Voyé. 1990. From pillar to postmodernity: The changing situation of religion in Belgium. *Sociological Analysis* 51:S1-S13.

———. 1991. Western European Catholicism since Vatican II. In *Vatican II and US Catholicism*, edited by H. R. Ebaugh, 205-31. Greenwich, CT: JAI Press.

———. 1996. Europäische Katholiken und die katholische Kirche nach dem Zweiten Vatikanischen Konzil. In *Vatikanum II und Modernisierung: Historische, theologische und soziologische Perspective*, edited by F. X. Kaufmann and A. Zingerle, 209-32. Paderborn: Schöningh.

Dobbelaere, K., and W. Jagodzinski. 1995. Religious cognitions and beliefs. In *Beliefs in government, Volume 4: The impact of values*, edited by J. W. van Deth and E. Scarbrough, 197-217. Oxford: Oxford University Press.

Durkheim, E. 1969. *The division of labor in society*. New York: Free Press.

Fenn, R. K. 1978. *Toward a theory of secularization*. Storrs, CT: Society for the Scientific Study of Religion.

Habermas, J. 1982. *Theory des kommunikativen Handelns*. Volume 2: *Zür Kritik der funktionalitischen Vernunft*. Frankfurt: Suhrkamp.

Hadden, J. K. 1987. Toward desacralizing secularization theory. *Social Forces* 65: 587-611.

Halman, L. 1991. *Waarden in de westerse wereld*. Tilburg: Tilburg University Press.

Halman, L., and R. de Moor. 1993. Religion, churches, and moral values. In *The individualizing society: Value change in Europe and North America*, edited by P. Ester et al., 37-65. Tilburg: Tilburg University Press.

Hammond, P. E., ed. 1985. *The sacred in a secular age*. Berkeley: University of California Press.

Inglehart, R. 1990. *Culture shift in advanced industrial society*. Princeton, NJ: Princeton University Press.

Jagodzinski, W., and K. Dobbelaere. 1993. Der Wandel kirchlicher Religiosität in Westeuropa. *Kölner Zeitschrift für Soziologie und Socialpsychologie*. 33:68-91.

————. 1995. Secularization and church religiosity. In *Beliefs in government, Volume 4: The impact of values*, edited by J. W. van Deth and E. Scarbrough, 76-119. Oxford: Oxford University Press.

Kaufmann, F. X. 1979. *Kirche begreifen: Analysen und Thesen zur gesellschaftlichen Verfassung des Christentums*. Freiburg: Herder.

Kuhn, T. S. 1970. *The structure of scientific revolutions.* Chicago, IL: University of Chicago Press.

Laermans, R. 1992. *In de greep van de "Moderne Tijd." Modernisering en verzuiling, individulisering en het naoorlogs publieke discours van de ACW-vormingsorganisaties: een proeve tot cultuursociologische duiding.* Leuven: Garant.

Laeyendecker, L. 1992. Kerkelijke vernieuwingsbewegingen in de Katholieke Kerk. In *Godsdienst in Nederland*, edited by H. Schaeffer, 104-12. Amersfoort: De Horstink.

Lechner, F. J. 1991. The case against secularization: A rebuttal. *Social Forces* 69: 1103-19.

Luckmann, T. 1967. *The invisible religion: The problem of religion in modern society.* New York: Macmillan.

————. 1979. The structural conditions of religious consciousness in modern societies. *Japanese Journal of Religious Studies* 6: 121-37.

————. 1990. Shrinking transcendence, expanding religion? *Sociological Analysis* 50: 127-38.

Lübbe, H. 1975. *Säkularisierung: Geschichte eines ideen-politischen Begriffs.* Freiburg: Karl Alber.

Luhmann, N. 1977. *Funktion der Religion.* Frankfurt: Suhrkamp.

————. 1982. *The differentiation of society.* New York: Columbia University Press.

Martin, D. A. 1978. *A general theory of secularization.* Oxford: Blackwell.

Parsons, T. 1967. Christianity and modern industrial society. In *Sociological theory: Values and sociocultural change*, edited by E. A. Tiryakian, 33-70. New York: Harper & Row.

Rokkan, S. 1977. Towards a generalized concept of "Verzuiling": A preliminary note. *Political Studies* 25: 563-70.

Shiner, L. 1967. The concept of secularization in empirical research. *Journal for the Scientific Study of Religion* 6: 207-20.

Stark, R., and W. S. Bainbridge. 1987. *A theory of religion.* New York: Lang.

Stolzenberg R. M. *et al.* 1995. Religious participation in early adulthood: Age and family life cycle effects on church membership. *American Sociological Review* 60: 84-103.

Tschannen, O. 1992. *Les théories de la sécularisation.* Geneva: Librairie Droz.

Voyé, L. 1995. From institutional Catholicism to "Christian inspiration": Another look at Belgium. In *The post-war generation and establishment religion: Cross-cultural perspectives*, edited by W. C. Roof *et al.*, 191-204. Boulder, CO: Westview Press.

Waege, H. 1997. *Vertogen over de relatie tussen individu en gemeenschap.* Leuven: Acco.

Wallis, R. 1984. *The elementary forms of the new religious life.* London: Routledge and Kegan Paul.

Weber, M. 1920. *Gesammelte Aufsätze zur Religionssoziologie.* I. Tübingen: Mohr.

Wilson, B. R. 1969. *Religion in secular society: A sociological comment.* London: Watts.

————. 1976. Aspects of secularization in the West. *Japanese Journal of Religious Studies* 3: 259-76.

————. 1982. *Religion in sociological perspective.* Oxford: Oxford University Press.

3

Secularization, R.I.P.

Rodney Stark*

University of Washington

From the beginning, social scientists have celebrated the secularization thesis despite the fact that it never was consistent with empirical reality. More than 150 years ago Tocqueville pointed out that "the facts by no means accord with [the secularization] theory," and this lack of accord has grown far worse since then. Indeed, the only shred of credibility for the notion that secularization has been taking place has depended on contrasts between now and a bygone Age of Faith. In this essay I assemble the work of many recent historians who are unanimous that the Age of Faith is pure nostalgia — that lack of religious participation was, if anything, even more widespread in medieval times than now. Next, I demonstrate that there have been no recent religious changes in Christendom that are consistent with the secularization thesis — not even among scientists. I also expand assessment of the secularization doctrine to non-Christian societies showing that not even the highly magical "folk religions" in Asia have shown the slightest declines in response to quite rapid modernization. Final words are offered as secularization is laid to rest.

For nearly three centuries, social scientists and assorted western intellectuals have been promising the end of religion. Each generation has been confident that within another few decades, or possibly a bit longer, humans will "outgrow" belief in the supernatural. This proposition soon came to be known as the secularization thesis, and its earliest proponents seem to have been British, as the Restoration in 1660 led to an era during which militant attacks on faith were quite popular among fashionable Londoners (Durant and Durant 1965). Thus, as far as I am able to discover, it was Thomas Woolston who first set a date by which time modernity would have triumphed over faith. Writing in about 1710, he expressed his confidence that Christianity would be gone by 1900 (Woolston 1733). Half a century later Frederick the Great thought this was much too pessimistic, writing to his friend Voltaire that "the Englishman Woolston . . . could not calculate what has happened quite recently. . . . It [religion] is crumbling of itself, and its fall will be but the more rapid" (in Redman 1949: 26). In response, Voltaire ventured his guess that the end would

* I would like to thank Andrew Greeley, with whom I have long been exchanging citations on the nonexistence of an Age of Faith in European history.

come within the next 50 years. Subsequently, not even widespread press reports concerning the second "Great Awakening" could deter Thomas Jefferson from predicting in 1822 that "there is not a young man now living in the United States who will not die a Unitarian" (Healy 1984: 373). Of course, a generation later, Unitarians were as scarce as ever, while the Methodists and Baptists continued their spectacular rates of growth (Finke and Stark 1992).

Subsequent prophets of secularization have been no less certain, but they have been somewhat more circumspect as to dates. Thus, just as Jefferson's prophesy failed, back in France, Auguste Comte announced that, as a result of modernization, human society was outgrowing the "theological stage" of social evolution and a new age was dawning in which the science of sociology would replace religion as the basis for moral judgments. But, Comte did not say exactly when all this would be accomplished. In similar fashion, as often as Frederich Engels gloated about how the socialist revolution would cause religion to evaporate, he would only say that it would happen "soon." In 1878 Max Müller (p. 218) complained that:

> Every day, every week, every month, every quarter, the most widely read journals seem just now to vie with each other in telling us that the time for religion is past, that faith is a hallucination or an infantile disease, that the gods have at last been found out and exploded.

At the start of the twentieth century, A. E. Crawley (1905: 8) reported that "the opinion is everywhere gaining ground that religion is a mere survival from a primitive . . . age, and its extinction only a matter of time." Several years later, when Max Weber explained why modernization would cause the "disenchantment" of the world, and when Sigmund Freud reassured his disciples that this greatest of all neurotic illusions would die upon the therapist's couch, they too would be no more specific than "soon."

A generation later, however, "soon" became "underway" or "ongoing." For example, the distinguished anthropologist Anthony F. C. Wallace (1966: 264-265) explained to tens of thousands of American undergraduates that "the evolutionary future of religion is extinction," and while he admitted that it might require "several hundred years" to complete the process, it already was well underway in the advanced nations. And throughout his illustrious career, Bryan Wilson (1982: 150-151) has described secularization as "a long term process *occurring* in human society" and pointed out that "the process implicit in the concept of secularization concedes at once the idea of an earlier condition of life that was not secular, or that was at least much less secular than that of our own times."

Then in 1968, in contrast to all of this intellectual pussy-footing, Peter Berger (1968: 3) told the *New York Times* that the by "the 21st century, religious believers are likely to be found only in small sects, huddled together to resist a worldwide secular culture." Unleashing his gift for memorable imagery, Berger said that "the predicament of the believer is increasingly like that of a Tibetan astrologer on a prolonged visit to an American university." In light of the recent lionization of the Dalai Lama by the American media and his cordial welcome to various campuses, Berger's simile now admits to rather a different interpretation. In any event, when his prediction had only three years left to run, Berger gracefully recanted his belief in secularization (as I discuss at the end of this essay). I quote his statements during the 1960s only because they so fully express the mood of the times, a mood that I shared (cf., Stark 1963).

Notice five things about all of these secularization prophesies.

First, there is universal agreement that modernization is the causal engine dragging the gods into retirement. That is, the secularization doctrine has always nestled within the broader theoretical framework of modernization theories, it being proposed that as industrialization, urbanization, and rationalization increase, religiousness *must* decrease (Hadden 1987; Finke 1992). Keep in mind that modernization is a *long, gradual, relatively constant process.* Wars, revolutions, and other calamities may cause an occasional sudden blip in the trend lines, but the overall process is not volatile. If secularization is the result of modernization or, indeed, is one aspect of it, then secularization is not volatile and, rather than proceeding by sudden fits and starts, it too will display a long-term, gradual, and relatively constant trend of religious decline, corresponding to similar upward trends in such aspects of modernization as economic development, urbanization, and education. In terms of time series trends, modernization is a long, linear, upward curve, and secularization is assumed to trace the reciprocal of this curve, to be a long, linear, downward curve. Indeed, since modernization is so advanced in many nations that "postmodernism" is the latest buzzword, it must be assumed that secularization is at least "ongoing" to the extent that a significant downward trend in religiousness can be seen.

The *second* thing to notice about the secularization prophecies is that they are *not* directed primarily toward institutional differentiation — they do not merely predict the separation of church and state or a decline in the direct, secular authority of church leaders. Their primary concern is with *individual piety,* especially *belief.* Thus, Jefferson predicted the next generation would find Christian beliefs, and especially faith in the divinity of Jesus, implausible and would limit themselves to the minimalist conception of God sustained by Unitarians. What most concerned Engels were not bishops, but the religious "fantasies" of the masses. Freud wrote about religious illusions, not about church taxes, and Wallace (1966: 265) asserted that "belief in supernatural powers is doomed to die out, all over the world" because, as Bryan Wilson (1975: 81) explained, "The rational structure of society itself precludes much indulgence in supernaturalist thinking."

This is very significant because in recent years secularization has been defined in several ways (Hanson 1997; Tschannen 1991; Dobbelaere 1987; Shiner 1967) and, unfortunately, this permits some proponents of the thesis to shift definitions as needed in order escape inconvenient facts (cf., Dobbelaere

1987, 1997; Lechner 1991, 1996; Yamane 1997). One definition, often referred to as the macro version (cf., Lechner 1996), identifies secularization as *de-institutionalization* (Dobbelaere 1987; Martin 1978). This refers to a decline in the social power of once-dominant religious institutions whereby other social institutions, especially political and educational institutions, have escaped from prior religious domination.

If this were all that secularization means, there would be nothing to argue about. Everyone must agree that, in contemporary Europe, for example, Catholic bishops have less political power than they once possessed, and the same is true of Lutheran and Anglican bishops (although bishops probably never were nearly so powerful as they now are thought to have been). Nor are primary aspects of public life any longer suffused with religious symbols, rhetoric, or ritual. These changes have, of course, aroused scholarly interest, resulting in some distinguished studies (Casanova 1994; Martin 1978). But, the prophets of secularization theory were not and are not merely writing about something so obvious or limited. At issue is not a narrow prediction concerning a growing separation of church and state. Instead, as we have seen, from the start the prophets of secularization have stressed personal piety, and to the extent that they expressed macro interests it has been to claim that they are so linked that a decline in one necessitates a decline in the other. Thus, if the churches lose power, personal piety will fade; if personal piety fades, the churches will lose power. Indeed, Peter Berger, long the most sophisticated modern proponent of the secularization thesis, was entirely candid on this point. Having outlined the macro aspects of secularization, Berger (1967: 107-108) noted:

> Moreover, it is implied here that the process of secularization has a subjective side as well. As there is a secularization of society and culture, so there is a secularization of consciousness. Put simply, this means that the modern West has produced an increasing number of individuals who look upon the world and their own lives without the benefit of religious interpretations.

As noted, recently Berger (1997) gracefully withdrew his support for the theory of secularization. I cite this passage from his earlier work not to emphasize my previous disagreement with Berger, whose work I always have much admired, but as a contrast to the recent tactic by other proponents of secularization, who seek to evade the growing mountain of contrary evidence by pretending that the theory merely pertains to deinstitutionalization and any trends in personal piety are irrelevant. Let me note Karel Dobbelaere's breathtaking evasion in his article in this issue, "the religiousness of individuals is *not* a valid indicator in evaluating the process of secularization." Such revisionism is not only historically false, it is insincere. Those who employ it revert to celebrating the demise of individual piety whenever they see a fact that seems to be supportive or whenever they believe they are speaking to an audience of fellow devotees. Thus, at a conference in Rome in 1993, Lilliane Voyé and Karel Dobbelaere

(1994: 95) explained that because science is "a thoroughly secular perspective on the world" and has come to dominate the educational curricula, this has resulted in "desacrilizing the content of learning and the world-view of students." Citing earlier essays by Dobbelaere, they went on to claim:

> the successful removal by science of all kinds of anthropomorphisms from our thinking have transformed the traditional concept of "God as a person" into a belief in a life-force, a power of spirit and this has also gradually promoted agnosticism and atheism — which explains the long-term decline of religious practices.

Exactly! That is precisely what the secularization thesis has always been, and Voyé and Dobbelaere's empirical claims, if true, would fully satisfy Woolston's prophesy — albeit a bit late. But, as will be seen, it isn't so. What *is* so, is that secularization predicts a marked decline in the religiousness of the individual.

The *third* thing to notice about the secularization thesis is that, implicit in all versions and explicit in most, is the claim that of all aspects of modernization, it is science that has the most deadly implications for religion. For Comte and Wallace, as for Voyé and Dobbelaere, it is science that will free us from the superstitious fetters of faith. Or, in the odd formulation by Bryan Wilson (1968: 86), "Christianity, with the impact of scientific and social scientific hindsights, has lost general theological plausibility." If this is so, then scientists ought to be expected to be a relatively irreligious lot. But, as will be seen, scientists are about as religious as anyone else, and the presumed incompatibility between religion and science seems mythical.

Fourth, secularization is regarded as an absorbing state — that once achieved it is irreversible, instilling mystical immunity. However, events and trends in eastern Europe and the nations of the former Soviet Union do not support these expectations. Instead, as Andrew Greeley (1994: 272) so aptly put it, after more than 70 years of militant efforts by the state to achieve secularization, "St. Vladimir has routed Karl Marx."

Fifth and finally, while most discussions of secularization focus on Christendom, all leading proponents of the thesis apply it globally. Thus, it is not merely belief in Christ that is "doomed to die out," but, as Wallace explained in the passage quoted above, "belief in supernatural powers," and this is going to happen "all over the world." Hence, Allah is fated to join Jehovah as only "an interesting historical memory." However, no one has bothered to explain this to Muslims, as will be seen.

Now for specifics.

THE MYTH OF RELIGIOUS DECLINE

Many scholars appear to believe that if rates of individual religious belief and participation for most nations of northern and western Europe were graphed, they would be reciprocal to the trends in modernization. Beginning with high levels of faith and practice at the end of the eighteenth century, the master trends are assumed to have been ever downward, culminating in very low current levels of religiousness. And the latter are regarded as but insignificant residuals, soon to disappear too (Wilson 1966, 1982; Bruce 1995; Lechner 1991, 1996). For evidence in support of these claims, we are directed to note a steep decline in church attendance in much of Europe and to infer from this an erosion of individual faith as well, on the grounds that participation is low because of a lack of the beliefs needed to motivate attendance. These views are wrong in all respects.

David Martin (1965) was the first contemporary sociologist to reject the secularization thesis outright, even proposing that the concept of secularization be eliminated from social scientific discourse on the grounds that it had served only ideological and polemical, rather than theoretical, functions and because there was no evidence in favor of any general or consistent "shift from a religious period in human affairs to a secular period" (Martin 1991: 465). And, astounding as it may seem, the secularization thesis has been inconsistent with plain facts from the very start. For example, having noted the popularity of the secularization doctrine among eighteenth-century philosophers, Alexis de Tocqueville then commented:

> Unfortunately, the facts by no means accord with their theory. There are certain populations in Europe whose unbelief is only equalled by their ignorance and debasement; while in America, one of the freest and most enlightened nations in the world, the people fulfill with fervor all the outward duties of religion ([1840] 1956: 319).

In the more than 150 years since Tocqueville made those observations, not only has American religiousness not gone into decline, the rate of church membership actually has more than trebled (Finke and Stark 1992), while other indices of commitment have held steady or have risen modestly (Greeley 1989). Moreover, although the American case continues to offer a devastating challenge to the secularization doctrine, it fails in Europe too. First, there has been *no demonstrable long-term decline in European religious participation!* Granted, participation probably has varied from time to time in response to profound social dislocations such as wars and revolutions, but the far more important point is that religious participation was very low in northern and western Europe many centuries before the onset of modernization.

The second reason to reject claims about the secularization of Europe is that current data do not reveal the arrival of an age of "scientific atheism." *Levels of subjective religiousness remain high* — to classify a nation as highly secularized when the large majority of its inhabitants believe in God is absurd. Indeed, the important question about religion in Europe is, as Grace Davie (1990b: 395) put it, not why do people no longer believe, but why do they "persist in believing but see no need to participate with even minimal regularity in their religious institutions?" Of these two major bases for rejecting claims about the secularization of Europe, the claim that religious participation was never very high in northern and western Europe is the one that must strike most readers as dubious.

THE MYTH OF PAST PIETY

Everyone "knows" that once upon a time the world was pious — that in olden days most people exhibited levels of religious practice and concern that today linger only in isolated social subcultures such as the Amish, ultra-orthodox Jews, or Muslim fundamentalists. But, like so many once-upon-a-time tales, this conception of a pious past is mere nostalgia; most prominent historians of medieval religion now agree that there never was an "Age of Faith" (Morris 1993; Duffy 1992; Sommerville 1992; Bossy 1985; Obelkevich 1979; Murray 1972; Thomas 1971; Coulton 1938). Writing in the eleventh century, the English monk William of Malmesbury complained that the aristocracy rarely attended church and even the more pious among them "attended" mass at home, in bed:

> They didn't go to church in the mornings in a Christian fashion; but in their bedchambers, lying in the arms of their wives, they did but taste with their ears the solemnities of the morning mass rushed through by a priest in a hurry (in Fletcher 1997: 476).

As for the ordinary people, during the middle ages and during the Renaissance, the masses rarely entered a church, and their private worship was directed toward an array of spirits and supernatural agencies, only some of them recognizably Christian (Gentilecore 1992; Schneider 1990; Delumeau 1977; Thomas 1971). Alexander Murray's assessment of medieval Italian religious life is typical: "substantial sections of thirteenth-century society hardly attended church at all." The Dominican prior Humbert of Romans in his handbook *On the Teaching of Preachers*, Murray notes, advised his friars that "reaching the laity involves catching them at markets and tournaments, in ships, and so on," which Murray interprets as "a fair enough sign that they were not to be caught in churches." Indeed, Humbert frankly acknowledged that the masses "rarely go to church, and [when they do attend] rarely to sermons; so they know little of what pertains to their salvation." Finally, Humbert admitted that the regular clergy were so involved in gambling, pleasure, and "worse things," that they too "scarcely come to church." In similar terms, Blessed Giordano of Rivalto reported that, upon arriving in Florence to preach, he suggested to a local woman that she take her daughter to church at least on feast days, only to be informed that "It is not the custom" (Murray 1972: 92-94). The anonymous English author of *Dives and Pauper* ([circa 1410] 1976: 189) complained that "the people these days . . . are loath to hear God's Service. [And when they must attend] they come late and leave early. They would rather go to a tavern than to

Holy Church."[1] In about 1430, St. Antonino (in Coulton 1938: 192) wrote that Tuscan peasants seldom attend mass and that "very many of them do not confess once a year, and far fewer are those who take communion. . . . They use enchantments for themselves and for their beasts . . . being ignorant, and caring little for their own souls or for keeping God's commandments, which they know not." Antonino went on to blame most of this on "the carelessness and evil conscience of their parish priests."

In further support of these reports, an extensive survey of surviving parish churches in various parts of Europe reveals them to be too small to have held more than a tiny fraction of local inhabitants (Brooke and Brooke 1984). Indeed, it wasn't until the late middle ages that there even were more than a few parish churches outside of the cities and larger towns (not counting the private chapels maintained for the local nobility), at a time when nearly everyone lived in rural areas (Morris 1993). Moreover, as Eamon Duffy noted, a large percentage of what rural parishes did exist lacked a pastor much of the time. He estimated that during the sixteenth century, for example, at least 25 percent of the parishes in the Diocese of Strasbourg and up to 80 percent in the Diocese of Geneva had no clergy. To make matters worse, even where there was an assigned pastor, "Absenteeism was rife" (Duffy 1987: 88). The bishop's visitation of 192 parishes in Oxfordshire during 1520 found 58 absentees (Coulton 1938: 156). Indeed, P.H. Sawyer (1982: 139) noted that in northern Europe "Bishops who never visited their sees were not unknown." Indeed, many such dioceses were given to papal protégés without any obligation to reside (Coulton 1938).

That religious participation was lacking even in the cities is not very surprising when we realize that going to church in, say, the fifteenth century, required the average person to stand in an unheated building to hear a service which was conducted entirely in incomprehensible Latin by priests who may indeed not have been speaking Latin at all, but many of whom were simply mumbling nonsense syllables. The Venerable Bede ([730] 1955: 340) advised the future bishop Egbert that because so few English priests and monks knew any Latin "I have frequently offered translations of both the [Apostle's] Creed and the Lord's Prayer into English to many unlearned priests." In 1222 the Council of Oxford described the parish clergy as "dumb dogs" (Coulton 1938: 157). Almost a thousand years after Bede's efforts to teach clergy at least the Lord's Prayer, nothing had changed. William Tyndale noted in 1530 that hardly any of the priests and curates in England knew the Lord's Prayer or could translate it into English. This was confirmed when in 1551 the Bishop of Gloucester systematically tested his diocesan clergy. Of 311 pastors, 171 could not repeat the Ten Commandments and 27 did not know the author of the Lord's Prayer (Thomas 1971: 164). Indeed, the next year Bishop Hooper found "scores of

---

[1] My translation from Middle English.

parish clergy who could not tell who was the author of the Lord's Prayer, or where it was to be found" (Coulton 1938: 158). Across the channel, St. Vincent de Paul discovered in 1617 that his local priest knew no Latin, not even the words of absolution (Delumeau 1977). Similarly, in 1547 Archbishop Giovanni Bovio, of the Brindisi-Oria diocese in southern Italy, found that most of his priests "could barely read and could not understand Latin" (Gentilcore 1992: 42).

Clerical ignorance is not surprising when we recognize that "there were virtually no seminaries" and therefore most priests "learned rubrics" and a "smattering of Latin" as an apprentice to "a priest who had himself had little or no training." In the fifteenth century, St. Bernardino of Siena observed a priest "who knew only the Hail Mary, and used it even at the elevation of the Mass" (Duffy 1987: 88). Eamon Duffy (1992) has effectively demonstrated the ignorance of the parish clergy from the contents of the very first "primers" for clergy that began to be distributed in the fourteenth and fifteenth centuries. That booklets, most of them written in the local language rather than in Latin and prepared for those who already were serving as clergy, were limited to the most elementary aspects of doctrine and practice — for example, simple lists of the sacraments and of the sins that should be confessed — shows that church officials thought most serving clergy knew considerably less than a modern 10-year-old attending parochial school.

Given such clerical ignorance, it is no wonder that the masses knew next to nothing in terms of basic Christian culture. The Lateran Council of 1215, in addition to requiring all Catholics to confess and to take communion at least once a year during the Easter season, proposed that a massive campaign of elementary religious instruction of the laity be undertaken. Thus, at the Council of Lambeth in 1281, the English bishops responded by adopting the *aim* of teaching the laity the Lord's Prayer, Hail Mary, and the Apostle's Creed. Later this was expanded to include the Ten Commandments, the Seven Works of Mercy, the Seven Sacraments, and the Seven Deadly Sins (Duffy 1992). Similar plans to catechize the laity were adopted throughout Europe. Despite these very modest goals, it seems unlikely that many of the laity, other than members of the educated elite, ever mastered these simple lessons — since so many priests did not. As Colin Morris (1993: 232) put it, "Ignorance of the formal content of faith was general." Morris then recounted an instance of a village priest who managed to teach many in his congregation to recite the "Our Father" in Latin, noting that they had not the slightest idea of what it meant (possibly the priest didn't either). Other examples come from investigations of scores of incidents involving religious apparitions (mostly of Mary) in Spain during the fourteenth and fifteenth centuries. These hearings revealed that most parishioners reporting such visions were ignorant of the Ten Commandments and the Seven Deadly Sins. It wasn't merely that they could not recite them, but that they were entirely ignorant of their contents. A typical instance involved a man who claimed frequent visions of Mary and who, during an interrogation in 1518, was asked if he knew the Ten Commandments and the Seven Deadly Sins. "He said he did not know any of these in whole or in part. . . . He was asked if pride or envy or lust or killing a man or insulting someone with offensive words was a sin, to each of these he replied that he did not know. He was asked if theft was a sin, and he said that, God preserve us, theft was a very great sin" (in Christian 1981: 154).

It must be noted too, that even when people back then did go to church they often did so unwillingly and behaved very inappropriately while there. The eminent historian Keith Thomas not only noted that in late medieval times "it is problematical as to whether certain sections of the population [of Britain] at this time had any religion at all," but "that many of those who did [go to church] went with considerable reluctance." When the common people did show up in church, often under compulsion, they so misbehaved "as to turn the service into a travesty of what was intended" according to Thomas. Presentations before ecclesiastical courts and scores of clerical memoirs report how "Members of the population jostled for pews, nudged their neighbours, hawked and spat, knitted, made coarse remarks, told jokes, fell asleep, and even let off guns." Church records tell of a man in Cambridgeshire who was charged with misbehaving in church in 1598 after his "most loathsome farting, striking, and scoffing speeches" had resulted in "the great offence of the good and the great rejoicing of the bad" (Thomas 1971: 159-162). A man who issued loathsome farts in church today surely would not draw cheers from part of the congregation in any British church, even if he accompanied his efforts with scoffing speeches.

An additional sign of the times was that people often did gather regularly and eagerly within churches, but to conduct entirely unreligious activities. The Archbishop of Florence denounced the Tuscan peasants of his diocese because "in the churches themselves they sometimes dance and leap and sing with women" (in Coulton 1938: 193). Indeed, through the centuries there was a constant flow of complaints and threats directed toward local parishes, and, often enough even toward those in charge of cathedrals, to cease using them primarily for indoor marketplaces and for storage of crops and sheltering livestock. For example, between 1229 and 1367 in England alone there were eleven episcopal "fulminat(tions) against holding markets . . . in churches" (Coulton 1938: 189).

Summing up his survey of popular religion in thirteenth-century Italy, Alexander Murray (1972: 83) disputed "the notion of an Age of Faith." Instead, he pointed out (1972: 106), 'The friars [of that era] were not typical figures in a freakish age, but, morally, freakish figures in a typical age. Their mendicant life was a lasting wonder to contemporaries. They were a small minority: 'Virgins are few, martyrs are few, preachers are few,' said Fra Giordano."

To be sure, there were periodic explosions of mass religious enthusiasm in medieval times as new sectarian movements — including the Waldensians and the Albigensians — attracted large followings (Lambert 1992). However, as I have clarified elsewhere, such outbursts are not to be expected where conventional religious organizations are strong, but only where religious apathy and alienation are widespread (Stark 1996a, 1996b). That is, religious rebellions during medieval times offer additional testimony against images of widespread involvement in *organized* religion.

As Europe passed out of medieval times, religious participation seems not to have improved — however, the statistics on religious behavior do. Some of the best of these can be found in the reports written by various Anglican bishops and archbishops following lengthy visitation trips to their parishes. Thus the Oxford diocesan visitations report that 30 parishes in Oxfordshire drew a *combined total* of 911 communicants in 1738, based on the four "Great Festivals" — Easter, Ascension, Whitsun, and Christmas. This turnout amounted to far less than five percent of the total population of these parishes taking communion during a given year. Other visitation reports yield similarly low rates of participation in communion over the remainder of the eighteenth century (Currie *et al.* 1977). Indeed, Peter Laslett (1965) reported that only 125 of 400 adults in a particular English village took Easter communion late in the eighteenth century and went on to note "much smaller attendances" in other villages. Incredibly, Laslett uses these data to demonstrate the *unanimity of faith* in this era — the title of his book is *The world we have lost.*[2] Were these twentieth-century statistics, they would be cited routinely as proof of massive secularization.

If we use 1800 as the benchmark, then church membership in Britain is substantially higher today. In 1800, only 12 percent of the British population belonged to a specific religious congregation. This rose to 17 percent in 1850 and then stabilized — the same percentage belonged in 1990 (Stark and Iannaccone 1995). In his remarkable reconstruction of religious participation in the British communities of Oldham and Saddleworth, Mark Smith (1996) found there had been no change between 1740 and 1865 — a period of intensive industrialization. As will be noted, Laurence Iannaccone (1996) has reconstructed a time series that does show a modest decline in church attendance in Britain during the twentieth century. This finding is offset both by the lack of similar declines in most other European nations, as well as by studies suggesting recent increases in church participation in lower-class, British urban neighborhoods, which had long been notable for their very low rates of attendance (G. Smith 1996). The "market" theory of religiousness developed in my earlier publications (Stark 1985, 1998b; Stark and Iannaccone 1993, 1994; Finke and Stark 1988, 1992) is compatible with religious *variation*: with increases as well as decreases in religiousness, indeed its usual prediction is for relatively stable levels

---

[2] He also wrote (p.7) that "All our ancestors were literal Christian believers, all of the time."

of religious commitment in societies. In contrast, the secularization thesis is incompatible with either stability or increase: it requires a *general, long-term pattern of religious decline*. It makes no provision for reports such as that of Gabriel La Bras (1963) that French Catholics today participate more willingly and frequently, with far greater comprehension of what they are doing, than was the case 200 years ago.

The evidence is clear that claims about a major decline in religious participation in Europe are based in part on very exaggerated perceptions of past religiousness. Participation may be low today in many nations, but not because of modernization; therefore the secularization thesis is irrelevant. But, what about *very* recent times, maybe the secularization theorists simply were premature in their predictions? As mentioned, Laurence Iannaccone (1996) has been able to use survey data to reconstruct church attendance rates for 18 nations (most of them European) beginning in 1920. In 15 of the 18 nations Iannaccone could detect no trends even vaguely consistent with the secularization thesis: only in East Germany, Slovenia, and Great Britain did he observe downward trends that could possibly be claimed as support for secularization, and the British trend may already have been reversed, while the declines in Slovenia and East Germany began with the imposition of Communist regimes.

Little wonder, then, that historians have long expressed dismay at "un-historically minded sociologists" for clinging to the myth of Europe's lost piety, complaining that "not enough justice has been done to the volume of apathy, heterodoxy, and agnosticism that existed long before the onset of industrialization" (Thomas 1971: 173). For, as Andrew Greeley (1995: 63) put it so crisply, "There could be no de-Christianization of Europe . . . because there never was any Christianization in the first place. Christian Europe never existed."

THE FAILURE TO CHRISTIANIZE

This raises a most significant question: Why wasn't the Christianization of Europe accomplished? At the start of the fourth century Christianity was an immense *mass* movement sweeping over the Roman Empire, and by the middle of the century a majority of the population probably had been converted (Stark 1996a). What happened then? The failure of the early church to Christianize the outer reaches of the empire and the rest of Europe is entirely in keeping with the market model of religiousness (Stark 1985; Stark and Iannaccone 1994; Stark 1998b). The Christianity that triumphed over Rome was a mass social movement in a highly competitive environment. The Christianity that subsequently left most of Europe only nominally converted, at best, was an established, subsidized, state church that sought to extend itself, not through missionizing the population, but by baptizing kings (Davies 1996: 275) and then canonizing them as national saints (Vauchez 1997). That is, the Christianity that prevailed in Europe was an elaborate patchwork of state churches that settled for the allegiance of the elite and for imposing official requirements for conformity, but that made little sustained effort to Christianize the peasant masses (Duffy 1987; Greeley 1995). Thus, it isn't merely that the state churches of Scandinavia and northern Europe currently lack the motivation and energy to fill their churches, they have *always been like this*. The "Christianization" of a Norse kingdom, for example, often involved little more than the baptism of the nobility and legal recognition of the ecclesiastical sovereignty of the church. This left the task of missionizing the masses to a "kept" clergy whose welfare was almost entirely independent of mass assent or support, with a predictable lack of results.

Indeed, corruption and sloth, as well as power struggles and enforced conformity, became prominent features of the Christian movement in the fourth century, almost immediately upon its having become the official state church (Johnson 1976). Contrary to received wisdom, the conversion of Constantine did not cause the triumph of Christianity. Rather, it was the first and most significant step in slowing its progress, draining its vigor, and distorting its moral vision. Most of the evils associated with European Christianity since the middle of the fourth century can be traced to establishment.

The "conversion" of Scandinavia is instructive. Denmark was the first "Christian" nation in the north, as a succession of kings accepted, rejected, or were indifferent to Christianity, culminating in the ascension of the devout Christian, Knut the Great, in 1016 (Sawyer 1982; Roesdahl 1980; Jones 1968; Brøndsted 1965). This now is regarded as the "official" date of the Christianization of Denmark. However, most historians do not equate this with the Christianization of the Danish people, writing instead that this followed only "gradually" (Brøndsted 1965: 310) and noting that the conversions of the monarchs were "[n]ever the result of popular demand" (Sawyer 1982: 139).

Next came the "Christianization" of Norway. Olaf Tryggvason, an English-educated, Christian convert, seized the throne of Norway in 995 whereupon he attempted to covert the country by force, killing some who resisted and burning their estates. These and other repressive measures aroused sufficient opposition to defeat him in the Battle of Svolder (about the year 1000) during which he died. Fifteen years later, Olaf Haraldsson, who had been baptized in France, conquered Norway, and he too used fire and sword in an effort to compel Christianization. And he too provoked widespread hatred leading to rebellion, and was driven into exile. When he attempted to return leading a new army raised in Kiev, he was defeated and killed at the Battle of Stikklestad in 1030. Despite this, he soon was canonized as St. Olaf and is credited with the Christianization of Norway, which seems to have consisted primarily of the reimposition of Olaf's official policies of intolerance (Sawyer 1982; Jones 1968).

The conversion of Iceland followed a somewhat similar pattern as both

Norwegian Olafs successively extended their efforts at forced conversion upon their colony. At a meeting of the Althing in 1000 the Icelanders yielded to Norwegian pressure by adopting the law "that all people should become Christian and those who here in the land were yet unbaptized should be baptized." *But*, the law read on: "people might sacrifice to the old gods in private" (Byock 1988:142). Although paganism subsequently was outlawed, aspects of paganism still linger among Icelanders, and their Christianization never resulted in more than the most minimal participation in the church.

The Swedish court remained pagan into the twelfth century, and Finland remained officially pagan until the thirteenth (Sawyer 1982; Brøndsted 1965). It seems revealing as to the lack of effort to Christianize the general population that no missionaries were even sent to the Lapps until the middle of the sixteenth century (Baldwin 1900). In reality, it is not clear when popular paganism actually began to wane in Scandinavia and, as in the case of Iceland, there is reason to suppose it never did entirely disappear (Sawyer and Sawyer 1993). The famous Christian missionary to Scandinavia, Adam of Bremen, wrote at length of ceremonies (including human sacrifices) conducted in the luxurious pagan temple of Uppsala (Sweden) during the eleventh century (Jones 1968; Brøndsted 1965). Indeed, it seems to have been typical for the Norse to "convert" by including Christ and various Christian saints (especially Olaf) into the pagan pantheon. Thus, it was written in the Icelandic *Landnámabók* that Helgi the Lean "was very mixed in his faith; he believed in Christ, but invoked Thor in matters of seafaring and dire necesssity" (in Brøndsted 1965: 306). Johannes Brøndsted (1965: 307) noted that "a change of gods at the summit of society might occur easily enough; but lower down on the scale there was a natural resistance." Indeed, Brøndsted suggests that the conversion of Scandinavia occurred "only . . . when Christianity took over old [pagan] superstitions and useages and allowed them to live under a new guise." Thus, the popular Christianity that eventually emerged was a strange amalgam, including a great deal in the way of pagan traditions and celebrations, some of them only thinly Christianized (Davies 1996). Consequently, as Andrew Greeley (1996: 66) has pointed out, Christian commitment was never deep enough in northern Europe to generate much mass attendance, nor "deep enough to survive changes in the religious affiliation of their political leaders during the Reformation, sometimes back and forth across denominational lines."

Both of Greeley's points are easily demonstrated quantitatively. I began with the 16 nations of western Europe.[3] For each, I calculated the number of centuries since their supposed Christianization (20 minus the century), with

---

[3] (Century of supposed Christianization) Austria (9), Belgium (7), Denmark (11), Finland (13), France (6), Germany (9), Great Britain (9), Iceland (11), Ireland (5), Italy (4), Netherlands (8), Norway (11), Portugal (4), Spain (4), Sweden (12), and Switzerland (8).

values ranging from 16 for Italy down to 7 for Finland (Davies 1996; Barrett 1982; Sawyer 1982; Roesdahl 1980; Shepherd 1980; Jones 1968; Brøndsted 1965). This variable is based on the assumption that the more recent the Christianization, the more superficial. Turning to the 1990-1991 World Values Surveys, I created a variable based on the rate of church attendance. As would be predicted, the duration of Christianization is extremely highly correlated with contemporary rates of church attendance (.72). In similar fashion, the most plausible measure of participation in the Reformation (since some of these modern nations include many areas that were independent states in the sixteenth century) is the percent Catholic, which I took from the 1996 *Catholic Almanac*. Again, as predicted, this variable is very highly correlated (.89) with the duration of Christianization.

SUBJECTIVE RELIGIOUSNESS

Steve Bruce of the University of Aberdeen has long been one of the most die-hard proponents of the secularization thesis. Recently, even he admitted that, in terms of organized participation, the Golden Age of Faith never existed. Indeed, Bruce (1997: 674) proposes that the medieval church was not even especially concerned to bring the people to mass as "was clear from the very architecture of churches and forms of service." But, rather than giving up on the secularization thesis, Bruce now claims that the Golden Age of medieval religiousness was subjective, that people strongly embraced supernatural beliefs, Christian or otherwise. Put another way, Bruce now claims that even if the medieval masses seldom went to church, most people in this era still must be regarded as religious because they believed. I agree. Certainly most people in medieval times seem to have held religious beliefs, even if these were somewhat vague and included as much magic and animism as Christianity, and thus through belief, if not through practice, these were *religious* societies (cf., Duffy 1992), keeping in mind that a substantial proportion of medieval populations did not take their religious beliefs very seriously. Nor must we forget that a significant number, probably about the same as today, rejected religious beliefs. As Franklin Baumer (1960: 99) put it, "Contrary to popular supposition there was plenty of scepticism in the Middle Ages, and some of it was quite radical." Judging from the prevalence of blasphemous graffiti on the walls of Pompeii, the same must be said of the Greco-Roman era (MacMullen 1981; Stark 1996a).

Nevertheless, I too assume that belief was widespread, and I interpret the prevalence of religious beliefs as representing a *potential demand* for organized religion in these societies — a potential in the sense that it awaited activation by such aggressive suppliers as the Waldensians. However, rather than restoring a benchmark of past piety against which to demonstrate the secularization of modern-day Europe, the same observation applies with equal force *today*. That is, while rates of religious participation are far lower in Europe than in the United

States, differences are small when comparisons are based on subjective measures of faith (Stark and Iannaccone 1994; Stark 1998a).

My colleagues and I are hardly the first to notice this phenomenon. There is a substantial British research literature on what Grace Davie (1990a, 1990b, 1994) refers to as "believing without belonging." In a recent addition to this literature, Michael Winter and Christopher Short (1993: 635, 648) summed up: "What is clear is that most surveys of religious belief in northern Europe demonstrate continuing high levels of belief in God and some of the more general tenets of the Christian faith but rather low levels of church attendance." They add that their research has "revealed a relatively, and perhaps surprisingly, low level of secularization" — and perhaps for that reason their work has not been much cited by other European social scientists. But it is true, nonetheless: subjective religiousness remains high in the nations most often cited as examples of secularization, places where it is claimed that people have outgrown religion for good. It seems useful to examine one case in greater detail.

Because Iceland has been proposed as the first fully (or nearly fully) secularized nation on earth (cf., Tomasson 1980), it seems an appropriate test case. The claim that Iceland is extremely secularized is taken as self-evident on the basis of its empty churches — about 2 percent attend weekly. Nevertheless, on the basis of extensive fieldwork, William Swatos (1984) reported high levels of in-the-home religion in Iceland today, high rates of baptism, that nearly all weddings occur in church, and that "affirmations of personal immortality are typical" in newspaper obituaries, which usually are written by a close friend of the deceased rather than by a newswriter. It is hardly surprising, therefore, that the 1990 World Values Surveys report that 81 percent of Icelanders express confidence that there is life after death, 88 percent say they believe humans have a soul, and 40 percent believe in reincarnation. And when asked "How often do you pray to God outside of religious services?" 82 percent said they prayed sometimes, and one of four said they did so "often." Moreover, only 2.4 percent of the population of Iceland say they are "convinced atheists." Surely this is not what usually is meant by a "secularized society." Moreover, that 4 in 10 believe in reincarnation serves to remind us that the secularization theory never has been limited to Christianity; *all* beliefs in the supernatural are pertinent and even a massive shift from belief in Jesus to the worship of the goddess Kali would not constitute secularization. It is worth noting, therefore, that spiritualism also is extremely widespread in Iceland, popular even among leading intellectuals and academics (Swatos and Gissurarson 1997). In light of these data, claims that Iceland is the first secularized nation seem as fatuous as do the claims, once so popular among western leftists, that true Communism was being achieved in China under Mao's leadership.

RELIGION AND SCIENCE

If secularization is to show up anywhere it *must* show up among scientists! In an earlier study, my colleagues and I examined evidence that the conflict between religion and science is largely fictional and that scientists are not notably irreligious, being as likely to attend church as is the general public. Even more revealing is the fact that among American academics, the proportion who regard themselves as religious is higher the more scientific their field. For example, physical and natural scientists, including mathematicians, are more than twice as likely to identify themselves as "a religious person" as are anthropologists and psychologists (Stark *et al.* 1996, 1998). But, aren't some scientists militant atheists who write books to discredit religion — Richard Dawkins and Carl Sagan, for example? Of course. But, it also is worth note that most of those, like Dawkins and Sagan, are marginal to the scientific community for lack of significant scientific work. And possibly even more important is the fact that theologians (cf., Cupitt 1997) and professors of religious studies (cf., Mack 1996) are a far more prolific source of popular works of atheism.

Recently, quite amazing time series data on the beliefs of scientists were published in *Nature*. In 1914 the American psychologist James Lueba sent questionnaires to a random sample of persons listed in *American Men of Science*. Each was asked to select one of the following statements "concerning belief in God" (all italics in the original):

1. I believe in a God to whom one may pray in the expectation of receiving an answer. By *"answer," I mean more than the subjective, psychological effect of prayer.*
2. I do not believe in God *as defined above.*
3. I have no definite belief regarding this question.

Leuba's standard for belief in God is so stringent it would exclude a substantial portion of "mainline" *clergy.*[4] It obviously was an intentional ploy on his part. He wanted to show that men of science were irreligious. To his dismay, Leuba found that 41.8 percent of his sample of prominent scientists selected option one, thereby taking a position that many would regard as "fundamentalist." Another 41.5 percent selected the second option (many of whom, as Leuba acknowledged, no doubt believed in a somewhat less active deity), and 16.7 percent took the indefinite alternative. Clearly, these results were not what Leuba had expected and hoped. So he gave great emphasis to the fact that, as measured, believers were not in the majority and went on to express his faith in

---

[4] In a 1968 sample of Protestant clergy in California, only 45 percent of pastors of the United Church of Christ could agree "I know God really exists and I have no doubts about it" (Stark *et al.* 1971). Of Methodist clergy, 52 percent agreed. Notice that this item is much less stringent than the one used by Leuba since clergy were free to define God as they wished. Given that the majority of these same clergy doubted the divinity of Jesus, one must suppose that many of them asserted their beliefs in a rather remote and vague conception of God, not one who hears and answers prayers.

the future, claiming that these data demonstrated a rejection of "fundamental dogmas — a rejection apparently destined to extend parallel with the diffusion of knowledge" (1916: 280).

In 1996 Edward J. Larson and Larry Witham (1997) replicated Leuba's study exactly. They found that nowadays 39.3 percent of eminent scientists selected option one, which is not significantly different from the 41.8 percent who did so in 1914. This time 45.3 percent chose option two, and 14.5 percent took option three. Thus, over an 82-year period, there has been no decline in a very literal belief in God among scientists. Secularization, indeed!

EASTERN REVIVALS

The collapse of Soviet Communism had many remarkable consequences, not the least of which was to reveal the abject failure of several generations of dedicated efforts to indoctrinate atheism in eastern Europe and the former Soviet Union. As Andrew Greeley (1994: 253) put it, "Never before in human history has there been such a concerted effort to stamp out not merely *a* religion, but all trace of religion. . . . Atheistic Communism thought of itself as pushing forward the inevitable process of secularization in which religion would disappear from the face of the earth — a process which, in perhaps milder form, is an article of faith for many dogmatic social scientists."

And the results? Atheists are few, not more prevalent than in western Europe or, indeed, in the United States. In most of these countries the majority pray, and by 1990 church attendance already had recovered to levels comparable to western Europe. Moreover, church attendance continues to rise, as do other forms of religiousness. In Hungary, for example, monthly church attendance rose from 16 percent in 1981 to 25 percent in 1991, while the percent attending less than once a year fell from 62 percent to 44 percent. Meanwhile, the percent of Hungarians who said they were "convinced atheists" fell from 14 to 4. In Russia, 53 percent of respondents said they were not religious in 1991. In only five years this fell to 37 percent.

By any measure, major religious revivals are underway during these early days of the post-Communist era in the old Soviet bloc. This seems to have taken most social scientists entirely by surprise (as have *all* recent signs of religious vitality). As Mary Douglas pointed out as long ago as 1982:

> No one, however, foresaw the recent revivals of traditional religious forms. . . . According to an extensive literature, religious change in modern times happens in only two ways — the falling off of traditional Christian churches [or whatever the traditional religious expressions of a society], and the appearance of new cults, not expected to endure. No one credited the traditional religions with enough vitality to inspire large-scale political revolt . . . the explicitly Catholic uprising in Poland, which evokes deep Western admiration, was as unpredicted as the rise of the fundamentalist churches in America.

It would be needlessly vindictive for me to quote various social scientists who once were certain that "enlightened" educators in "socialist" nations were "freeing children" from the grip of superstition and launching a new era of permanent secularity. But, my will-power does not go so far as to prevent a bit of crowing, hence I quote a paper I initially presented at a conference in 1979:

> [S]ecular states cannot root out religion, and . . . to the extent that they try to root it out, they will be vulnerable to religious opposition. . . . Lenin's body may be displayed under glass, but no one supposes that he has ascended to sit on the right hand, or even the left hand, of Marx. And, dams along the Volga do not light up the meaning of the universe. Moreover, repressive states seem to increase levels of individual deprivation and, in so doing, to fuel the religious impulse. In making faith more costly, they also make it more necessary and valuable. Perhaps religion is never so robust as when it is an underground church (Stark 1981: 175).

And so it was.

ISLAM

The evidence examined thus far has been limited to Christian nations. Now let us shift to religious trends in Islam. In extraordinary contradiction to the secularization doctrine, there seems to be a profound *compatibility* of the Islamic faith and modernization — several studies from quite different parts of the world suggest that Muslim commitment *increases* with modernization!

In a study of Muslims in Java, Joseph Tamney (1979, 1980) found that religious commitment was positively correlated with education and with occupational prestige. That is, people who had attended college and/or held high status occupations were substantially more likely to pray the required five times a day, to give alms, and to fast in accord with orthodox Islamic practice than were Muslims with little education and/or low status occupations. Tamney also recognized that his findings implied that Muslim practice would increase as modernization proceeded. In a subsequent work, Tamney (1992) has analyzed the "resilience" of religion, how it has been able to adjust to challenges of modernity.

A study of the leading Muslim "fundamentalist" movement in Pakistan found that the leaders are highly educated (all having advanced degrees), and supporters of the movement are drawn overwhelmingly from "the new middle class" (Ahmad 1991). This is confirmed by data on Turkish students based on an actual time series. Since 1978 there has been a remarkable *increase* in the proportion of students at the University of Ankara who hold orthodox Islamic beliefs, and in 1991 the overwhelming majority of students held these views. Thus, in 1978, 36 percent of students expressed firm belief that "there is a Heaven and a Hell," while in 1991 three-fourths held this view. As Kayhan Mutlu (1996: 355) explained, faith in "the essential elements of Islamic beliefs is becoming widespread among the university students i.e., the prospective elites, in Ankara." These students are the future political and intellectual leaders of the nation, including its future scientists and engineers. Moreover, Turkey is, by most measures, the most modernized of Islamic nations and, beginning in the 1920s, experienced decades of official state secularity and semi-official irreligion, although these policies have waned in recent times (for reasons entirely clear in the data).

Of course, these Islamic data are fragmentary. On the other hand, no informed observer even needs data such as these to detect the thunderous vitality of contemporary Islam and to realize that it is in direct proportion to modernization.

ASIAN "FOLK" RELIGIONS

Following World War II, all observers expected rapid and profound religious changes in Asian religions, especially in Japan and in the rapidly westernizing Chinese enclaves, such as in Taiwan, Hong Kong, and Malaysia. More specifically, it was assumed that the traditional, and highly magical, "folk" religions found in these settings would rapidly give way to modernity (Chen 1995; Tan 1994). Summing up the scholarly consensus, John Nelson (1992: 77) noted that "Shinto religious practices would seem a highly likely candidate for extinction within Japan's high-tech consumer society." But, that's not what happened. In Taiwan today, there are proportionately more folk temples than there were a century ago, and a larger proportion of the population (about 70 percent) frequent these temples than ever before (Chen 1995). In Hong Kong, traditional Chinese folk religion also flourishes, with the Temple of Wong Tai Sin, "a refugee god" imported from China in 1915, having the largest following (Lang and Ragvald 1993). In Malaysia, the Chinese folk religion "continues to thrive" (Tan 1994: 274). Meanwhile, in Japan, Shinto is very vigorous (Nelson 1992). In all four contexts an "old fashioned," traditional faith has proved so adaptable as to come to be seen as *especially suitable* for modern life. That is, folk religion does not linger among elderly, uneducated peasants, but flourishes among the young, successful, educated urbanites (Chen 1995; Tan 1994; Lang and Ragvold 1993; Nelson 1992). Consequently, in Japan "it is commonplace that new cars be blessed at a [Shinto] shrine, that new residences, offices, or factories be built after exorcism ceremonies purify and calm the land and its deity, that children are dedicated there" (Nelson 1992: 77). Indeed, Shinto rituals seem to play a more prominent role in Japan today than in the pre-World War II days, back when the Emperor was thought to be divine and Shinto was the state religion. That Shinto was strengthened by being disestablished is entirely in accord with the market theory of religion.

WHAT ABOUT CHANGE?

Recently I spoke to a group of Christian historians, some of whom found it very difficult to accept that secularization is not far along. One mentioned that religiousness rose precipitously in Germany in the latter half of the nineteenth century only to fall substantially in the twentieth. Another went on at length about doctrinal changes over the past several centuries, and another chided me for failing to see secularization in the decline in belief in witchcraft. I had some difficulty in seeing how some of this related to the secularization thesis until I realized that these remarks came from people who somehow believed that this article proposes that there is no such thing as religious *change!* Of course, religion changes. Of course, there is more religious participation and even greater belief in the supernatural at some times and places than in others, just as religious organizations have more secular power in some times and places than in others. Of course, doctrines change — Aquinas was not Augustine, and both would find heresy in the work of Avery Dulles. But change does not equate with decline! If next year everyone in Canada became a pious Hindu this could have many interpretations, but secularization would not be among them. Indeed, what is needed is a body of theory to explain religious *variation*, to tell us when and why various aspects of religiousness rise and fall, or are stable (Stark 1998b). In that regard, the secularization theory is as useless as a hotel elevator that only goes down.

CONCLUSION

Let me emphasize that no one can *prove* that one day religion will not wither away. Perhaps the day will come when religion has been relegated to memory and museums. If so, however, this will not have been caused by modernization, and the demise of faith will bear no resemblance to the process postulated by the secularization doctrine. Therefore, once and for all, let us declare an end to social scientific faith in the theory of secularization, recognizing that it was the product of wishful thinking. As a requiem, I offer final remarks by three distinguished scholars: an anthropologist, then a medieval historian, and finally by a sociologist.

Mary Douglas (1982: 29) has argued forcefully and persuasively against the secularization doctrine as having "been constructed to flatter prejudged ideas" which will need to be discarded "when religious sociology modernizes." It simply is not true, Douglas notes, that modern life contrasts sharply with life in simple societies when it comes to the prevalence of religious belief. With Clifford Geertz (1966), she recognizes that unbelief is not uncommon in pre-literate societies or, indeed, in Old Testament times:

> Uncritical nostalgia for past ages of faith being out of place in religious studies, let us note at once that there is no good evidence that a high level of spirituality had generally been reached by the mass of mankind in past times. . . . Nor does [anthropology] teach that modern times show a decline from ancient standards of piety.

Alexander Murray (1972: 106), having demonstrated that the original sources are nearly unanimous in their admission of widespread irreligiousness in medieval times, then asked whence came the notion of the Age of Faith. He concluded:

> The scientific enlightenment was tempted to conceive faith not as a virtue, but as an original sin, from which the Messiah of knowledge came to rescue it. It follows from that view that, in the olden days, men must have believed all the Church told them. This paper has tried to shake the historical part of that conception.

And finally, Peter Berger (1997: 974):

> I think what I and most other sociologists of religion wrote in the 1960s about secularization was a mistake. Our underlying argument was that secularization and modernity go hand in hand. With more modernization comes more secularization. It wasn't a crazy theory. There was some evidence for it. But I think it's basically wrong. Most of the world today is certainly not secular. It's very religious.

After nearly three centuries of utterly failed prophesies and misrepresentations of both present and past, it seems time to carry the secularization doctrine to the graveyard of failed theories, and there to whisper "*requiescat in pace.*"

REFERENCES

Ahmad, M. 1991. Islamic fundamentalism in South Asia: The Jamaat-i-Islami and the Tablighi Jamaat of South Asia. In *Fundamentalisms observed*, edited by M. E. Marty and R. Scott Appleby, 457-528. Chicago, IL: University of Chicago Press.

Anonymous. [circa 1410] 1976. *Dives and pauper*. London: Oxford University Press.

Antonino, St. [circa 1430] XXXX. *Summa major*.

Baldwin, S. L. 1900. *Foreign missions of the Protestant churches*. Chicago, IL: Missionary Campaign Library.

Barrett, D. B. 1982. *World Christian encyclopedia*. Oxford: Oxford University Press.

Baumer, F. L. 1960. *Religion and the rise of skepticism*. New York: Harcourt, Brace.

Bede. [730] 1955. *Ecclesiastical history of the English people*. London: Penguin.

Berger, P. 1967. *The sacred canopy*. Garden City, NY: Doubleday.

———. 1968. A bleak outlook is seen for religion. *New York Times*, 25 April, 3.

———. 1979. *The heretical imperative: Contemporary possibilities of religious affiliation*. New York: Doubleday.

———. 1997. Epistemological modesty: An interview with Peter Berger. *Christian Century* 114: 972-75, 978.

Bossy, J. 1985. *Christianity in the West: 1400-1700*. New York: Oxford University Press.

Brøndsted, J. 1965. *The Vikings*. Baltimore: Penguin.

Brooke, R., and C. Brooke. 1984. *Popular religion in the Middle Ages*. London: Thames and Hudson.

Bruce, S. 1992. *Religion and modernization*. Oxford: Clarendon.

———. 1995. The truth about religion in Britain. *Journal for the Scientific Study of Religion* 34: 417-30.

————. 1997. The pervasive world-view: Religion in pre-modern Britain. *British Journal of Sociology* 48: 667-80.

Byock, J. L. 1988. *Medieval Iceland: Society, sagas, and power.* Berkeley: University of California Press.

Casanova, J. 1994. *Public religions in the modern world.* Chicago, IL: University of Chicago Press.

Chen, H. 1995. The development of Taiwanese folk religion, 1683-1945. Ph.D. diss., University of Washington.

Christian, Jr., W. A. 1981. *Apparitions in late medieval and renaissance Spain.* Princeton, NJ: Princeton University Press.

Comte, A. 1830-1842. *Cours de philosophie positive.* Paris: Bachelier. 1896. *The positive philosophy.* Translated and edited by Harriet Martineau. London: George Bell and Sons.

Coulton, G. G. 1938. *Medieval panorama.* Cambridge: Cambridge University Press.

Crawley, A. E. 1905. *The tree of life.* London: Hutchinson.

Cupitt, D. 1997. *After God: The future of religion.* London: Weidenfeld and Nicolson.

Currie, R., A. Gilbert, and L. Horsley. 1977. *Churches and churchgoers: Patterns of church growth in the British Isles since 1700.* Oxford: Clarendon Press.

Davie, G. 1990a. "An ordinary God": The paradox of religions in contemporary Britain. *British Journal of Sociology* 41: 395-420.

————. 1990b. Believing without belonging: Is this the future of religion in Britain? *Social Compass* 37: 455-69.

————. 1994. *Religion in Britain since 1945: Believing without belonging.* Oxford: Blackwell.

Davies, N. 1996. *Europe: A History.* Oxford: Oxford University Press.

Delumeau, J. 1977. *Catholicism between Luther and Voltaire: A new view of the Counter-Reformation.* Philadelphia, PA: Westminster Press.

Dobbelaere, K. 1987. Some trends in European sociology of religion: The secularization debate. *Sociological Analysis* 48: 107-137.

Douglas, M. 1982. The effects of modernization on religious change. In *Religion and America: Spirituality in a secular age,* edited by M. Douglas and S. M. Tipton, 25-43. Boston: Beacon Press.

Duffy, E. 1987. The late middle ages: Vitality or decline. In *Atlas of the Christian Church,* edited by H. Chadwick and G. R. Evans, 86-95. New York: Facts on File.

————. 1992. *Stripping of the altars.* New Haven, CT: Yale University Press.

Durant, W., and A. Durant. 1965. *The age of Voltaire.* New York: Simon and Schuster.

Finke, R. 1992. An unsecular America. In *Religion and modernization,* edited by S. Bruce, 145-169. Oxford: Clarendon.

Finke, R., and R. Stark. 1988. Religious economies and sacred canopies: Religious mobilization in American cities, 1906. *American Sociological Review* 53: 41-9.

————. 1992. *The churching of America, 1776-1990: Winners and losers in our religious economy.* New Brunswick, NJ: Rutgers University Press.

Fletcher, R. 1997. *The barbarian conversion.* New York: Holt.

Geertz, C. 1966. Religion as a cultural system. In *Anthropological approaches to the study of religion,* edited by M. Banton, 1-46. London: Tavistock Publications.

Gentilcore, D. 1992. *Bishop to witch.* Manchester, UK: Manchester University Press.

Greeley, A. M. 1989. *Religious change in America.* Cambridge, MA: Harvard University Press.

————. 1994. A religious revival in Russia? *Journal for the Scientific Study of Religion* 33: 253-72.

————. 1995. *Religion as poetry.* New Brunswick, NJ: Transaction Publishers.

Hadden, J. K. 1987. Toward desacralizing secularization theory. *Social Forces* 65: 587-611.

Hanson, S. 1997. The secularization thesis: Talking at cross purposes. *Journal of Contemporary Religion* 12: 159-79.

Healy, R. M. 1984. Jefferson on Judaism and the Jews: "Divided we stand, united, we fall!" *American Jewish History* 78: 359-74.

Iannaccone, L. R. 1996. Looking backward: Estimating long-run church attendance trends across eighteen countries. Paper presented at the annual meeting of the Society for the Scientific Study of Religion.

Johnson, P. 1976. *A history of Christianity.* New York: Harper & Row.

Jones, G. 1968. *A history of the Vikings.* London: Oxford University Press.

Lambert, M. 1992. *Medieval heresy: Popular movements from the Gregorian Reform to the Reformation,* 2nd ed. Oxford: Blackwell.

Lang, G., and L. Ragvold. 1993. *The rise of a refugee god: Hong Kong's Wong Tai Sin.* Oxford: Oxford University Press.

Larson, E. J., and L. Withan. 1997. Belief in God and immortality among American scientists: A historical survey revisited. *Nature* 386: 435.

Laslett, P. 1965. *The world we have lost.* London: Keagan Paul.

Le Bras, G. 1963. Dechristianisation: Mot fallacieus. *Social Compass* 10:448-51.

Lechner, F. J. 1991. The case against secularization: A rebuttal. *Social Forces* 69: 1103-19.

———. 1996. Secularization in the Netherlands? *Journal for the Scientific Study of Religion* 35: 252-64.

Leuba, J. H. [1916] 1921. *The belief in God and immortality.* Chicago, IL: Open Court.

Mack, B. L. 1996. *Who wrote the New Testament?: The making of the Christian myth.* San Francisco, CA: HarperSanFrancisco.

MacMullen, R. 1981. *Paganism in the Roman Empire.* New Haven, CT: Yale University Press.

Martin, D. 1965. Towards eliminating the concept of secularization. In *Penguin survey of the social sciences,* edited by J. Gould. Harmondsworth, UK: Pengiun Books.

———. 1978. *A general theory of secularization.* New York: Harper & Row.

———. 1991. The secularization issue: Prospect and retrospect. *British Journal of Sociology* 42: 465-74.

Morris, C. 1993. Christian civilization (1050-1400). In *The Oxford history of Christianity,* edited by J. McManners, 205-42. Oxford: Oxford University Press.

Müller, F. M. 1878. *Lectures on the origin and growth of religion.* London: Longmans Green.

Murray, A. 1972. Piety and impiety in thirteenth-century Italy. *Studies in Church History* 8: 83-106.

Mutlu, K. 1996. Examining religious beliefs among university students in Ankara. *British Journal of Sociology* 47: 353-59.

Nelson, J. 1992. Shinto ritual: Managing chaos in contemporary Japan. *Ethnos* 57: 77-104.

Obelkevich. J. 1979. *Religion and the people, 800-1700.* Chapel Hill: University of North Carolina Press.

Redman, B. R. 1949. *The portable Voltaire.* New York: Penguin.

Roesdahl, E. 1980. The Scandinavians at home. In *The Northern World,* edited by D. M. Wilson, 145-58. New York: Harry N. Abrams.

Sawyer, P. H. 1982. *Kings and Vikings: Scandinavia and Europe, AD 700-1100.* London: Methuen.

Sawyer, P., and B. Sawyer. 1993. *Medieval Scandinavia: From conversion to reformation, circa 800-1500.* Minneapolis: University of Minnesota Press.

Schneider, J. 1990. Spirits and the spirit of capitalism. In *Religious orthodoxy and popular faith in European society,* edited by E. Badone, 24-53. Princeton, NJ: Princeton University Press.

Shepherd, W. R. 1980. *Shepherd's historical atlas,* 9th ed. Totowa, NJ: Barnes & Noble.

Shiner, L. 1967. The concept of secularization in empirical research. *Journal for the Scientific Study of Religion* 6: 207-20.

Smith, G. 1996. The unsecular city: The revival of religion in East London. In *Rising in the East: The regeneration of East London,* edited by T. Butler and M. Rustin. London: Lawrence and Wishart.

Smith, M. 1996. *Religion in industrial society: Oldham and Saddleworth 1740-1965.* Oxford: Oxford University Press.

Sommerville, C. J. 1992. *The secularization of early modern England.* New York: Oxford University

Press.

Stark, R. 1963. On the incompatibility of religion and science: A survey of American graduate students. *Journal for the Scientific Study of Religion* 3: 3-20.

———. 1981. Must all religions be supernatural? In *The social impact of new religious movements*, edited by B. Wilson, 159-77. New York: Rose of Sharon Press.

———. 1985. From church-sect to religious economies. In *The sacred in a secular age*, edited by P. E. Hammond, 139-49. Berkeley: University of California Press.

———. 1996a. *The rise of Christianity: A sociologist reconsiders history*. Princeton, NJ: Princeton University Press.

———. 1996b. Why religious movements succeed or fail: A revised general model. *Journal of Contemporary Religion* 11: 133-46.

———. 1998a. *Sociology*, 7th ed. Belmont, CA: Wadsworth.

———. 1998b. Explaining international variations in religiousness: The market model. *Polis*. Special Issue.

Stark, R., B. D. Foster, C. Y. Glock, and H. E. Quinley. 1971. *Wayward shepherds: Prejudice and the Protestant clergy*. New York: Harper & Row.

Stark, R., and L. R. Iannaccone. 1993. Rational propositions about religious groups and movements. In *Handbook of cults and sects in America*, edited by D. G. Bromley and J. K. Hadden, 241-61. Greenwich, CT: JAI Press.

———. 1994. A supply-side reinterpretation of the "secularization" of Europe. *Journal for the Scientific Study of Religion* 33: 230-52.

———. 1995. Truth? A reply to Bruce. *Journal for the Scientific Study of Religion* 34: 516-19.

Stark, R., L. R. Iannaccone, and R. Finke. 1996. Religion, science, and rationality. Papers and proceedings of *American Economic Review*: 433-437.

———. 1998. Rationality and the religious mind. *Economic Inquiry* 36: 373-89.

Swatos, Jr. W. H. 1984. The relevance of religion: Iceland and secularization theory. *Journal for the Scientific Study of Religion* 23: 32-43.

Swatos, Jr., W. H., and L. R. Gissurarson. 1997. *Icelandic spiritualism: Mediumship and modernity in Iceland*. New Brunswick, NJ: Transaction Publishers.

Tamney, J. B. 1979. Established religiosity in modern society: Islam in Indonesia. *Sociological Analysis* 40: 125-35.

———. 1980. Fasting and modernization. *Journal for the Scientific Study of Religion* 19: 129-37.

———. 1992. *The resilience of Christianity in the modern world* Albany: State University of New York Press.

Tan, C. B. 1994. Chinese religion. In *Religions sans Frontieres*, edited by R. Cipriani, 257-289. Rome: Dipartimento per L'Informazione e Editoria.

Thomas, K. 1971. *Religion and the decline of magic*. New York: Scribner.

Tomasson, R. F. 1980. *Iceland*. Minneapolis: University of Minnesota Press.

Tocqueville, A. de. 1956. *Democracy in America*. 2 vols. New York: Vintage.

Tschannen, O. 1991. The secularization paradigm: A systematization. *Journal for the Scientific Study of Religion* 30: 395-415.

Vauchez, A. 1997. The saint. In *The medieval world*, edited by J. L. Goff, 313-45. London: Parkgate Books.

Voyé, L., and K. Dobbelaere. 1994. Roman Catholicism: Universalism at stake. In *Religions sans frontières?*, edited by R. Cipriani, 83-113. Rome: Dipartimento per L'Informazione e Editoria.

Wallace, A. F. C. 1966. *Religion: An anthropological view*. New York: Random House.

Wilson, B. 1966. *Religion in secular society*. London: Watts.

———. 1968. Religion and the churches in contemporary America. In *Religion in America*, edited by W. G. McLoughlin and R. N. Bellah, 77-84. Boston: Houghton Mifflin.

———. 1975. The debate over secularization: Religion, society, and faith. *Encounter* 45: 77-84.

———. 1982. *Religion in sociological perspective*. Oxford: Oxford University Press.

Winter, M., and C. Short. 1993. Believing and belonging: Religion and rural England. *British Journal of Sociology* 44: 635-51.

Woolston, T. 1733. *Works of Thomas Woolston.* London: J. Roberts.

Yamane, D. 1997. Secularization on trial: In defense of a neosecularization paradigm. *Journal for the Scientific Study of Religion* 36: 109-22.

4

Secularization in a Context of Advanced Modernity

Liliane Voyé

Université Catholique de Louvain, Belgique

In Europe, the general trend of secularization continues. It is attested by the loss of authority of the Catholic church on the societal level and in societal subsystems. This trend is confirmed by the decline of personal religiosity (beliefs, church practice, and moral attitudes). However, the situation is more complex than that: some paradoxes should be stressed. Not infrequently religious authorities are considered to be experts on ethical matters and are requested by civil authorities to give advice; popular religious practices are re-legitimized; at different territorial levels, Catholicism — and to a lesser extent other Christian religions — is invoked to affirm the specific identity of a city, a region, and even of Europe. The courts now-a-days sometimes take into account religious identities and their particularistic exigences and characteristics. Consequently, religious institutions — and most specifically the Catholic church — appear to be a resource used on the levels of the society, subsystems, and the individual. However, its impact is subject to the fact that its specific religious character — to wit its doctrine and specific moral standards — is watered down. This in itself may be considered a consequence of secularization.

As described by Dobbelaere (1981), secularization — considered as a process on the macro-level — is in general still an unquestionable fact in Europe. Functional differentiation is persisting; the organized world is based on impersonal roles and on contractual patterns. The privatization of religion signifies not only that institutional religion loses its capacity to exercise an impact on public affairs but also that religion is considered as a matter of personal choice. This choice is enlarged by the numerous opportunities which have appeared in the "religious market" and, among other things, by the development of New Religious Movements. Such a context stimulates the relativization of religious messages, and their acceptance appears to be more and more oriented to a "this worldly" end, to the immanent level of everyday reality.

However, at the same time that unbelief is growing and the numbers of the unchurched are increasing (Jagodzinski and Dobbelaere 1995b; Dobbelaere and Jagodzinski 1995), different facts testify that religion is not absent from the scene. Considering Europe, we can see that many individuals seem to set up some kind of "religious patchwork," using various existing resources which they compose according to their own needs, views, and experiences (Voyé 1995). At different levels, it appears also that the religious reference is used to affirm a territorial identity (Voyé 1996) and so to differentiate oneself from others considered as dangerous or inferior or simply as different. We may also see that the autonomy of the different functions — notably, the political and the juridical functions — is not always as radical as it was supposed to be in the first phase of modernity.

Taking into account this apparent paradox — the confirmation of the process of secularization and the effective presence of religious references not only at the individual level but also at the macro level — I advance some reflections which — considering the European case and the Catholic church — might suggest that the actual situation is not exactly the same as it was twenty-five years ago, i.e., when Dobbelaere defined secularization as he did. We are no longer in the heart of a triumphant modernity, and this induces different effects in the religious field as in any other field.

To develop this point of view, I will discuss some aspects of what I will call "advanced modernity" — considered more as a factual situation than as a theory — and I will try to show how these aspects modify the position of the religious field, without invalidating the effects of secularization. In contrast to what is often suggested, there is no *retour*, no return to a pre-modern situation. I suggest, rather, that institutional religion may no longer presume to impose its views, its doctrine, its morals, its rules, either in public affairs or on individuals who claim their autonomy. To be listened to, religious spokespersons have to modify their discourse and its presentation. The religious actor has also to re-legitimize some religious dimensions which, during modernity, were eliminated or at least reduced in order to rationalize religion. To survive or to have a chance still to play a role in society, the religious actor will offer himself as a resource for other systems, i.e., to develop its "performances" (Luhmann 1990) — by showing its capacity to solve problems generated in other fields but not solved there. And we shall see that the political field in particular, at various levels, not only accepts this but sometimes requires it directly.

In this perspective, I review several points that I consider a consequence of a context of advanced modernity, without pretending to be exhaustive. A first characteristic is the relative scepticism toward science, because of its "perverse effects," its incapacity to solve every problem (contrary to what was hoped for during modernity), and its long-term character. This induces two possibilities for religious performances: one on the level of the political field, which is supposed to regulate science and its applications, and one on the individual level. Then, I will take into account the disrepute into which the state has fallen and the correlative growing importance of Europe, on the one side, and of "regions," "nations," and different particular identifications on the other. For these last two levels, the Catholic church is foremost in offering its resources. I will then consider the actual trend which tends to evolve from laws considered as general and substantial to laws which take into account particular and situational aspects — among others, those of religious diversity. At the same time, the state, being in search of allies, tends to reaffirm its ancient collusion with the main Christian religions.

AN ETHICAL EXPERTISE

During modernity, science was a kind of "grand narrative," as Lyotard says (1979), i.e., science offered itself and was looked upon as the means to solve each and every material, physical, psychological, and social problem. Through science, the world would become better and better for everyone in every domain. This narrative is actually put into question from different points of view. It is more and more often apparent that science has perverse effects and that in itself it induces new problems.

Some recent advances in science effectively confront society with the question of the limits which should eventually be prescribed for the applications of scientific knowledge. Let us simply think about the domain of procreation and about the technique of "cloning" or about the genetic manipulations concerning different kinds of food — but also of human beings.

Scientific advances require more and more urgently regulations which define limits that should not be transgressed. But who will set these limits, who will elaborate appropriate regulations? Clearly, this is the responsibility of the political actor who has to translate them into laws. But this actor is not well equipped for the task. If, before modernity, ethics were generally within the complete control of religious actors, secularization has changed this tradition. Now ethical questions appear everywhere, in public debates as well as on the public agenda. One can read or hear in the mass media discussions on the ethics of the arts and of sports, on business and bank ethics, on the ethics of education and of humanitarian help, and so forth.

This proliferation of ethical questions induces a twofold comment. First, it is clear that there no longer exists a universally accepted ethic such as was inspired by a religious doctrine and which rested therefore on a few general principles considered as timelessly valid, everywhere, for each and every situation (Jagodzinski and Dobbelaere 1995b). Now it seems as if each field needs its own specific ethical rules. Second, these diversified ethical rules are considered as a matter for discussion and debate, in which one refers to the particularism of concrete situations and not to a rule given in advance by a transcendental power. So we moved from a universalistic and substantial ethic to a situational and "procedural" ethic, which takes into account the practical data and the point of view of the people (directly) concerned (de Sousa Santos 1988, 1990).

At the same time, and apparently contradicting the logic of this evolution, however, when ethical questions arise, religious actors are very often requested to give their advice as experts in moral domains. Several governments — in

Belgium, France, the Netherlands — have for instance created "ethical commissions," asking for the elaboration of rules concerning bio-ethical questions (such as abortion, genetic manipulations, euthanasia, therapeutic relentlessness, and so on). A large number of members of these commissions are representatives of the major traditional (i.e., essentially Christian) religions. Nobody, no political party or ideological group, seems to object to this, and the media present it as something natural and normal. So, even if we live in a secularized world and if functional differentiation tends to confine religion to its own field, it appears that no institution other than religion has developed a competence in the ethical field (which previously was the monopoly of religion). Other fields — and most of all the political field, which has to regulate by law the various issues as they appear — provide no credible alternative: it is considered that one finds people with a certain competence in ethical matters only in the religious field (and in some cases also in the academic world).

Such a resort is clearly facilitated by the fact that, on the religious side — and more specifically in the Catholic church — the discourse has changed. The church presents itself as "dedogmatized" and "deconfessionalised." Instead of speaking of "the laws of God," "the rules of the church," more and more frequently representatives of the Catholic church refer to "human rights" and to "human values," without mentioning a specific doctrinal background. Using such neutral language, the Catholic church seems to enlarge its credibility in the eyes of the political actors. Politicians then feel no objection to using the competence which this church pretends to have ("we are experts in humanity") and is largely recognized as having.

We have here an example of what Luhmann (1990) calls "a performance": the religious field may play a role outside its own realm when it can offer to another field a service that the latter is unable to produce by itself. The radical functional differentiation is then shaken, and religious thinking may regain some influence on the orientations of society.

A "MAGICAL" SUBSTITUTE

The fact that science may have perverse effects and that its advances require the formulation of ethical limits is not the only aspect of science which induces some kind of appeal addressed to religion. Indeed, contrary to what was hoped for during modernity, one is confronted with the incapacity of science to solve every problem (let us think about poverty, war, or illness and death for instance). Science has also a long-term and general character; from the point of view of individuals, i.e., very often science has no direct significance for them since its developments have no immediate applicability, being unable to offer the urgent answer required by concrete and particular problems that people have to face here and now. Confronted with a fatal illness — cancer or AIDS, for instance — the individual is not comforted by knowing that, within some years, there will probably be medicine to cure it.

This fact stimulates people to look for a solution elsewhere (or at least a hope of solution), which they do not find in science. In this respect, popular religion appears as an important resource. People go on pilgrimages, for instance, first of all hoping to solve or to avoid health difficulties for themselves and their nearest relatives and friends, to reconstruct familial harmony, to find a job, or to pass exams (Voyé 1992).

If religious places, figures, and objects are today instrumentalized in this way, it is clearly because the confidence with which modernity regards science, on one hand, and the welfare state, on the other, is not fully realized: science is now suspected of having perverse effects, of creating different kinds of new problems, and of being unable to solve *hic et nunc* the everyday pressing problems of the people. As regards the welfare state, it is to some degree discredited everywhere in Europe, because it appears that it has not solved all the problems it claimed to solve, and because the economic situation requires the reduction of the benefits paid to people in different situations and of various public services. The current reign of doubt and insecurity induces people to seek elsewhere a response for which, in modernity, they would have searched first of all in science or/and in the benevolence of the state. This is the case not only of individuals confronted by the hazards of their personal everyday life: there exist many testimonies showing that people with important responsibilities, notably in business or finance, are searching for responses in their professional affairs along nonrational lines, such as practices of popular religion or cartomancy, and astrology (Brun 1989). The shaking of the confidence in rational thinking — which was promoted by modernity — thus induces the reappearance of many kinds of nonrational practices, which affords an opportunity for popular religion to regain a popularity and a legitimacy which modernity intended to eradicate.

One may object to this argument that this appeal to popular religion does not signify that people will re-activate their involvement in the institutional church. Popular religion has its own logic, which makes it nearer to "magic" than to religion, in the sense of the Weberian perpective. The rites and practices of popular religon are used, most of all in case of need, *au coup par coup*, without any continuity and without any particular doctrinal reference. The devotions it presupposes seek to influence "the gods" less through veneration than to constrain them through gifts and offers. Whatever historical links it may have with the church and with its religious expressions, popular religion is evolving along an autonomous path. Nevertheless, the appeal to rites and practices of popular religion is, for the religious actor, another device with which to play a role in this secularized society, if he is willing to re-legitimize different practices which were previously denounced in the name of the rationality and of the "purity" of religiousness.

AN IDENTITY REFERENT

These first two points that we have examined to show that secularization does not signify a radical elimination of religion have to be considered in relation to some disappointments generated by the utopian hope put into science. Another character of the current situation may explain other appeals made to religion: appeals that express at different levels a quest for identity in circumstances where states lose their capacity to generate the commitment which they were once supposed to command.

The disintegration of the welfare state and the numerous "affairs" in which important political figures from the most important democratic parties were implicated led to the state falling into disrepute: people no longer have confidence in the state and identify less and less with it. This fact is corroborated by the current context of globalization which induces a significant decrease of the power of the states as they were conceived during the nineteenth century. In Europe, states lose progressively their main prerogatives, which were to control their borders, to raise armies, and to mint coins. Above all, states are becoming completely unable to regulate the economic system, which knows no borders, or to compensate for the social damage caused by the development of a worldwide capitalist system. In this "global circumstance," where so called national-states appear less and less able to induce a collective identity, we notice in Europe a double quest: the one essentially sought by the authority which is governing Europe and encountering an explicit proposal from the Catholic church; the other relatively spontaneously arising from people themselves.

"A Christian Europe"

In contradiction to the purpose of the fathers of the European idea, the construction of a unified Europe seems until now to have focused mainly if not solely on the economic perspective. Such a purpose, however, is not very readily able to mobilize citizens, most of all if it is gradually built in an economically troubled period which is now the case. In this context, the Catholic church tends to propose an alternative image of Europe: that of a "Christian Europe," where people share the same fundamental values and the same worldview, which are different from those found in other parts of the world, particularly in the Arabic and Muslim world. Many examples may illustrate this point. For instance, one needs only to think about the great gatherings of youth convened by the Pope, e.g., in Loreto (Italy) and in Santiago di Compostella (Spain), where he insisted on the major role that Christianity had played in the construction of a specific European culture and of the values of freedom, equality, and fraternity, which he declared to be typical of this part of the world (Voyé 1997). Very recently, a document from the Vatican emphasized the fact that Maestricht — the city where an important advance was made for the unification of Europe — was especially connected with the Catholic church: in 1947, the city received the statue of the Virgin Mary of Fatima. This was the first journey of this statue, which went there to celebrate the end of World War II and to signify the fraternity between European countries. It was added that it was certainly not a coincidence that this treaty was signed in Maestricht, but an important symbol of the links existing between Europe and the Catholic church. The same publication underlined also that when, in May 1997, the hermitage of Gibraltar — dedicated in 1309 by the king of Castilla to "Our Lady of Europe" — was returned to the church by the British Army, the Pope emphasized the importance to have such a place at the end of the continent "to help Europe to remember its Christian legacy" (Bulletin d'information du Conseil Pontifical pour la Pastorale du Tourisme, June and September 1997). The European flag — blue with a crown of stars at the center — is also seen by some as an involuntary (?) borrowing from a Catholic symbol: it is indeed the same as that of the Virgin Mary, as Vincent notices (1993: 79-81).

These are only a few examples among many others, which attest the congruence of two intentions. There exists an explicit intention by the Catholic authorities to offer their religion as the European religion and to insist on the old links between this church and Europe (Luneau and Ladrière 1989; Willaime 1991; Lefort 1996). For their part, the European authorities consider Christianity (and most of all Catholicism) as an intrinsic part of Europe. Indeed, the overture for identification advanced by the Church has not only been well received by the European political authorities, but they have expressly requested this religious support in order to help them to "give a soul to Europe," as it was put by former president Delors, anxious to win the population over to the idea of the political unification. Other countries in non-Christian parts of the world have often perceived this affinity. For instance, the refusal to start negotiations toward the entrance of Turkey into the European Community was explicitly interpreted in that country as a clear indication that "Europe intended to be a Christian club" and therefore feared the arrival of a large Muslim country.

Let me add here an important remark. The expression "Christian" Europe which is regularly used would be better replaced by that of "Catholic" Europe. Indeed, if the Roman Catholic church as such is very positively concerned about the construction of Europe, the same is not absolutely true for the other branches of Christianity. Certainly, each of them says that it sees in a unifed Europe a greater chance for peace and an opportunity to develop eucumenism. But at the same time, the non-Catholic Christian churches develop an ambiguous feeling when they consider the connotations attached by the Catholic church to its vision of Europe.

Since the beginning, the Protestants have had a relatively sceptical and distant attitude toward Europe. Three main concerns motivate this difference with the Catholic church. First, in Europe, historical Protestantism is intrinsically linked with the affirmation of national and regional identities, and it has no one central authority (Willaime 1995: 313). The reservations of the Protestant churches are also linked to two facts: it was Catholic social-democratic figures who were at the origin of the European project; among the twelve first countries involved, seven are quasi-exclusively Catholic ones and two others are mixed — so whereas Catholicism represents 60 percent of the population in this Europe, Protestantism concerns only 16 percent, which induces easily the image of a "Vatican Europe." Last but not least, Protestants disagree with the Pope's proposal to "re-Christianize secularized Europe" because they recognize that the Enlightenment permitted the manifestation of essential values found in the Gospel and because they see the differentiation between state and church as valuable (Willaime 1995:320). As with the Protestant churches, the Orthodox church is also more or less reluctant to see Europe extending, as the Pope puts it, "from the Atlantic Ocean to the Ural Mountains," because it fears the dominance of Catholicism, which it considers as too liberal, and because it represents itself as invested with the moral duty to entertain and protect the specificities of the Eastern countries, hoping to avoid "the materialist drift" experienced by the West. Regarding the Anglican church, the deep connection it has with the state provokes the fear that, with the efflux of time, Europe will reduce the specific identity of the country and the legitimacy of this particular church (Voyé 1997).

The European field is thus relatively free for the strategy of the Catholic church, which clearly occupies it. This church also has other means to occupy the European field, at another level.

Particular Territorial Identities and the Rediscovery of the Subject

As is clearly underlined by Roland Robertson, the actual global circumstance supposes "a two-fold process . . .the universalization of particularism and the particularization of universalism. [That induces] a conception of the world as a series of culturally equal, relativized, entities or ways of life. . . .Globalization. . . relativizes and equalizes all socio-cultural formations . . . [and induces] the insistence on heterogeneity and variety." In such a context, the questions of "identity, tradition, and the demand for indigenisation" become crucial. The same diagnosis is proposed by Alain Touraine.

> If it is true that we live together on the same planet, it is just as true that everywhere, one may see a reinforcement and a multiplication of identity — conferring groups, of associations grounded in a common belonging, of sects, cults, nationalisms. . . . When we are all together, we have almost nothing in common and when we share beliefs or one specific history, we reject those who are different from us. . . . We see the dislocation of these unities — political, territorial, social and cultural as well — that we called societies, civilizations, or simply countries. We see the division between, on one side, the objectivised world of the signs of globalization and, on the other side, unities of values, cultural expressions, places of memory (1997: 14-15).

These different kinds of particularism, which are stimulated by the global circumstance and the correlated disintegration of previous locations of identification and commitment, provoke a quest for symbols capable of expressing specificities and differences. And here also the Catholic church has everywhere in Europe a wealth of resources to propose: the cult of a specific saint or of a particular image of the Virgin Mary is frequently used as a means of expressing a local or regional identity, a particular profession, or a specific personal problem (of health or love, for instance). These diverse modalities of popular religion, related to Catholicism, appear as many possibilities of expressing the current rediscovery of the individual subject both in different concrete aspects — such those we have just seen — and in itself.

This rediscovery of the individual in itself tends also to induce some regeneration of popular religion not only to affirm one or another kind of collective identity but also to express the rediscovery of the pluridimensionality of the human being. Indeed, the emphasis which modernity put on formal rationality induced an image of the human being underlining essentially, if not solely, its capacity to think, to use its reason to organize its life and to control its relations to others and to the world. This view seems to be actually contradicted by the importance given to the body and to the emotions (Champion and Hervieu-Léger 1990). Here again, "popular religion" finds an opportunity to be functional. Popular religion is not only instrumental for the lower strata, characterized more or less by naïvete and simple mindedness: research shows that neither social class nor educational level discriminates in this field. If popular religion may take various forms according to these variables, it is evident that, in each social "milieu," people are turning to some kind of popular religion, particularly at certain times and in relation to their family and friends (Voyé 1998). The specificity of popular religion rests essentially not on a well constructed discourse but rather on concrete gestures, and involves the various senses.

It is probably this character which explains why popular religion was rejected and considered not legitimate during the period in which positivist rationalist thought was promoted, and when, in the religous field, "profoundness" of faith, stripped of profane parasites or interferences, was insisted upon. Immediately after Vatican II, different changes in the Catholic church attest to that. Parish priests depreciated popular religion — e.g., statues of the saints were removed from the churches, praying the rosary was considered an infantile practice, and the demand for benedictions (of houses, cars, pets, etc.) discontinued. "Solemn communion" at the age of 12 was stripped of its festive character; children had all to wear the same religious robes and to "profess" their faith (Bonnet 1973; Pannet 1974). A new term emerged: "the protestantization of the Catholic church." The building of new churches was also inhibited since they took too much space, were too costly, and were underused; consequently it was considered nonrational from an economic point of view. A very interesting example of this is given by the relocation of the French-speaking part of the *Catholic* University of Louvain: a new city — and not only a new campus — was built; however, students and professors rejected the proposal that a church should be built and that space should be reserved in the center of the town for a church to be built in the future.

Advanced modernity seems to give new legitimation to popular religion: it emphasizes the fact that sense is imprinted in the body and that corporeal practices such as pilgrimages, requests for blessings, offerings to saints, the wearing of medals, and the possession of sacred images, have to be considered more seriously than is suggested by purely rationalist evaluations. Faith passes not only through the mind: it may also be expressed and entertained by using the body and material objects.

Once again this will underline the fact that popular religion is something other than the doctrinal and ethical "grand narrative" promoted by the institutional church; it is even the case that sometimes they contradict one another. But, as I have said, places and actors are often the same, even if the "logic of appropriation" of the saints and the Virgins, of gestures and objects, departs from the "logic of production" of their origin. This resort to religious "products" generated by the church favors the preservation of a link between this church and individuals who, otherwise, would look elsewhere in hope of answers.

A GENERAL AND SUBSTANTIAL LAW QUESTIONED BY DIFFERENT RELIGIOUS REGULATIONS

Advanced modernity is also characterized by a tendency to dehomo-genization in various domains and by a refusal — implicit or explicit — to abandon one's own specific characteristics. In the Western European countries, for instance, immigrants seek to hold onto their particular culture, whereas before the aim was that they should be integrated into the culture of the country in which they lived. This claim seems to be increasingly translated in diverse fields, notably in law.

The emergence of modern states has brought about in each of them the elaboration of a prescriptive and normative law, considered as applicable to everyone, without taking into account any distinctions, including religious distinctions. In more recent times, it appears regularly that judges take religious rules into consideration in pronouncing their verdicts. Two examples may illustrate this. Recently, in France, a young Jewish man, working in a Jewish restaurant, had to go to Israel where his father had died; he remained there for three weeks as is prescribed by Jewish law or at least is considered as normal. When he came back, he was dismissed for unjustified absence. He went to the court and he won the action since the judge ruled that the owner of the restaurant, who respected the Jewish prescription concerning *kosher* food, had also to accept these specific rules in respect of funerals. The other example concerns the wearing of the Islamic veil. Because a Belgian school had refused to permit the veil, the parents of the girl went to court; they lost the action but the judge stipulated that this decision was taken because the girl had the possibility to go to another school where the veil was permitted and because it appeared that some respected Islamic authorities do not consider that wearing the veil to be a strict koranic obligation. Apart from the existence of an alternative school, it appears clearly that the judge had taken into account the advice of well-recognized religious authorities to pronounce his sentence. So, as is underlined by L.L. Christians (1996), these examples illustrate the fact that, recently, "a phenomenon of internormativity" is appearing: the judiciary takes into consideration the particularistic laws of the different religious groups which are present in the country, but solely as the definition of the religious norm is given by the religious institution and not the self-definition proposed by the believer.

These examples are interesting because they illustrate two things. First, from the juridical point of view in general, they show the current tendency toward "inter-legalism" (de Sousa Santos 1988:164): there is now a recognition of the coexistence, in one geopolitical space, of different juridical orders; and this is a kind of revolution if one considers the previous affirmation of one unique law to ensure democracy and to defend the existence of the state. It also underlines an important change in social functioning: instead of a "technical bureaucratic and violent application of the law," which characterized modernity, we are now confronted — so says de Sousa Santos (1990: 41) — with an "ethical know-how," taking into account "communal" interpretations and criteria which have nothing to do with the state and its claim strictly to regulate its own territory. For the religious field, the fact that courts more and more often take into consideration particular religious regulations and consult religious authorities indicates not only that the religious dimension is officially recognized as legitimate in itself but also that the religious field deserves to be taken into consideration beyond its own borders and to succeed in gaining special facilities or exemptions (Wilson 1996).

But the courts may take different positions. In the examples above, the court decided on religious matters after consulting the religious authorities. On the contrary, in July 1997, the court of Lyon (France) decided that it was incompetent to say if Scientology was or was not a religion; other examples, e.g., in Germany, point in the same direction. The judge affirmed that, in the name of the principle of the separation of state and church, which is a basic rule of the Republic, he was not empowered to decide on religious matters. So in this case, the court did not decide but recognized the autonomy of the religious field and its right and responsibility of self-regulation.

There is nevertheless an ambiguity in the recognition of religious particularities. Recently, in different Western European countries (France, Belgium, Germany), the governments have created "parliamentary commissions" to consider the necessity and possibility of legislating about sects and new religious movements. In France and Belgium, these commissions have consulted, among others, representatives of the Catholic church and, in the French report, it clearly appears that members of the commission take this church, and only this church, as their reference in defining what is and what is not a religion (Voyé 1996: 103-125). If finally, these commissions have decided to apply the existing laws and, in Belgium, to add a few articles to the criminal law, it seems that the creation and the work of these commissions call for some comments.

The fact that the parliaments have created such commissions indicates that the legislators do not consider religion as a totally private matter. Certainly, they try also to regulate other "private" matters — such as smoking — but in the case of religion it is clear, and it was directly said, that religion is also seen as a field capable of having an influence on society considered as a political body. The reports clearly indicated that some new religious movements might be dangerous for public security and for the state, because, for instance, some of these movements have connections with political parties and have members who have responsible jobs in high administration. It is interesting to note that this kind of reproach is never addressed to the mainstream religions. On the contrary: in Belgium, there exists a Catholic party which has been in power almost without interruption since the origin of the Belgian state, and in France, every time there is a new prime minister or a new president, the media insist on reporting the fact that he has a Catholic or a Protestant background. Thus, it seems that there exists a kind of affinity, a tacit complicity between the political state and one (or two) religion(s) which is (are) traditionally the religion(s) of the country: everything goes on as if an implicit alliance existed, which is a security for both parties. This is confirmed at another level by the current preoccupation of the European Commission in thinking about religions in Europe. In a recent meeting organized by the "Prospective Tank" of this Commission (Firenze, 26-27 April 1996: "The Religious Factor and the European and World Geostrategy"), it was explicitly stated that the Commission needed to know its religious interlocutors and that these were representatives of only the traditional religious institutions and, at the highest level, the representatives of the Christian churches. These churches thus seem to have a kind of prejudice of legitimacy, which places them in a privileged position in the view of those in politics.

CONCLUSION

As we have said, secularization is, in general, on the societal level still an unquestionable fact in Europe. But the advanced modern context is modifying the modalities through which secularization manifests itself. Certainly, the institutional Catholic church has lost its former capacity to be a "sacred canopy" at the societal level and of imposing its disciplinary power on individuals.

Nevertheless, some kind of dedifferentiation is appearing, notably between the political and the juridical fields, on the one side, and the religious field, on the other. But this presupposes that the institutional religious actor transforms his discourse. Instead of a dogmatic, confessional, and disciplinary message, he has to propose a general ethical message; consequently the Church has lost its own typical characteristics and is becoming more and more undifferentiated from both other religious and from agnostic or atheistic perspectives. This message may no longer be an imperative one: it has to present itself as a kind of guidance that people or institutions may or may not follow. The Catholic authorities have also to recognize that other religions may regulate some parts of the population when these people have a different cultural and religious background. Catholic authorities no longer have a monopoly of moral regulation in a specific territory: it is no longer, we might say, the "right of the territory" but the "right of the blood" which prevails. This is an important change for the Catholic church which always organized its pastoral work on a territorial basis.

Concerning individuals, we have seen that it is primarily different expressions of popular religion which are considered as relevant for concrete everyday life problems. But we know that popular religion is not absolutely regulated by institutional authority: it has its own logic. Some of its manifestations may even contradict the views of the church, and the church authorities may be reluctant regarding some aspects of popular religion. Furthermore, some popular religious expressions appear to be more or less compatible with forms which emerged in the *nébuleuse mystico-esotérique* in general. No distinction is clearly or always made between all such practices that are perceived as potentially helpful in everyday life.

Consequently, on the societal as well as on the individual level, the religious institution — and more specifically the Catholic church — may pretend to be a resource only when it more or less renounces its specific creeds and practices, in other words, its proper identity, and insofar as it refers to the expectations of other fields or of "ordinary" people. This seems to indicate that the process of secularization is still advancing, but also that the religious field and religious actors have regained the right to express themselves legitimately on the public scene, insofar as they abandon any dogmatism and as far as they serve interests outside their own field.

REFERENCES

Bonnet S. 1973. *A hue et à dia: les avatars du cléricalisme sous la Vème République*. Paris: Cerf.

Brun, C. 1989. *L'irrationnel dans l'entreprise*. Paris: Balland.

Champion, F., et D. Hervieu-Léger. 1990. *De l'émotion en religion. Renouveaux et tradition*, Paris: Centurion.

Christiaens, L. L. 1996. Approches juridiques de la normativité religieuse, Conférence, UCL.

De Sousa Santos, B. 1988. Una cartografia simbolica das representaçoes sociais: o caso do direito. *Revista Critica de Ciêncas Sociais* 24: 139-172.

————. 1990. O estado e o direito na transiçâo post-moderna: para um novo senso comum sobre o poder e o direito. *Revista Critica de Ciêncas Sociais* 30: 13-43.

Dobbelaere, K. 1981. Secularization: A multi-dimensional concept. *Current Sociology* 29(2): 1-213.

Dobbelaere, K., and W. Jagodzinski. 1995. Religious cognitions and beliefs. In *Beliefs in government: The impact of values*, edited by J.W. van Deth and E. Scarbrough, 197-217. Oxford: Oxford University Press.

Jagodzinski, W., and K. Dobbelaere. 1995a. Secularization and church religiosity. In *Beliefs in government: The impact of values*, edited by J.W. van Deth and E. Scarbrough, 76-119. Oxford: Oxford University Press.

————. 1995b. Religious and ethical pluralism. In *Beliefs in government: The impact of values*, edited by J.W. van Deth and E. Scarbrough, 218-249. Oxford: Oxford University Press.

Lefort, B. 1996. Présence des Religions. Envoi. In *Cahiers d'Europe* 1: 5-9.

Luhmann, N. 1990. *Essays on self-reference*. New York: Columbia University Press.

Luneau, R., and P. Ladrière. 1989. *Le rêve de Compostelle*, Paris: Centurion.

Lyotard, J. F. 1979. *La condition postmoderne*. Paris: Minuit.

Pannet, R. 1974. *Le catholicisme populaire: 30 ans après "La France pays de mission?*, 3rd ed. Paris: Centurion.

Robertson, R. 1992. *Globalization*. London: Sage.

Touraine, A. 1997. *Pourrons-nous vivre ensemble?* Paris: Fayard.

Vincent, G. 1993. *Religions et transformations de l'Europe*. Strasbourg: Presses Universitaires de Strasbourg.

Voyé, L. 1992. Religion populaire et pèlerinages en Europe. In *Actes du 1er Congrès Mondial de la Pastorale des Sanctuaires et des Pèlerinages, Conseil Pontifical pour la pastorale des Migrants et des Itinérants*, Rome: Conseil.

————. 1995. From institutional Catholicism to "Christian inspiration." In *The post-war generation and establishment religion: Cross-cultural perspectives*, edited by W. C. Roof, J. W. Carroll, and D. A. Roozen, 191-206. Boulder, CO: Westview Press.

————. 1996. Sous le regard du sociologue: Le rapport de la Commission d'enquête parlementaire française sur les sectes. In *Pour en finir avec les sectes. Le débat sur le rapport de la Commission parlementaire*, edited by M. Introvigne and J.G. Melton, Milano: Cesnur – di Giovanni.

————. 1997. Religion in modern Europe: Pertinence of the globalization theories? In *Globalization and indigenous culture*, edited by N. Inoue, 154-186. Tokyo: Institute for Japanese Culture and Classics, Kokugakuin University.

————. 1998 Uitwissing of nieuwe legitimatie van de volksreligie? Een sociologische benadering. In *Volksreligie, liturgie en evangelisatie*, edited by J. Lamberts, 129-151, Leuven: Acco.

Willaime, J. P. 1991. *Jean-Paul II et l'Europe*. Paris: Cerf.

————. 1995. Le Protestantisme face à la construction de l'Europe. In *Le politique et le religieux*, edited by F. Alvarez-Pereire. Louvain: Peeters.

Wilson, B. 1996. Religious toleration, pluralism, and privatization. In *Religion and modernity: Modes of coexistence*, edited by P. Repstad. Oslo: Scandivian University Press.

5

Secularization from the Perspective of Globalization

Peter Beyer
University of Ottawa

The perspective of globalization often treats global social reality as a single global society. The question of secularization must therefore be addressed primarily to that society and not in the first instance to a regional or cultural subunit of it. Following Dobbelaere's three-dimensional model of secularization, it is argued that world society is for the most part secularized in the dimension of "laicization," but not in those of "religious change" or "religious involvement." The three dimensions vary independently just as the corresponding Luhmannian types of social system, interaction, organization, and societal system do. The approach permits the analysis of regional differences without thereby having to put forward one or another of these as normative for the society as a whole. In this light, four forms of religion are analyzed for their likely dominance in global society, namely the collective cultural, the organized, the politicized, and the individualistic. The conclusion is that global society offers the most favorable conditions for the last three, but that overall the future of religion in this society is fundamentally unpredictable for social theory.

The term globalization, much like that of secularization, is subject to a variety of meanings which, while perhaps not contradictory, also do not necessarily imply each other. Without clarity at the beginning as to what we mean by globalization, therefore, the same sort of confusion is likely to result that has so often plagued discussions of secularization: different people use the word in different ways all the while assuming that we all mean the same thing. Moreover, globalization has already become, like secularization, a charged term laden with implicit or explicit commitment as to whether the process is good or bad, whether it should or should not happen. This feature has the tendency to politicize discussions involving either term, a perhaps unavoidable outcome, but one about which it is best to be aware.

GLOBALIZATION AND GLOBAL SOCIETY

I begin, therefore, with statements of what I mean by globalization. First and foremost, I mean that my primary unit of analysis is a single, globally extended society. That, of course, assumes or hypothesizes that there is such a society. More important, however, it implies a concept of society that, above all, does not accept the straightforward equation of societal boundaries with state boundaries. From this perspective, we can and at times must speak about, for instance, society in the United States or society in China because states are powerful forces in the contemporary world and it makes a difference whether one is in China or in the United States. Indeed, much of the debate about secularization has centered on matters such as "church/state relations" or "market regulation," for which state boundaries are of course decisive. Nonetheless, to accept without further qualification that the category of society as such coincides self-evidently with that of (nation-)state is to make the mistake of adopting uncritically certain nonscientific, but culturally powerful, self-descriptions as the basis for a key sociological concept. The globalization perspective that I take here therefore accepts state boundaries as *one* of the differences within global society that makes a difference when one asks the question of secularization. Yet it is not the only such important difference: others are the difference among religions, among religious organizations, among regions, and among cultures; none of these necessarily follows state boundaries. Overall, however, the principal question that I ask is whether global society as a whole is secularized or secularizing. Sectional differences are part of that larger question.

The insistence on global society as the primary unit of analysis points to a particular perspective on globalization that allows this unit to appear precisely as a society. For this purpose I rely on the adaptation of various concepts taken from the social theories of Niklas Luhmann (1975, 1982, 1995, 1997). These include above all the notion that a society is bounded by the range of the communicative processes that constitute it, not by the range of political surveillance nor by a sense of commonality or belonging that its participants supposedly share. Other critical notions are those of functional societal systems and, for the purposes of examining the question of secularization, his tripartite typology of social systems: interaction, organization, societal systems. To the latter I add a fourth type, the social movement. In this respect, my view is more or less in accord with that presented by Karel Dobbelaere in his chapter. Accordingly, I see the structural basis of global society as the global extension of communication based primarily but not exclusively on a set of independent but also interdependent technical, instrumental, or functional societal systems. These institutional systems include, among others, the capitalist economic system, the political system of states, the scientific/technological system, the system for mass information media, systems for academic education and medicalized health, and a religious system of religions. Here cannot be the place for a closer examination of any of these, nor for justifying this view of the structural bases of globalization (see Beyer 1994, 1998). I should, however, point out that these systems are not all that there is to globalization or to global society. A more complete presentation would have to include, at the very least, the complex cultural dimensions of the historical process (see Robertson 1992; Featherstone 1990, 1995), especially the diverse ways in which these systems receive cultural respecification in different regions of the world.

Looking at global society in terms of these societal systems articulates rather directly with standard theories of secularization such as those of David Martin (1979), Bryan Wilson (1966), Peter Berger (1967), Thomas Luckmann (1967), Talcott Parsons (1966), Luhmann (1977), and, of course, Dobbelaere (1981). In particular, the focus on functionally differentiated societal systems as a key moment of globalization parallels the notion that secularization refers to the consequences for religion of the dominance in modern societies of this form of differentiation. The central idea is that, as the *other* societal systems render themselves more independent of religious determination — certainly in their internal operations — religious institutions are at the very least challenged to recontextualize and even restructure themselves in terms of that new situation. As José Casanova (1994) has argued, it is this meaning of the concept of secularization that is and probably always has been of the greatest relevance for analyses of the contemporary social world. The global perspective I am offering here, therefore, has the question of secularization built into it at the very foundation of the analysis. For consideration of the more precise consequences for religion, however, we must, with Dobbelaere, use a multidimensional view of secularization, above all to avoid the simplistic notion that such functional secularization necessarily implies the straightforward decline of institutional religion.

Following Dobbelaere's well-known work on the multidimensionality of the notion (1981; see also Simpson 1988), secularization can refer to three relatively independent dimensions: that of societal systems (laicization), that of religious organizations (religious change), and that of individual religious involvement. The controversies and misunderstandings surrounding secularization most often seem to center on the last dimension, in particular whether or not in modern societies (or, in the present context, in global society) individual people are abandoning religious practice, in part as a reflection of their loss of religious consciousness. Recognizing that the three dimensions can and do vary independently gives one significantly better depth of field in the analysis of religious change in the modern world since it permits us to see different aspects of the question in their specificity, not just as an automatic reflection of the others. Moreover, reference to Luhmann's three types of social systems allows a clearer way of understanding the socio-structural bases of this independent variation. Societal system, organization, and interaction are not just points on a singular macro to micro continuum: they are different ways of constructing social systems. As such, changes in one do not necessarily imply parallel changes in the other two; but neither is such mutual conditioning excluded. As a hypothesis, then, we would test the secularization thesis separately and in conjunction at the level of societal systems (first dimension), at the level of organizational and social movement systems (second dimension), and at the level of interactions and interaction networks (third dimension; cf., Luhmann 1982).

GLOBAL SOCIETY AND SECULARIZATION THEORY

If we now ask the question of secularization of global society, one of the main consequences is that we will take the world as a whole as our empirical testing-ground and subunits of it only in the context of that whole. Thus, from a global perspective the notion that "local" factors are sufficient for understanding the religious situation in any region, country, or other geographical division is no longer a justifiable assumption. No longer can we limit ourselves, for instance, to western countries because these have supposedly become "modern" while the rest of the world remains in a "pre-modern" state. The theory of secularization will stand, fall, or transform in a field of vision that includes not only Europe, Australasia, and North America, but also all of Asia, South America, and Africa. In addition, how a religious institution appears in any given region has to be tested and understood also in terms of non-regional, that is global, influences.

To take one obvious example, the Roman Catholic church is quite clearly a global religious organization that cannot be identified with any of its regional manifestations; nor is it simply the sum of these (see Casanova 1997). The global character finds its reflection in organizational policies ranging from the nature of its ritual offerings to the way it relates to governments and responds to changes in local religious involvement. Accordingly, Roman Catholicism itself is a relatively consistent independent variable when it comes to understanding religious involvement; just as there is a consistency in the way this organization, as an institutional manifestation of the global religious system, relates to political, economic, health, educational, media, and other societal systems. Such observations do not negate the importance of a whole host of more local factors such as cultural particularities and relative minority/majority status. They point out, however, that not only can we not have a proper understanding of secularization and Roman Catholicism without at least the addition of a global perspective, but that implicitly the secularization debate has been forced to do this all along (see, e.g., Chaves and Cann 1992; Verweij et al. 1997).

Similarly, the religion of immigrant groups may look locally like cultural adaptation; but very often such religious expression is also tied into transnational and global movements, leading to developments in terms of both points of reference. To take one or two examples: recent Muslim migrants to Europe and North America have been forming different sorts of religious institutions, often congregational and multifunctional, in their new locations. These forms can be understood to a large extent in local terms. Yet at least in part, the proliferation of these organizational and involvement manifestations owes its strength and other of its features to global characteristics of contemporary Islam. These include the availability of a range of social resources: everything from money and books to "anti-secular" (that is, de-differentiating) theologies and the global cultural example of Islamic strength or resurgence. Even among non-migrants, such as African-American Muslims, these same factors undoubtedly affect the form — for example, greater "orthodoxy" — and the strength of local religious movements (cf., Haddad and Smith 1994). Again, therefore, such factors affect all three dimensions of what secularization theory looks at.

A third example concerns Pentecostalism. Like Roman Catholicism and Islam, this is a global movement with at least as striking local variations. It seems to be strong and growing in a great many regions of the world, in some more than others (cf., Cox 1995). Trying to understand Pentecostal organizational and involvement growth in terms of only one region or country at a time is quite clearly inadequate in light of the global character of the phenomenon (see Poewe 1994). Thus, to take but one instance, Pentecostalism is growing in almost all regions of Canada, but this seems to be paltry when compared to what is happening in Latin America. Therefore, differences between the region that coincides with the Canadian state and that which we call Latin America do have an impact. Yet how does one understand the fact that Pentecostalism is such a significantly growing religious movement in so many regions of the world at the same time? To what elements does that global growth correspond? As with Roman Catholicism, both local and global factors are evidently involved. To attempt an understanding of this movement with relation to the questions of secularization solely on an isolated country-by-country basis is not only to underestimate sub-national local variation but, more important, to miss the dynamic features of Pentecostalism that make it a growing worldwide religious phenomenon: it seems to respond to critical features of global society, as well as those of local regions or countries. Or, to put the matter in another way, this time using the language of current rational choice approaches to religion, a global perspective asks us to look at the religious market as global, as well as local or national. And to repeat, part of my main point is that the debate about secularization has been doing this implicitly for quite some time simply because the data make it almost unavoidable.

Looking at the question of secularization from a global perspective, and in light of the concrete examples that I have just given, one is led to at least one rather obvious conclusion. If we include Iran, Korea, and India in our view along with the United States and Sweden, it seems evident that the notion of secularization as a straightforward loss for religion of all societal influence or significance does not apply to global society as a whole. Indeed, few observers anywhere are willing to defend the hypothesis that, globally speaking, we live today in a secularized society in that sense. The distinction among dimensions of secularization should, however, induce caution in letting the matter rest there. It may be that globally, at the level of individual involvement and orientations, religion is as strong or weak as it has ever been. Yet that idea does not address the question of the social forms of religion and the broader societal influence and significance of those social forms. For these social forms are what, sociologically speaking, religion is. It is these that the sociological theory of secularization addresses primarily. Individual religious consciousness must, sociologically speaking, remain strictly derivative. Put somewhat differently, if the religious institutions that bring about the convergence of religious communication (and, only thereby, consciousness) in specific social forms of religion are relatively weak in one society as opposed to another (and I remind the reader that in the present context *society* is quite expressly *not* a synonym for *country*), then it is meaningful to speak about the secularization of the former in comparison with the latter. Attention to the different dimensions of secularization with respect to global society can serve to clarify this statement.

As I indicated above, the societal dimension of secularization refers to the effects on religious forms and influence of a dominance of functionally differentiated societal systems. What secularizes at this level are the *other* societal systems, meaning that religious communication directly determines at best *only one* such system among others. The secularization thesis would then hypothesize the decline of overall societal influence of religion as a result of this circumstance, not its disappearance or even necessarily overall decline in *all* dimensions. In a context of *competition*, not among religions, but among different technically and instrumentally oriented societal systems, the one for religion will have difficulty being among the more determinative.[1] Thus, for example, a region of global society which is "underdeveloped" in terms of political power, economic wealth, educational attainment, technological sophistication, mass media presence, or health institutions is one that, from the perspective of social power, most observers would consider disadvantaged and marginalized. In that light, the secularization thesis would ask: How many of these observers would put into this category a region where religious institutions are weak or declining? If the answer to this question, based on empirical observation, is that few would, then the secularization thesis would be pointing to an important sociological aspect of that society. I should note that this scenario quite expressly includes the possibility that quite a few observers would consider the "religiously weak" regions *religiously and morally* insufficient and perhaps even doomed in the future because of their religio-moral weakness; but that is another way of making the same point: it is *only* by religious and religiously dependent criteria that such regions are weak. Such considerations, however, point to only part of the picture.

---

[1] This argument is, of course, equivalent to transposing the question of secularization to that of *privatization*. I avoid that formulation here because the term privatization is subject to at least as much varied meaning as secularization, and therefore its use would require me to devote considerable space to a preliminary discussion of this term as well. Elsewhere, I have done the reverse — avoided the term secularization to talk only about privatization (see Beyer 1994: chapter 3).

A further important point is that any secularization thesis, whether applied locally or globally, will have very little cogency if we adopt a too functional conception of religion. If, for instance, whatever makes for societal integration, community solidarity, worldview, or speculation about "ultimate reality" is to be counted as religion, then it is located so closely to the very existence of social groups and the act of reflection on the human condition that religion will be influential in any society by definition. For secularization to have real meaning, therefore, we have to adopt a more substantive idea of religion, one that includes both the necessary presence in religious activity of postulated supraempirical, supernatural or divine agency, and above all the supposition by human religious actors that such agencies (whether personal or not) can and do communicate or are more generally accessible as sources of information. Such a substantive conception would also have to include authoritative institutions that carry, control, and are primarily charged with such communication.

In sum then, secularization at the level of global society must address the question of religious influence and importance with multiple dimensions in mind, with a substantive or institutional conception of what will count as religion, and therefore with a focus on the fate of the social forms of religion in this society. Only with these assumptions can we coordinate what it is that we are talking about. What arises from such a perspective, however, is not a straightforward picture of either the confirmation or the falsification of a thesis of religious decline; nor, for that matter, one of religious resurgence. Instead, I would suggest, what we get is a fairly complex and *unpredictable* picture. As Karel Dobbelaere states in his chapter, secularization, from a multidimensional and institutional perspective, becomes a descriptive and not a predictive hypothesis. Even if we were to agree that, thus far, the dominance of a functionally differentiated system at the global societal level has led to the decline in the broader social influence of religious institutions relative to other functionally oriented institutions, that does not mean that we can say with any assurance that this situation will continue as long as the structure of global society is as it is. That, of course, is already a significant retreat from a strong version of secularization, which insists that modernization means the inevitable decline and even disappearance of religion, in whatever form.

RELIGION IN GLOBAL SOCIETY

Turning now to the question of the social forms of religion in global society, we can perhaps divide the possibilities into four general heuristic types or alternatives for creating and maintaining religious convergence or authority that can be broadly powerful and influential in the day-to-day workings of global society. First, historically one of the most common is what I wish to call the "collective cultural" type, in which religion is not clearly differentiated from other aspects of culture and is simply the religious dimension of collective cultural life. Examples are the religions of small scale societies, most popular religion, and religious expressions that maintain their patterns and convergence by local custom and tradition. This is a very interaction-based form of religion. Second, we have organized religion (including religious movements), a form that differentiates religious activity in terms of distinctions between members and nonmembers and the rules that define the difference. Monastic religion, religious orders, sects, denominations, and today many cultic and pilgrimage centers would fall in this category. The third model is that of politicized religion, which includes state enforced religious monopolies such as the classic "church," and instances in which religious prescriptions are made collectively binding through incorporation in political and legal structures. Finally, the limiting case of minimal or no convergence is individualized or small social-network religion, exemplified for instance in Luckmann's notion of "invisible religion" or *bricolage* (Luckmann 1967), and Stark and Bainbridge's idea of audience or client cult (Stark and Bainbridge 1985).

In global society as a whole, all four of these types have their place and importance. In light of the density of global communication, however, the collective cultural type is probably disfavored simply because it relies heavily on the lack of both religious and secular alternatives to maintain convergence. It is, of course, still widely present, not just in comparatively isolated regions, but also in the world's large urban areas. Here as well, local traditions have a way of perpetuating themselves. People do not change their religious habits all that easily. Cultural traditions, including religious ones, maintain themselves through families and other interaction-based social networks without the assistance of overarching systems, organizations, or social movements. Indeed, the increasing availability of religious alternatives can just as easily lead to the reassertion of one's traditional religious identity. Getting to know "the other" does not necessarily mean becoming more like that other; it can also lead to the clearer understanding of the difference of oneself (see Beyer 1997). Nonetheless, left to itself, this sort of religious continuity will probably eventually lead to greater and greater divergence unless institutions of religious authority can find ways of asserting or maintaining the convergence. That implies organizational (including social movements) and/or politico-legal strategies. For the purposes of the secularization thesis, this type would therefore appear under the analysis of one or more of the other three.

The other three types would seem, by contrast, to be greatly favored in a global society dominated by technical societal systems and by undeniable cultural and religious pluralism. Individualized religiosity is a clear possibility in the majority of the world's regions, but I leave this aside because this form cannot, almost by definition, generate the kind of religious convergence that would seem to be a condition for the possibility of the broad social influence of the religious modality. Put somewhat differently, and following Luckmann (1967), a dominance of "invisible" religion is tantamount to secularization in a quite strong sense because there would be insufficient concentration of communicative resources to mount a serious effort at broad societal influence of religious tendencies as religion.

As for politicized religion, I have argued elsewhere (1994) that this is probably the prime way for religious institutions and authorities to gain the sort of influence that would negate any version of the secularization thesis. Nonetheless, a key part of that argument is that the possibilities in this direction have thus far been restricted, above all by the limitations of the most important structure of the global political system, the nation-state. States are geographically limited in their surveillance capacities, and in the context of the global state system, extending religious prescriptions beyond borders is problematic except insofar as state authorities avail themselves of the same techniques as are available to any nongovernmental movement or organization. Indeed, with the exception of a number of Islamic countries such as Iran, Saudi Arabia, and Pakistan, politicizing religion in order to generate a religious monopoly is in global terms comparatively rare or at least difficult to maintain. We thus arrive at organized religion as the one form with the most possibilities and perhaps even the most interest as far as the secularization thesis is concerned.

Organized religion has the distinct advantage of not having to rely directly on other societal systems nor on circumstances that are difficult to maintain in a richly connected global society. Unlike the politicized option, it does not have to depend on control of the political and legal systems, nor on their express support for religious authority. Unlike the collective cultural type, it does not rely on a relatively homogeneous religious environment. In fact, the organization is a type of social system that can, through its membership rules and internal structures, ignore other social boundaries, even those defined by geography and powerful systems such as states and the global economy. Social movements have similar advantages. Organizations allow, from a global society perspective, relatively arbitrary communicative convergence simply because the members agree on the rules that define it. And in modern global circumstances, most organizations are not totalistic, allowing their members to lead much or most of their lives outside the organizational structures. This feature is part of the flexibility of the organization that makes it such a widespread type of social system under modern and global circumstances. From the Roman Catholic church to Soka Gakkai, from Agudat Israel to worldwide Buddhist orders, organization is one, and possibly even the prime, systemic face of religion in today's world.

The advantages of organizations and social movements have a reverse face, however. Unlike societal systems such as economy, state, or science, organizations and movements can be endlessly multiplied; they foster pluralism in religion, indeed they are largely the way that we give form and face to religious pluralism. While that is a strength from some perspectives — notably in current rational choice theories of religion — in other respects it points precisely to what the secularization thesis is talking about, at least in its societal dimension. If we reduce the secularization thesis to the simplistic prediction that religion will disappear in modern and global society, then the continued strength and vitality, at the least, of organized religion belies it rather straightforwardly. If, on the other hand, we look at religion as a societal system in comparison and to some degree in competition with other societal systems, notably politics, law, economy, science, mass media, education, and medicine, then the picture is quite different. Without overarching structures beyond movements and organizations, structures that bring about a broader convergence of communication such as happens in these latter systems, religion is at a distinct disadvantage. It is in this sense that pluralism points to secularization; for there are currently no such overarching structures for religion. There are just religions and their myriad independent subdivisions in whatever form. At bottom, for religion there is no "discipline of the market," a lack for which we find ironic evidence in the inability thus far for proponents of rational choice approaches to religion to find any satisfactory measure of "competitiveness" other than "success" in terms of strictly organizational or social movements measures. Religion has, for instance, no global bodies of note, other than those for individual religions; it has no broadly accepted standards of attainment such as generating the latest scientific or medical advance, scoring high or low on educational attainment tests, or even, as in the world of sport, world championships. It has no equivalent of interchangeable currencies or capital markets, and only very rudimentary parallels to political diplomacy. These and others like them are, of course, technical measures and procedures, and one might argue that such things should not apply to religion. That, however, is simply a reflection of the fact that the society is dominated by technically oriented systems.

Looked at from a somewhat different angle, the prevalence of organizational and politicized religion as forms for producing convergent religious authority means that the strength of religion in global society is unlikely to yield any discernible pattern over the medium to long term. Only two possibilities are easy to exclude: the outright disappearance of either religion as such or authoritative religions, and the emergence of a victorious world religion that effectively absorbs or supersedes all the others. Within those broad extremes exists a great variety of possibilities. If we accept that politicization is both difficult and effectively limited to individual states, if we accept further that the reliance on organizational and social movement forms can lead to very diverse regional results ranging from little authoritative religion and *bricolage* to multiple strong religious organizations and even regional monopolies, then the global picture from the perspective of secularization theory will continue to be extremely varied with no discernible global pattern. Religion, in other words, is *optional* at the level of global society. It can be locally strong or weak, by whatever institutional measure, with no necessary consequences in other functional systems. If educational attainment, economic performance, saturation of mass media, strength of legal system and government can be correlated with health (for example infant mortality, average life expectancy), or any other combination of these, the same cannot be said for religion. People can go to church in droves in the United States or stay away in droves in Europe. Iran can set up a theocratic state and China can claim an atheistic one. As far as religion is concerned, at the level of global society, there are quite a number of likely regional outcomes; therefore it makes little sense to see one region or another as the *exception* because, on the basis of current evidence, both contemporary and historical, there does not seem to be a clear trend. Following this suggestion, the whole question of exceptionalism would in effect become moot, and it would become so on the basis of secularization theory. This brings me, in a concluding argument, to the matter of the explanatory status of secularization theory — and, for that matter, of its supposed rivals.

THE USE OF SECULARIZATION THEORY

As I have argued, versions of secularization theory which have predicted that modern societal conditions mean the necessary decline of religion in all dimensions have been proved wrong. Such strong versions were in any case rarely the rule among sociologists of religion. If Berger (1967), Luckmann (1967), and Wallace (1966) could be accused of that in the 1960s and 1970s, others such as Parsons (1966), Luhmann (1977), and Martin (1979) could not. The aspect of the secularization thesis that is, I suggest, still valuable is the portion of the analysis which looks at the consequences for religion of a dominance of functional differentiation (see Casanova 1994). The institutional or societal dimension of secularization continues to be a way of gaining insight into what is happening to religion not only under modern, but also under global conditions. Yet even here, we must bear in mind that secularization is a very high level, macrotheoretical construct. As such, its value is not and never has been in *predicting outcomes*, but rather in offering a useful *description of the societal situation* in which we find ourselves with respect to religion. Put in another way, the secularization thesis explains why and how religion as an arena of human endeavor faces peculiar challenges in contemporary global society; it cannot, however, predict how the observable responses in the religious domain will fare, simply because at that macrosocial level there are far too many variables at play. One of the advantages of moving the question of secularization to the global level is that this limitation of the theory becomes that much more obvious. It is from this perspective that I must by and large agree with Karel Dobbelaere's assessment: secularization is useful as a descriptive term, much like the idea of globalization and its various attendant theories. Its "truth" or "falsity" is therefore in the cogency of its descriptions and in the kinds of questions it allows us to ask, not in its predictive capacity. In this respect, probably its main strength is that it encourages us to ask the question of social form and social influence of religion and religions, and not just that of quantitative presence or absence. It sharpens our awareness of distinctions between religiousness and religion, between religious orientation or religious action and religious authority. As such, it is well worth maintaining in the sociological arsenal as a way of seeing the contemporary, modern, and global situations — as long as we understand that neither it nor any other theoretical approach deserves to monopolize our sociological vision.

REFERENCES

Berger, P. 1967. *The sacred canopy: Elements of a sociological theory of religion.* Garden City, NY: Doubleday Anchor.

Beyer, P. 1994. *Religion and globalization.* London: Sage.

———. 1997. Identity and character as elective strategies. *International Journal on World Peace* 14 (4): 13-39.

———. 1998. The modern emergence of religions and a global social system for religion. *International Sociology* 13: 151-72.

Casanova, J. 1994. *Public religions in the modern world.* Chicago, IL: University of Chicago.

———. 1997. Globalizing Catholicism and the return to a "universal" church. In *Transnational religion and fading states*, edited by S. H. Rudolph and J. Piscatori, 121-43. Boulder, CO: Westview.

Chaves, M., and D. E. Cann. 1992. Regulation, pluralism, and religious market structure. *Rationality and Society* 4: 272-90.

Cox, H. 1995. *Fire from heaven: The rise of Pentecostal spirituality and the reshaping of religion in the twenty-first century.* Reading, MA: Addison-Wesley.

Dobbelaere, K. 1981. Secularization: A multi-dimensional concept. *Current Sociology* 29 (2): 1-213.

Featherstone, M., ed. 1990. *Global culture: Nationalism, globalization, and modernity.* London: Sage.

———. 1995. *Undoing culture: Globalization, postmodernism, and identity.* London: Sage.

Haddad, Y. Y., and J. I. Smith, eds. 1994. *Muslim communities in North America.* Albany: State University of New York Press.

Luckmann, T. 1967. *The invisible religion: The problem of religion in modern societies.* New York: Macmillan.

Luhmann, N. 1975. Die Weltgesellschaft. In *Soziologische Aufklärung II: Aufsätze zur Theorie der Gesellschaft*, 51-71. Opladen: Westdeutscher.

———. 1977. *Funktion der Religion.* Frankfurt: Suhrkamp.

———. 1982. *The differentiation of society.* New York: Columbia University Press.

———. 1995. *Social systems.* Stanford, CA: Stanford University.

———. 1997. *Die Gesellschaft der Gesellschaft.* Frankfurt: Suhrkamp.

Martin, D. 1979. *A general theory of secularization.* Oxford: Blackwell.

Parsons, T. 1966. Religion in a modern pluralistic society. *Review of Religious Research* 7: 125-46.

Poewe, K., ed. 1994. *Charismatic Christianity as a global culture.* Columbia: University of South Carolina Press.

Robertson, R. 1992. *Globalization: Social theory and global culture.* London: Sage.

Simpson, J. H. 1988. Religion and the churches. In *Understanding Canadian society*, edited by J. Curtis and L. Tepperman, 345-69. Toronto: McGraw-Hill Ryerson.

Stark, R., and W. S. Bainbridge. 1985. *The future of religion: Secularization, revival, and cult formation*. Berkeley: University of California Press.

Verweij, J., P. Ester, and R. Nauta. 1997. Secularization as an economic and cultural phenomenon: A cross-national analysis. *Journal for the Scientific Study of Religion* 36: 309-24.

Wallace, A. F. C. 1966. *Religion: An anthropological view*. New York: Random House.

Wilson, B. 1966. *Religion in secular society: A sociological comment*. London: Watts.

6

Religion in Modernity as a New Axial Age: Secularization or New Religious Forms?

Yves Lambert[*]

Groupe de Sociologie des Religions et de la Laïcité
CNRS-EPHE, Paris

This article proposes a general model of analysis of the relations between religion and modernity, where modernity is conceived as a new axial age. Modernity appears to have four principal types of religious effects: decline, adaptation and reinterpretation, conservative reaction, and innovation. It produces secularization as well as new religious forms, in particular: worldliness, dehierarchization of the human and the divine, self-spirituality, parascientificity, pluralism, and mobility. Two thresholds of secularization are distinguished: (1) autonomization in relation to a religious authority and (2) abandonment of any religious symbol. I conclude that the first threshold has largely been crossed, but not the second one, except in some domains (science, economics) or for only a minority of the population. This is because of the adaptation of the great religions to modernity, of fundamentalist reactions, and of the spread of new religious forms.

Instead of approaching the question of secularization directly, I will begin with a general model of analysis of the relations between religion and modernity. This model is based on a comparative analysis of oral religions, religions of antiquity, religions of salvation, and the transformations linked to modernity. In itself, secularization is not the object of this work, but if we proceed correctly, it should allow us to evaluate the scope of secularization without entering into the debates and emotions to which this thesis has given rise in the past thirty years. A large portion of the article will thus be devoted to an analysis of the relation between religion and modernity. It characterizes modernity as a new axial period, reviews the global analyses of the religious consequences of modernity, presents a model of analysis and several religious forms typical of modernity, and provides empirical illustrations. We shall then examine the conclusions which

[*] *Many thanks to A. T. Larson and S. Londquist, for the translation of the French original; to A. Blasi, J. Ruane and W. H. Swatos for the revision; and, for their comments and criticisms, to: F. Champion, M. Cohen, K. Dobbelaere, D. Hervieu-Léger, F. Lautman, D. Olson, J.-M. Ouédraogo, G. Michelat, J. Ruane, J. Sutter, W. H. Swatos, and L. Tomasi.*

can be drawn from this analysis as far as secularization is concerned and compare them to the data obtained from the 1981 and 1990 World Value Surveys (WVSs), and the 1991 International Social Survey Programme (ISSP) survey dedicated to religion.

Obviously, our conclusion depends in part on the ways in which we define modernity, religion, and secularization. Without wishing to enter into the debate on these questions, I will explain my definitions with the aim of clarifying my approach and indicating the limits of my analysis. For religion, I understand it in the most common sense of a group, organization, or institution considering itself as such. This excludes "secular religions" but does not prevent us from finding a religious dimension present in such ideologies. More precisely, I will consider "religious" any practice or belief which refers to a superempirical reality, i.e., a reality radically exceeding the objective limits of nature and man, provided that there is a symbolic relationship between man and this reality; "objective" is used in the sense of the scientific process which characterizes the point of view of the social sciences. This definition allows us to deal with "parallel beliefs" which are currently increasing in importance (telepathy, astrology, fortune telling, spiritism, cosmic consciousness, energies, near death experiences, and so on). They refer to a superempirical reality, and they will be considered as religious if they include a symbolic relationship with man, which is the case of spiritism but not of astrology, which will be considered as parareligious. For secularization, Peter Berger's (1967) definition seems to be the most relevant to our purpose, and I will operationalize it by distinguishing two thresholds of secularization: (1) an autonomization in relation to religious authority while religious symbols remain salient and (2) an abandonment of religious symbols.

MODERNITY AS A NEW AXIAL PERIOD

Several historians and philosophers have stressed the key role that certain periods in history have played in developing techniques, political structures, or worldviews which were to dominate the foreground of the next centuries or millennia before being, in turn, questioned, then replaced, or altered and inserted into new systems. "Man seems to have started again from scratch four times," Karl Jaspers wrote (1954: 37-38): with the Neolithic age, with the earliest civilizations, with the emergence of the great empires, and with modernity. Each of these axial turns produced a general reshaping of the "symbolic field," to use Pierre Bourdieu's term, and a great religious commotion which led to disappearances, redefinitions, and emergences. Each period finally led to new religious configurations, respectively: oral agrarian religions, religions of antiquity, religions of salvation (universalist religions), modern changes. Of the religions of antiquity, only Judaism and Hinduism survived the preceding axial age, abeit greatly changed and keeping typically pre-universalist traits (at least up to modernity): a large number of prohibitions, important domestic rites, transmission by descent. We may assume that modernity also stands as a major challenge to established religions as well as a potential source of religious innovation, especially if it is about to be radicalized and generalized, as Giddens argues (1991). In addition, the hypothesis of modernity as a new axial turn leads us to consider very long-term effects; this enables us to perform comparative research, and proposes an interpretation accounting not only for religious decline, but also for revivals, mutations, and inventions.

The concept of "axial age" has been used to refer to one historical period: the emergence of universalism, philosophy, great religions, early science (see, e.g., Jaspers 1954; Bellah 1976: 20-50; Eisenstadt 1986; Hick 1989: 21-35). This is especially true of the sixth to fifth centuries BCE, which were a key stage in this process (Deutero-Isaiah, the era of Pericles, Upanishads, Jain, Buddha, Confucius, Lao-Tze), of which Christianity and Islam are offsprings. This age is considered as "axial" because we continue to be its heirs, particularly through the great religions. However there is no reason that we cannot also consider the Neolithic age, the earliest civilizations, the great empires, and modernity as such axial ages, since they too mark a general reshaping of collective thought. Therefore, our definition of "axial age" (or axial period) shall include these four ages. At its beginning, an axial age is a kind of cinematic fade; it is marked by critical moments of crisis and shifts of thought which lead to a reshaping of the symbolic field which creates a new period of stability. These critical phases vary in duration from, for example, a thousand years for universalism (from the sixth century BCE to the emergence of Islam) to several millennia for the Neolithic age (from its first emergence to its eventual global expansion and triumph).

Jaspers, while in fact considering modernity as being a new axial period, regarded the turn taken by modernity in the nineteenth century as the harbinger of a probable "second axial period" (Jaspers 1954: 38). He hesitated because globalization was not yet a widespread phenomenon when he first wrote this in 1949, although we can assume that this is the case today. Jaspers identified modernity with four fundamental distinguishing features: modern science and technology, a craving for freedom, the emergence of the masses on the historical stage (nationalism, democracy, socialism, social movements), and globalization. We find it relevant to add to this list the primacy of reason (a point that Jaspers implicitly includes in the four features), the development of capitalism, and functional differentiation (the rise of the modern state, and Parsons's and Luhmann's concept of differentiation of the spheres of activity in society).

This notion of axial age has not been utilized by sociologists to analyze modernity. However Arpád Szakolczai and Lászlo Füstös (1996) refer to the "axial age," and they use the concept of "axial moment" in ways that are relevant to this analysis. They define this notion as follows: "An axial moment occurs whenever there is a global collapse of the established order of things, including the political system, the social order of everyday life, and the system of beliefs — a very rare event — and a major spiritual revival. . . . Such a period happened in the first centuries (collapse of the Roman republic and rise of Christianity), in the fifth-seventh centuries (collapse of the Roman Empire and rise of Islam), in the fifteenth-sixteenth centuries (the waning of the Middle Ages, Renaissance, and Protestantism), and finally the two majors stages of the dissolution of absolutist politics and the traditional European social order, Enlightenment and socialism." Thus, that which they choose to define as an axial moment corresponds to key phases that occur within an axial age. For example, the rise of Christianity and of Islam are two key phases of the previous axial age (universalism), and the fifteenth-sixteenth centuries, the Enlightenment, and socialism (or more accurately the rise of industrial society) are the three key phases of modernity. Nonetheless, I believe that it is useful to employ the term "axial moment" to define such phases within an axial period.

In a very schematic fashion we can therefore periodize modernity. It begins with this axial moment of the fifteenth-sixteenth centuries, which is not only the beginning of what historians call "the modern age," but also that of modern science, and of the birth of capitalism and the bourgeoisie. But modernity only becomes a major phenomenon at the end of this period with the Enlightenment, the English and, especially, the American and French Revolutions, the birth of scientific method and thought, and the birth of industry (second axial moment). The third axial moment should include the development and triumph of industrial society and of capitalism (nineteenth-mid-twentieth centuries), first in England, and then throughout Europe and North America, the development of socialism, the building of the nation-state, the spread of nationalism and colonialism to its breaking point with the two world wars, and finally, decolonization, globalization and, in the West, the triumph of democracy, of the affluent society, and of the welfare state. Modernity also resulted in the Cold War and the threat of nuclear destruction. The 1960s are often considered as a turning point: the beginning of the so-called post-industrial, post-fordian society, the information or knowledge society, and the beginning of the moral revolution. Ever since, the tertiary sector has become increasingly dominant, intangible factors of production (information, communication, and knowledge) and new technologies (computers and electronics) have become more important; and the family is becoming less and less traditional. In addition, globalization is complete, the middle class is getting more and more powerful, new problems (unemployment and pollution) and new social movements (feminism, regionalism, ecology, etc.) are emerging, and finally, Communism has collapsed.

Are we still in the era of modernity or in postmodernity? I share the opinion of Anthony Giddens (1991:3) who writes that "rather than entering a period of post-modernism, we are moving into one in which the consequences of modernity are becoming more radicalized and universalized than before." In fact, that which is supposed to define postmodernity is far from featuring these fundamentally new traits that characterize an axial turn, but could constitute a new "axial moment" (as Szakolczai thinks) that could be explained in terms of generalized, radicalized, and reflexive modernity. The hallmark of postmodernity is the "disqualification of 'great narratives' ": great religions, great ideologies (nationalism, Communism, fascism), and the ideology of endless progress. But this only allows us to differentiate ourselves from the prior phase (axial moment) of modernity, and it is partly refuted by new forms of nationalism and by religious fundamentalism. The relativization of science and technology is not new, but is increasing precisely because the excesses and dangers of the former are becoming dramatically threatening (nuclear threat, pollution). One could continue and show that the other features attributed to postmodernity are the logical extension of trends within modernity, as are the nuclear threat and pollution: the detraditionalization of the life-world, the anti-authoritarian revolt, hedonism, new social movements, and above all, individualization. The same even holds true for the selective return to certain traditions, once modernity has prevailed over tradition, or for the repeated claim to local identities, which is a reaction against globalization. So I agree with Beckford's criticism (1996: 30-47) of the concept of postmodernity.

In spite of all of this, I remain open to the hypothesis that we should be on the edge of some form of postmodernity, at least in a deeply new moment in modernity, because the risk of irreparable pollution and, above all, of nuclear destruction is the most dramatic and the most radical fate we can imagine insofar as the very survival of the human species is at stake; this actually is a fundamentally new trait. Besides, if we consider modernity as a new axial period, we cannot know where we are in this process, so much the more as modernity involves permanent change, even change at an accelerated pace, so that it might not be followed by a phase of stabilization, as was formerly the case. Thus, it could create some kind of permanent turn. Anyway, since an axial turn is a cinematic fade in which older forms can coexist for centuries with new forms or survive by adopting new forms, it would be very difficult, while we are on the inside of this fade, to distinguish the decline of modernity from the birth of postmodernity. At present, we do not have the necessary distance to resolve the matter, but in any case, whether we are in postmodernity, late modernity, hypermodernity, or whatever other term one might choose, it does not change anything concerning our method of analysis.

GLOBAL ANALYSES OF THE DISTINGUISHING RELIGIOUS FEATURES OF MODERNITY

The intent of this section is to review the various claims that have been made concerning the effects of modernity on religion and the transformations that are taking place in religion. I will not attempt to link these analyses in a systematic way, as that is the task of the following section. " I am reasonably sure," said Bellah (1976: 39), that "even though we must speak from the midst of it, the modern situation represents a stage of religious development in many ways profoundly different from that of historic religion." In addition, as Gordon Melton (1998: 594) remarks,

> [D]uring the twentieth century, the West has experienced a phenomenon it has not encountered since the reign of Constantine: the growth of and significant visible presence of a variety of non-Christian and non-orthodox Christian bodies competing for the religious allegiance of the public. This growth of so many religious alternatives is forcing the West into a new situation in which the still dominant Christian religion must share its centuries-old hegemony in a new pluralistic religious environment.

Of course, no new world religion or spirituality has spread on a wide scale, and until now, the most visible novelty of the modern symbolic landscape has been the offspring of secular thoughts and worldviews (science, ideologies, ethics, human rights, etc.). However, we have also observed fundamental changes in the religious landscape, and we may be in a burgeoning phase of evolution. What do we learn from the global analyses of modernity as a new stage in the religious history of humankind or from analyses considering the modernist challenge to religion as a whole?

Jaspers (1954: 278-80) confined himself to some terse but insightful remarks: "If a transcendent aid does manifest itself," he predicted about completed modernity, "it can only be to free a man and by virtue of his autonomy," for "he that feels free lets his beliefs fluctuate, regardless of any clearly defined credo . . . in accordance with an unfettered faith, which escapes any specific definition, which remains unattached while retaining the sense of the absolute and seriousness, along with their strong vitality." This faith, he adds, " still has not found any resonance with the masses" and is "despised by the representatives of the official, dogmatic, and doctrinaire creeds." But "It is likely, therefore, that the Bible religion will revive and undergo modifications." So Jaspers emphasizes the will to be free, which fits rather well with contemporary comments on *individualization*, but it also is an interesting prediction about *fundamentalism* and evangelism. In addition, Jaspers's own beliefs represent a radical *demythologization*: he neither believed in divine revelations nor in the incarnation and resurrection of Jesus, whom he considered only as a spiritual genius. But he was convinced that there was a transcendent dimension in man, to be found within oneself and especially through the value of life and the need for achievement. So we could say that he added two more possible characteristics of religion in modernity, especially new forms of *monism* and *this-worldliness*.

Joseph M. Kitagawa (1967: 60-62) highlights three related characteristic traits: *man as the center*, *this-worldly soteriology*, and the *search for freedom* (rather than the preservation of order), which are close to those of Jaspers. He especially recalls that "all classical religions tended to take negative attitudes toward phenomenal existence and recognized another realm of reality," which was the most important, and that, "in this life, man was thought to be a sojourner or prisoner" yearning for heaven or nirvana which would release him from suffering, sin, imperfection, finitude. "[A] radical change has taken place in this respect in the thinking of modern people, in that they no longer take seriously the existence of another realm of reality. To be sure, they still use such expressions as paradise, Pure Land, Nirvana, and the Kingdom of God. These terms have only symbolic meaning for the modern mentality . . . [to which] this phenomenal world is the only real order of existence, and life here and now is the center of the world of meaning." Religions now are compelled "to find the meaning of human destiny in this world — in culture, society, and human personality" in order to fulfill the human vocation (e. g., Gandhi), which means soteriologies centered on this world.

According to Bellah (1976: 39-44), "the central feature of the change is the *collapse of the dualism* [my emphasis] that was so crucial to all the historic religions. . . . There is simply no room for a hierarchic dualistic religious symbol system of the classical historic type. This is not to be interpreted as a return to primitive monism: it is not that a single world has replaced a double one but that an infinitely multiplex one has replaced the simple duplex structure. . . . Behind the 96 percent of Americans who claim to believe in God," he adds, "there are many instances of a massive reinterpretation that leaves Tillich, Bultmann, and Bonhoeffer far behind. . . . The dualistic worldview certainly persists in the mind of many of the devout, but just as surely many others have developed elaborate and often pseudo-scientific rationalizations to bring their faith in its experienced validity into some kind of cognitive harmony with the twentieth-century world." This, he explains, is due to science and individualization, which reduces the distance between the terrestrial and the celestial, the human and the divine, the laity and the clergy.

This reminds us of Kitagawa, while his stress on *individualization* reminds us of Jaspers: "the symbolization of man's relation to the ultimate conditions of his existence," says Bellah, "is no longer the monopoly of any groups explicitly labelled religious . . . not only has any obligation of doctrinal orthodoxy been abandoned by the leading edge of modern culture, but every fixed position had become open to question in the process of making sense out of man and his situation . . . one might almost be tempted to see in Thomas Paine's 'My mind is my church' or in Thomas Jefferson's 'I am a sect myself' the typical expression of religious organization in the near future." He adds: "[E]ach individual must work out his own ultimate solutions, and the most the church can do is provide him a favorable environment for doing so, without imposing on him a prefabricated set of answers," knowing that he will have an "open and flexible pattern of membership." So we can also speak of *flexibility* and *revisability*. He sees the modern man as "a dynamic multidimentional self capable, within limits, of continual self-transformation and capable, again within limits, of remaking the world, including the very symbolic forms with which he deals with it . . . with growing awareness that it is *symbolism* and that man in the last analysis is responsible for the choice of his symbolism." In addition, he observes that "the search for adequate standards of action, which is at the same time a search for personal maturity and social relevance, is in itself the heart of the modern quest for salvation," which refers to *this-worldliness*. He concludes that the analysis of modern man as secular and nonreligious is fundamentally misguided, and that the present situation is actually "offering unprecedented opportunities for creative innovation in every sphere of human action."

Analyzing "modern religious attitudes," Hajime Nakamura (1986: 511-60) refers to similar traits except for the *collapse of dualism*. He also deepens the notion of *humanism* and identifies new traits: a movement toward equality, an approach more open to the masses and a *lay tendency* (which reminds us of Jaspers's emergence of the masses) and *pluralism*. His analysis encompasses Asia and Japan, giving evidence that some form of modernity has also appeared to the East. He points to the "denunciation of religious formalism and the stress on inner devotion," emphasizing pure heart, pure mind, pure faith, the anti-ritualistic and anti-magic, citing the Reformation, but also Hinduism (from Râmânanda, Caitanya, Kabir to Râmakrishna), Sikhism (Nânak), and Zen Buddhism (especially Shinran, who was compared to Luther). However he also stresses the typically modern *search for authenticity*, which we can add to the picture.

He speaks of this-worldliness in terms similar to Kitagawa's, underlining the "return to this-worldliness," the "rise in popularity of worldly activity and vocational ethics," and the denial of monasticism not only in Protestantism but also in Hinduism (among the masters already cited and Tulsî Das), Sikhism, and Buddhism (Suzuki Shôsan shows that to pursue one's vocation is to do the doings of a Buddha). He is close to Kitagawa about the "changing evaluation of man . . . man conceived as supreme and the stress on human love," hence, he adds, a new religious emphasis on "service to people." More than any of the other authors, he develops the "increased lay tendency of religion" (lay roles, married priests, etc.), the "accelerated approach to the masses" (use of vernacular language, service to people, etc.), and the "heightened movement toward equality of man and anti-discrimination," with its secular as well as religious forms, which we can link to Jaspers's ideas of freedom and emergence of the masses. We again meet the same tendencies in the East. In addition, he stresses the rise of the idea that each religion is valuable, i.e., the acknowledgment of *pluralism*, a typical global effect of modernity. Interestingly, he shows that all of these changes emphasize *positive and humanistic aspects of religion*, including the value of the body, at the expense of fear of damnation or asceticism, and that, as a result of the increased value of the human person, there is a new emphasis on religious ethical norms (Humanism, Enlightenment, and also Caitanya, Tulsî Dâs, etc.). But he adds that all these changes are more pronounced in the West.

Most other global analyses of the relationship between religion and modernity have focused on secularization and have stressed the following traits:

demonopolization, privatization, this-worldiness, laicization, decline, linked to the general processes of individualization, rationalization, and functional differentiation (Dobbelaere 1981; Tschannen 1992). Peter Berger (1967) has emphasized especially the rise of *secular worldviews, subjectivization* (individualization), and *pluralization.* Danièle Hervieu-Léger (1986) speaks of *deregulation, bricolage, pragmatism, subjectivism;* she also stresses (1993: 129-48) the fact that modernity makes secular promises it cannot keep, especially in its present deutopionised phase, which is favorable to religious restructurings, especially the development of an emotional community type of religion valuing personal experience. Françoise Champion (1993) finds *self-primacy, this-worldiness, optimism, alliance with science, love ethics* in the "mystic-esoterical nebula." Jean-Paul Willaime (1995) has shown that the fundamental features of modernity (he mentions *systematic reflexivity* [referring to Giddens], *functional differentiation, individualization, rationalization, globalization,* and *pluralism*) could fuel both religious decomposition and recomposition, the latter especially in ultramodernity because it reasserts the value of traditions, cultures, meaning, subjectivity. Lester Kurtz (1995) points out: (1) the *substitution* of religious traditions with rationalism, scientism, and individualism; (2) *secularization;* (3) the *revitalization* of traditional forms; (4) the construction of *quasi-religious forms,* such as civil religion or ideologies; (5) the creation of new forms of religious beliefs and practices through processes of *syncretism;* and he highlights the fact that pluralism can produce religious revitalization as well as relativization. As to postmodern analysts, they have highlighted *self-religion, bricolage, syncretism, pluralism, subjectivism, probabilism, mobility* (Flanagan and Jupp 1996).

A GENERAL MODEL OF THE RELATIONSHIPS BETWEEN RELIGION AND MODERNITY

What to do with so many overlapping concepts? Though probably nothing is missing from such a picture, it does not amount to a systematic model of the relationships between religion and modernity. To contribute to such a model, we will first analyze the religious effects of each of the distinguishing features of modernity: the primacy of reason, science and technology, the craving for freedom, the emergence of the masses, globalization, the development of the economy and modern functional differentiation — taking account also of their combined effects. This will permit us to identify four typical religious effects for each feature of modernity: decline, adaptation or reinterpretation, conservation, and innovation.[1] The way these factors have historically worked could explain the religious situation in each country. In the following section, I will focus on

---

[1] Conversely, we would analyze the influence of religion on the modernizing process, but for lack of space, we will not elaborate on this influence in this chapter.

several of the new religious characteristics I have highlighted: this-worldiness, optionality and self-spirituality, dehierarchization, parascientificity, pluralization and relativization, mobility and revisability, loosely organized networks. I will also include some of the results of the World Value Survey (WVS) and of the International Social Survey Programme (ISSP), not so much in order to test the model (since it is above all an historical model and these surveys were not designed to test its sociological relevance), but to illustrate it and prepare for the debate on secularization.

(a) The *primacy given to reason* has been an essential factor of modernity since it furnished a strong basis not only for the rapid growth of science, but also for individual liberty, the breaking with tradition, the autonomization of the economy, and the questioning of the legitimacy of an orderly society as well as of the monarchy. Reason introduced a notion of truth that rivaled religion and tradition. Ernst Troeltsch himself deeply emphasized this feature, following Max Weber. The effect of the ascendancy of reason upon religion was and still is considerable and fundamentally ambivalent. In fact, while on one hand reason can be seen as emanating from God or from a divine order, or at least as not being in contradiction to religion, on the other hand it can be seen as an effective tool in the war against religion and religious interpretations of the world. For example, Descartes believed that God created man and endowed him with reason and that this reason would lead back to God, although only through a religion purified by reason. For Diderot, by contrast, reason clearly demonstrated that religion was one of man's inventions. Weber showed how reason was a factor in the rationalization of religion, and studies on irreligion and the loss of faith illustrate the antireligious effects which are notably due to the influence of atheistic philosophies. In itself, we know that neither reason, nor science for that matter, can prove or invalidate the existence of God or of an impersonal divine figure; indeed, it can provide arguments for each side, hence we have this fundamental ambivalence. As a general rule, the more religion was linked to that which reason explicitly questioned, the more opposed the use of reason was toward religion; although the opposite is also true insofar as religion redefined itself in relation to these changes, indeed became itself an agent of them: demythologization, human rights, redefinition of the respective domains of religion and science, and so forth. In this respect, we could say that France and the United States are diametrically opposed.

We miss sociological data on the perceived role of reason and the correlation between reason and religion, which no study has yet tried to identify. Karel Dobbelaere and Wolfgang Jagodzinski (1995: 96-101, 210-14), in identifying the degree of rationalization with the degree of modernization (GDP per capita, level of education, social structure), have correlated these elements. The demonstration seems partly conclusive: among the ten countries surveyed, the least developed have the highest levels of religiosity, i.e., Ireland, followed by Spain and Italy; while the most developed have a moderate or low level of religiosity, i.e., Germany, followed by France and Sweden. But that would no longer be confirmed if the analysis took into account Luxembourg, Switzerland, Austria, Canada, and above all, the United States, which figure among the most developed nations and which have the highest levels of religiosity. In any case, and whatever the results might be, we would still be unable to prove much of anything, not only because these indicators are not precise enough with regard to the degree of rationalization, but also because rationalization in itself has a basically ambivalent effect; hence the nature of this relationship needs to be measured with more precise indicators. The same ambivalence holds true for the other factors of modernity, especially science.

(b) Obviously *science* might lead to atheism (scientism, materialism) as well as to reinterpretations (demythologization, critical exegesis), fundamentalist reactions (creationism), or innovations (deism, parascientific beliefs). From its origins in ancient Greece up to present time, science, in much the same way as reason, has always had a radically ambivalent effect on religion. Archimedes was convinced that the laws of arithmetic revealed the principles of the divine order of things, and Copernicus marveled at the laws of creation; believing in God, Galileo, Newton, and Einstein thought that if religious scriptures were at odds with science, they needed only to be reinterpreted. On the other hand, Democritus thought that the physical world rendered the divine vacuous; and when Napoleon asked the physicist Laplace, "And where is God in all of this?," Laplace replied, "My Lord, I haven't ever needed to concern myself with that hypothesis." Today, the Big Bang can be considered to be the last word in the explanation of the universe just as easily as it can be considered to be the hand of God. Finally, Buddhists believe that atomic theory confirms the philosophy of aggregation. From the beginning of modernity the major points of confrontation between science and Christianity have without a doubt been Galileo's condemnation, Darwinism, Positivism, and Marxism.

Among the religious innovations influenced by science, we could first mention the concept of an impersonal God, religious movements such as Christian Science, the Church of Scientology, the New Age, as well as parascience: astrology, telepathy, cosmic energies, waves, extraterrestrials, and near death experiences (NDEs), which are perceived as scientific by a majority of their believers. While astrology is in itself not a new domain of knowledge, its present interpretation is primarily parascientific. *Parascientificity* is a typically modern religious form. Elements borrowed from the human sciences have themselves led to the development of new spiritual movements such as Human Potential, Scientology, and Transcendental Meditation. There is a belief in the convergence of science ("sheer science," "new science") and spirituality in Buddhism, in the mystic-esoterical nebula, the gnose of Princeton, and many New Religious Movements (NRMs). In ultramodernity, the relativization of science and technology seems to be able to favor both a return to religious traditions, a spread of millenarianisms, and an increase of parascientific salvation

(Champion 1993); but, once again, we lack sufficient data to be able to answer this question.

We cannot speak of science without also mentioning technology. In revolutionizing the conditions and quality of life by the material improvements they have brought about (health, food, housing, transportation, media, leisure, etc.), science and technology have contributed to the Copernican revolution that made worldly happiness the ultimate goal in life, instead of other-worldly salvation. But neither science nor technology has been able to answer the ultimate questions (Where do we come from? Where are we going? What is the meaning of life? Why do we suffer and die?), nor have they been able to eliminate sickness, injustice, misery, unhappiness, and death. Here again, technology can result in a refusal of religion (materialism, for example), in a religious adaptation (this-worldliness, humanism, faith-healers), in a conservative reaction (Amish), or in innovations (UFOs, Electrometers in the Church of Scientology), but fundamentalist movements usually adopt modern technology if for no other reason than the diffusion of their message. The return to a system of beliefs that highlights the importance of this world is a consequence of all of the combined factors of modernity.

In spite of the lack of sociological data (once again), we can nonetheless obtain an indirect idea of science's impact thanks to a question on how the Bible is perceived (1991 ISSP survey), with the following answers being possible: "The Bible is the actual word of God and it is to be taken literally, word for word /The Bible is the inspired word of God but not everything should be taken literally, word for word /The Bible is an ancient book of fables, legends, history, and moral precepts recorded by man /This does not apply to me /Can't choose." We find that the first two answers, "actual word" /"inspired word," had rates of agreement of 13 percent and 40 percent respectively in the Western European sample group (from the highest which were found in Italy, 26 percent /51 percent, to the lowest in Denmark, 6 percent /17 percent); in the United States, 32 percent /47 percent; in Russia, 10 percent /16 percent; in Poland, 55 percent /26 percent, which was the only country where the first percentage is higher; in Israel, 25 percent /26 percent.[2] With the exception of Poland, the percentage of those choosing the answer "actual word" was higher for the older age groups and for those with lower levels of education. In addition, the answer was more frequent among farmers, the working classes, as well as in the lower-middle classes (Lambert 1998).

Although it is a less useful indicator, in the World Value Survey there is a question on the kind of God, with the distinction between "A personal God," (i.e., the "true" Christian answer); "A spirit or vital force," (which may be the

---

[2] In Western Europe, the 1991 ISSP Survey was conducted in Germany, Great Britain, Ireland, Italy, Norway, the Netherlands, and in the former Eastern Bloc countries (East Germany, Poland, Russia, and Slovakia).

origin or the architect of the universe, the energies, the divine within each creature, cosmic consciousness, and so forth); "I don't really think there is any sort of spirit, God, or life force" (and "don't know," "no answer"). In Western Europe, God is only slightly more considered as "a personal God," 36 percent, than as "a spirit or vital force," 34 percent (unbelief rates 11 percent) (Lambert 1995); in France, the figures are 20 percent and 32 percent respectively; and in the United States, 69 percent and 23 percent, which confirms the former difference between Europe and the United States. Moreover, 40 percent of American scientists claim to believe in God. The responses vary primarily according to age: in Europe, from the eldest to the youngest generations, the percentage of those choosing "personal God" decreases from 47 percent to 28 percent, but in the United States from 70 percent to 66 percent. Similarly, the decrease of the belief that "God really exists" is 41 percent to 25 percent, in Europe; 67 percent to 57 percent in the United States (ISSP). According to a 1994 survey conducted in France, the home of scientism (CSA-Le Monde-La Vie), only 27 percent believe in the Judeo-Christian conception of creation (20 percent of the 18-24 age group), and 49 percent say that they agree with the item "the more science progresses, the more difficult it is to believe in God" (64 percent for the 18-24 age group), which shows that the problem is not over.

(c) The primacy of reason has in itself been a factor in the desire for liberty insofar as it allows for individual autonomy in the face of tradition, political power, and religious authority. *Individual consciousness and freedom* may favor a rejection of religion, or a more personal religion, or a reaction through reaffirmation of collective identity, or (especially in ultramodernity) a turn to bricolages, syncretisms and inventions, and parallel beliefs. As we might expect, individual choice may lead to any possibility we can imagine vis-à-vis religion and the churches, and individualization can be considered as the main feature of the changes in the value system of high modernity (Ester *et al.* 1993).

Protestantism was the first widespread religious expression of the desire for liberty and freedom with its innovations that were at the time revolutionary: a more personalized faith, the possibility for the laity to read the Bible in the vernacular (as opposed to a Latin Bible reserved to scholars and members of the clergy), and the possibility to confess one's sins directly to God. In this new context of denominational plurality and religious wars, freedom of belief was the first important claim to individual liberty, and it took two to three centuries before it actually triumphed. This demand for individual liberty also took the form of economic freedom (freedom of trade and commerce), of a general freedom of thought (Enlightenment), and of political liberty (democracy, the emergence of the masses). Freedom of thought also led to deism, natural or civil religion, and allowed for the choice not to believe, something that was even more audacious. The Roman Catholic church condemned the French Declaration of Human Rights of 1789 and furthermore condemned freedoms of conscience and speech, as well as the principles of laicity and the separation between church and state, while in the encyclical *Quanta Cura* (1864), the Syllabus denounced 80 "modern errors," among which we have the following error: "The Supreme Pontiff can and must reconcile himself with and reach a compromise with progress, liberalism, and modern society." Insofar as modernity has triumphed in all areas of society, the Catholic church has finally recognized this evolution while nonetheless remaining critical of it (Vatican II). As we know, the United States has played a pioneering role not only with regard to religious freedom (from the founding of Rhode Island to the First Amendment to the Constitution), but also with respect to religious pluralism and denominational mobility, which can be seen as its logical consequences (cf., Melton 1998). The craving for freedom has conquered new areas such as sexuality and family life, and in doing so has fired the conflict between permissiveness and traditional ethics, and provoked a conservative reaction within the churches.

According to the WVS and ISSP surveys, the effects of individualization in late modernity are ambivalent, although rather unfavorable toward institutionalized religion. Dobbelaere's variable of a "Christian worldview" (WVS), which rests on the role attributed to God in the meaning of life, suffering, and death, finds itself negatively correlated, if only weakly, with the five criteria of individualization. On the other hand, the variable of "Christian religiosity," which is based in part on the feeling of being religious, prayer, and the ability to find strength and comfort in religion (which in fact goes far beyond the Christian framework), is negatively correlated with but three of these five criteria. Nonetheless, when we neutralize the effect of age, this negative correlation weakens and, if we continue with reincarnation, parallel beliefs, and religious liberalism, we obtain positive correlations, which would undoubtedly be the case with everything that gives expression to personal religious responsibility or auto-spirituality. Roland Campiche (1992) shows that individualization is also a fundamental tendency of Christian redefinition in Switzerland; we have been able to confirm this using the same data in the case of European youth (Lambert 1993; Lambert and Voyé 1997), and Jacques Janssen has also confirmed it with a survey on the Dutch youth (1998). Especially from the 1960s onward, with the baby-boom generation, these studies show that church members are becoming more and more autonomous in their religious and moral life (Roof 1993; Roof *et al.* 1995). For instance, the 1988-1989 Roof sample of 1,400 Americans born between 1946 and 1962 were asked to choose between the following items: "Going to church/synagogue is a duty and an obligation" and it "is something you do if you feel it meets your needs": 76 percent opted for the latter choice, and this feeling was echoed by two-thirds of those who consider themselves to be born-again Christians. It also holds true for the Catholics.[3]

---

[3] In the case of the United States, see for instance, the *National Catholic Reporter*, 8 October 1993.

The present effects of individualization on religious innovation can be illustrated by the spread of religious pluralism, denominational mobility, bricolage, and parallel beliefs, which are once again significantly visible in the post-war generations. In the Roof sample, for instance, 33 percent were loyal to the religion into which they were born, 42 percent had left their churches, and 25 percent had returned after a period of absence. Insofar as parallel beliefs (telepathy, astrology, etc.) are completely free, as they are not controlled by any institution or orthodoxy, they can be individually defined and may coexist with Christian beliefs. It is perhaps for this reason that they are more popular with the younger generation than with the older. According to the 1991 ISSP Survey which asked three questions on parallel beliefs, 34 percent of those between the ages of 18 and 29 believe (definitely or rather strongly) that "good luck charms do bring good luck," against 22 percent of those 60 or older; 39 percent and 26 percent respectively believe that "fortune tellers can foresee the future;" and 32 percent and 26 percent that "the horoscope affects the course of the future." We can also observe that the NRMs that are the most successful in the long run are those which are not perceived as being hostile to the desire for freedom (such as New Age movements or others which at least claim to develop personal abilities, such as Scientology), while the most rigid and closed "cults" tend to be declining in popularity.

The attitudes toward permissiveness can also be illustrated by the WVS. Karel Dobbelaere and Wolfgang Jagodzinski (1995: 218-49) have shown a relationship between "moral rigidity" (against underage sex, homosexuality, prostitution, abortion, and extramarital affairs) and Christian religiosity. This is the area where the differences according to church attendance and religious affiliation are the most pronounced. For instance, only 18 percent of those who attend church at least once a week agree with the idea of "complete sexual freedom," compared to 43 percent who practically never or never attend church. The corresponding percentages are 4 percent and 29 percent for "marriage is an outdated institution," 13 percent and 49 percent for abortion "when a married couple does not want to have any more children," and 70 percent and 47 percent are in favor of greater respect for authority. These results are similar in the United States, though the differences are reduced among groups.

(d) The *emergence of the masses on the historical stage* (nationalism, democracy, socialism, Communism, fascism, social movements) has also had contradictory effects on religion according to the historical role of churches, (i.e., support, neutrality, or rejection), as David Martin (1978) has pointed out. Let us just say that nationalism has not played a very important role in the evolution of religion because the churches have in general supported nationalistic claims. Nonetheless, examples such as the Pontifical State's opposition to the unification of Italy in the nineteenth century, which was one of the main reasons for Italian anticlericalism, can be cited. Countries such as Ireland and Poland, where religion has historically played an important role in preserving and affirming national identity, are found to have the highest rates of religiosity. The main challenges have been the changes from monarchical to democratic political system, and above all the rise of socialism and communism. On this issue the United States and France offer interesting points of comparison. In the United States, followers of the Protestant church have historically been the major force behind the fight for human rights; by contrast, in France the Catholic church, especially with regard to its internal hierarchy, has been monarchist and antirepublican up until the end of the nineteenth century, but French Protestantism, which had been long submerged by Catholicism, if not persecuted, favored democracy and laïcity. This phenomenon can aid in explaining the "war of the two Frances" (clerical/anticlerical; laïcity). While socialism and communism have never been very influential in the United States, they have deeply marked the history of France and have generally been the basis for the opposition in Europe between a nonreligious or slightly religious Left and a rather religious Right. Nonetheless, the Catholic church in France finally acknowledged the legitimacy of the socialist vote in 1972, while the Left acknowledged the legitimacy of Catholic education in 1984. In addition, in the United States, denominational belonging has been very influential in social integration. While these divisions are part of the historical past, their influence can still be seen today in regard to the levels of religiosity which vary according to social class and political preference. This heritage is found throughout Western Europe in the religious differences between the social-democratic and Christian-democratic parties. Finally, late-modernity has seen the collapse of Communism, religion's worst enemy in the twentieth century. Another consequence of the emergence of the masses is the general dehierarchization of the relationship between the laity and the clergy, the lay tendency, and the adoption of vernacular languages (from early Protestantism to Vatican II).

The rise of new social movements (counterculture, feminism, ecology, peace, regionalism) could have renewed the relevance, or underlined the failure, of religion according to this schema of support or hostility. However this does not seem to have been the case insofar as the churches, in not having much at stake in these areas, with some exceptions (abortion, married priests, women in the priesthood, etc.) have not taken any major stand and have given their members the right to choose; even feminism has found a voice in the churches. These movements have had the effects of innovation (countercultural movements were one of the main sources of the NRMs in the 1960s, and 1970s; ecology inspired Spiritual Ecology), of adaptation (ecology is becoming a significant concern for major religions), and consequently, of reaction (the Moral Majority).

On a political scale of Left-Center-Right, according to the 1990 WVS, in Europe, 16 percent of those who attend church at least once a week place themselves toward the left, compared to 45 percent of those who either never attend or only rarely attend; in the United States, these percentages are 9 percent and

28 percent respectively. These figures are nearly the same among young adults in the United States, while in the case of young European churchgoers, the rate rises to 28 percent, which testifies to the acceptance of the political left. In addition, when we compare the data collected in the 1981 WVS to those of the 1990 WVS, we observe that the differences in church attendance and religious affiliation between the lower and upper classes are tending to level out. This points to the fact that the basic principle of social antagonism linked to industrial society is in decline. Belonging to a trade union is more frequent among those who do not consider themselves to be regularly practicing, although this is not the case in the United States. As for the new social movements, we can observe very few differences, if any, between the regularly practicing and the nonpracticing or nonreligious in regard to the approval of and participation in movements such as "ecology, nature protection," "non-nuclear energy," "disarmament," "human rights," "women," or "anti-apartheid;" and this is true regardless of age (1990 WVS). This is, of course, with the exception of the most religious, who are less involved in women's movements (or in joining unofficial strikes or occupying buildings and factories, but this is very infrequent), but more involved in human rights organizations.

(e) The *development of capitalism* has itself been a factor of the rise of materialism as well as of reinterpretation such as this-worldliness. Economics was the first sphere of activity to acquire autonomy, and it contributed to the development of socialism and communism through proletarianization, as I have already discussed. Although it was in vain, the Catholic church had long been opposed to loans of money-bearing interest. This-worldliness allowed for the development of nonreligious materialism as well as for a religious reinterpretation in terms of vocational ethics, or a this-worldly spirituality, as was illustrated by the famous Weberian thesis. We can observe these two aspects from the very beginning of capitalism (merchant cities and states in the fifteenth-sixteenth centuries) until today. Another effect of capitalism, which is especially apparent in high-modernity in the United States, is the shift toward a market-type religious structure and a consumer-type attitude (Iannaccone 1992). As for the conservative reactionary effect, we could use the example of the Amish; examples of innovative effects include some televangelists or the spiritual way of making money that the Church of Scientology illustrates. Although more difficult to identify, I could also mention the role of spiritual complementation that religion might play in an affluent society, but once again we lack empirical data on these issues.

(f) *Functional differentiation* means modern state-building, differentiation between the public sphere and the private sphere, Luhmannian autonomization of the spheres of activity. Its first marked effect was to deprive religion of its monopoly in education and culture, and in legitimizing the sociopolitical order. It could favor a marginalization of the church and of religion; but in keeping them from legitimizing the dominant order, it could also favor a redefinition of their roles in education, culture, health, social aid and welfare, human rights, peace, and so on, in keeping with the more pluralistic context that is characteristic of high modernity (Casanova 1994; Beckford 1996). It also produces reactionary effects that aim to maintain or reconquer religion's hold on society (fundamentalist trends). According to Luhmann (1977, 1982), modern society is divided into subsystems which each have a specific function and relative independence: politics, economics, science, education, law, art, health, family, and religion. Religion is a subsystem which is defined by its spiritual function. Among these subsystems, Luhmann also distinguishes between those which are imposed or prescribed upon all members of society, which he qualifies as "professional," such as politics, economics, science, education, and law; and those that are optional or "complementary" such as art and, specifically, religion. Finally, he distinguishes between the dual functions of a subsystem, its internal (specific) function and its external function, which he calls "performance" and which denotes its influence upon other subsystems on their own terrain. The WVS and ISSP give interesting clues to measure the importance given to religion, the performance of religion for individuals, and the fundamentalist or secularist attitudes.

(g) Similarly, *globalization* could further a radical relativization of religions (insofar as their truths are incompatible), and promote worldwide diffusion and gatherings (missions, NRMs, papal visits, etc.), reinterpretations with a more pluralist view (all religions are acceptable), ecumenism and interreligious dialogues, fundamentalist reactions, innovations (borrowings, bricolage, syncretism). Each of these effects is growing more and more acute in the current phase of accelerated globalization (Beyer 1994), especially among the young. Combined with democracy, globalization facilitates the diffusion of new religions and NRMs or provokes defensive and, indeed, even aggressive reactions (Eastern Orthodoxy).

According to the 1981 European Value Survey, 25 percent (17 percent of 18-29 year olds) thought that there was only one true religion; 53 percent (56 percent of 18-29) said that there were interesting insights in all the great religions; and 14 percent (19 percent of 18-29) said that no religion has any truth to offer. In France, those who think that there is only one true religion dropped from one-half in 1952 to 14 percent in 1981 (11 percent of 18-29). In the 1988-89 Roof sample (1993), 48 percent of baby-boomers agreed that "All the religions of the world are equally true and good." At the same time, we observe a shift toward probabilism, especially among young adults: the answers "probably" (yes or no) are as important as the "certainly" answers for many beliefs. We shall consider fundamentalist attitudes in the last section. A good example of syncretism (or bricolage) is the overlapping of the notions of resurrection and reincarnation. In the 1990 WVS, in Europe, about 40 percent of those who believe in resurrection say that they also believe in reincarnation, and vice versa. The rate increases to 50 percent for young adults. Even the

Christian core does not escape this attitude although, according to interviews conducted in France, it appears that this group conceives of reincarnation as the resurrection of the body (a one-time reincarnation), while the others prefer to think of it as a multiple resurrection.

We might also consider the interrelations among these factors. For example, science, by furthering the primacy of reason in the face of a religious monopoly of authority, was able to create a favorable climate for individual freedom and the emergence of the masses on the historical stage. Science conveys an implicit empiricist pattern that may influence the importance of personal experience in modern religious attitudes (pragmatism, self-spirituality). Science and technology contributed to the development of the economy (by furnishing the fundamental material of its own expansion), to globalization (by being the most universalized forms of activity), and to functional differentiation (with science being one of the differentiated spheres). In this way they influenced religion's evolution with regard to these areas. While I could continue to expand on these notions, for want of space let us instead turn to some of the new forms of religion which are typical of modernity and high modernity.

SEVERAL NEW RELIGIOUS FORMS OF MODERNITY

While not claiming the list to be exhaustive, I will mention as forms that appear worth highlighting: (a) this-worldliness, (b) self-spirituality, (c) dehierarchization and dedualization, (d) parascientificity, (e) pluralistic, relativistic, fluctuating, seeking faiths, and (f) loose network-type organizations (indeed, religion without religion).

(a) *This-worldliness* especially as a consequence of science, freedom, emergence of the masses, and capitalism tends to delegitimize the religions of salvation as well as reorient them toward more earthly aims, as I have previously stated. The importance formerly given to an other-worldly salvation has collapsed (Walter 1996). This notion has even become problematic: for instance, the research group "Religious and Moral Pluralism in Europe" had to abandon a question on the idea of salvation because, according to the preliminary tests, it was understood by only a third of those questioned. In the case of a Breton parish, I observed that Catholicism had been de facto reinterpreted as a transcendental humanism, aimed toward earthly fulfillment, while open to an afterlife devoid of eternal damnation (Lambert 1985). This observation can probably be generalized. It seems that the function of the afterlife is mainly to free man from the fear of death. New millenarianisms, which propose an earthly fulfillment (Jehovah's Witnesses, Mormons, Adventists), are expanding in popularity. The idea of a covenant between the American people and God expresses a logic similar to the one found in the Old Testament, where the fidelity of the chosen people was the guarantee of their prosperity. Televangelists put forth an analogical argument by showing that the expiation of sin and fidelity to God are infallible ways of assuring heavenly grace and benediction, especially in matters of health, family, and employment. The book written by the televangelist Oral Roberts, who could be heard on the Euronews channel in 1998, is significantly titled: *God's Formula for Success and Prosperity*. Many NRMs, notably the most successful, like Scientology, New Age, Human Potential, have mundane purposes; the same is true for parallel beliefs, for instance, telepathy, astrology, or reincarnation (which is usually nothing more than the replaying of the game of life without any idea of karma). Wallis (1984) predicts a better future for world-affirming than for world-rejecting NRMs. An important consequence of this-worldliness is the disassociation between sin and guilt and one's fate after death (desoteriologization), which leads to the collapse of the concept of sin (hence the collapse of the practice of confession in Catholicism), or to a more worldly interpretation: sin distances one from God and prevents one from benefiting from His grace, from being fully happy, from communicating with the deep inner self, from finding earthly peace and harmony, and so forth.

(b) Beyond personal religious autonomy, pragmatism, and subjectivity, we can speak of *self-spirituality* where the desire for freedom and liberty then combines with empiricism, in a pluralistic environment. The supreme spiritual authority can be the inner self or some form of "divine within" (Holy Spirit, spark of the divine, parcel of the cosmic consciousness), or both. Even if external beliefs, scriptures, norms, or authorities are accepted, they must be legitimated through personal experience. In the 1988-1989 Roof sample, 31 percent of baby-boomers agree that "People have God within them, so Churches aren't really necessary." Self-spirituality is important in the mystical, psychological, and parascientific NRMs like Human Potential or the New Age (Champion 1993; Heelas 1996), in healing practices, or in many ordinary psychotherapies where the inner self is seen as an infallible source of guidance; a search for harmony usually follows certain rituals that dampen the potentially anarchic consequences, as is the case with New Age (cf., the Findhorn community rites of harmonization).

(c) It seems better to speak of *dehierarchization, dedualization, bringing nearer the human and the divine*, the layman and the priest, the body and the soul, than of collapse of the dualism in the way that Bellah emphasized, though the feeling of the *unicity of the cosmos, holism, monism*, is also a part of the picture and is becoming increasingly more important. The results are either nonbelief, an impersonal God, a more loving and blessing God, indeed, a divine Friend, or adopting monist beliefs. In Christianity, we can observe this bringing nearer the human with the divine from the birth of Protestantism to present Protestantism and to Vatican II Catholicism (use of vernacular language, emphasis on the goodness of God, the friendship of the Lord, instead of omnipotence, sin and hell; the French are allowed to address God with the familiar " tu" form after having begun with the formal "vous" form); Pentecostalism and the charismatic movement even experience the "God within" through the descent and active presence of the Holy Spirit. Monism is spreading in the West through esoteric groups, Eastern religions, many NRMs (TM, Divine Light Mission, International Society for Krishna Consciousness, Rajneeshees, which have an Eastern orientation, or New Age, Scientology, Human Potential) and many parascientific beliefs: astrology, telepathy, "waves," "energies." Holism, which is important in therapeutic, mystic, and esoteric groups (Beckford 1984), is a typical form of dedualization.

(d) Although we have already spoken about *parascientificity*, we *should* probably include something on science fiction and on phenomena such as the belief in NDE. The latter presents several very interesting traits: it is not based on a supernatural revelation nor on a personal illumination that is reserved to a chosen few, but rather on an experience which is accessible to anyone and everyone, and is supposedly verifiable. As we can see, this belief system is parascientific and democratic. It is also individualized and without constraint insofar as one is free to choose what he or she believes. It tries to enchant life by making death into something enchanting (this-worldliness). There is no conception of guilt, there is only responsibility (reviewing one's life). Finally, insofar as it can be grafted to any other system of religious belief and even to atheism, it is pluralist and universal in much the same way as human rights are. Appearing in 1969, it quickly spread throughout the United States and throughout the world, and its success suggests that it is indicative of high-modernity.

(e) Pluralism, relativism, probabilism, and pragmatism which are consequences of science, the desire for freedom (personal religious choice), democracy, globalization, and functional differentiation encourage *pluralistic, relativistic, ubiquitary forms of faith* with, in reaction, trends that reassert the certainties. Combined with an extreme from of demythologization, they can take on the appearance of a symbolist faith (for example, a faith that does not believe in the reality of the resurrection of Jesus Christ but believes that it is nonetheless a necessary symbol to give meaning to life). Combined with mobility, flexibility, and revisability, which are other typically ultramodern ideas related to freedom, pluralism, and accelerated change, they can lead to what Jaspers calls the floating faith or to what Roof (1993) describes as a seeker spirituality: to the question (1988-89 survey) "Is it good to explore many differing religious teachings and learn from them, or should one stick to a particular faith?," 60 percent prefer to explore. This notion of mobility is also prevalent among NRMs, as Eileen Barker (1986) observed about the Moonies, of whom, only one in twenty were still members two years after entering the movement. Some NRMs are intentionally very loosely organized so that they look like a spiritual self-service counter, a free resource, as in the New Age and the "mystic-esoteric nebula," where self-determination is sacred.

(f) These features, the very *loosely organized religious or spiritual networks*, such as psycho-spiritual healing or New Age groups, pose a previously unseen sociological problem: can we still speak of the "religious"with reference to these spiritual forms which are so vague and unstable? The hesitation between describing them as "religious" or "spiritual," and the preference many of their followers have for the term "spiritual," are in themselves significant of the fluidity of their boundaries. Is it indicative of a phase of growth or of decomposition in religion's evolution? The question is important, and it also addresses the way in which we interpret the notion of secularization. We shall return to it in the conclusion.

THE RETURN TO SECULARIZATION

This model can account not only for the religious losses, but also for adaptations, revivals, mutations, and inventions. Nothing permits us to announce a necessary link between modernity and a disappearance of religion or of the religious (except in their most traditional forms or as a monopoly), but rather of a religious reshaping within a general symbolic reshaping, including both secular and religious focuses. The present phase appears to be a burgeoning one, a sort of cinematic fade in which new forms supplement, redefine, or replace former ones, although not without some resistance (fundamentalism) or notable levels of nonbelief in some countries. It is possible that the current crisis of confidence in modernity will accelerate the reshaping of the spiritual. Now let us go to the heart of the question of secularization. I will treat this question in three steps. I will first clarify what we mean by secularization and show how the preceding model aids in this study. Then we will return to the WVS and ISSP analyses in order to define further the scope and limits of the functions of religion, as well as of fundamentalist and secularist attitudes. Finally, I will propose an assessment of secularization.

Two Thresholds of Secularization

To clarify our understanding of secularization, we can begin with Berger's definition (1967: 107-8): "By secularization, we mean the process by which sectors of society and culture are removed from the domination of religious institutions and symbols." He includes the secularization of consciousness, which "means that the modern West has produced an increasing number of individuals who look upon the world and their own lives without the benefit of religious interpretations." Much as Karel Dobbelaere does, this definition implicitly distinguishes between three levels of secularization: global (society), meso (culture), and individual, which I will also use.

Berger judiciously distinguishes between religious institutions and religious symbols, a distinction often practiced without being made explicit. We propose to conceptualize this distinction by differentiating between *two thresholds of secularization*, in the same way that Jean Baubérot (1990) makes the distinction between two thresholds of laicization (the Napoleonic Concordate and the separation between church and state). The first threshold will correspond to autonomization with respect to a religious institution or authority structure (institutional secularization), while religious symbols remain salient; and the second will refer to the complete abandonment of religious symbols (symbolic secularization). For example, when a state, school, or individual asserts his/her/its autonomy in relation to a religious authority while keeping a religious dimension, it is a case of the first threshold. If the above abandons all religious symbols (except as a cultural interest), it is a case of the second threshold; this abandonment can itself be benevolent, neutral, or hostile toward religion. From this point of view, laïcization (France) or pillarization (Belgium, the Netherlands) can be considered as the legal codification of a situation corresponding to the second threshold. The first threshold involves a loss of monopoly and authority but not necessarily a decline of religiosity. We do not consider this-worldliness as a form of secularization, since it was the principal orientation among oral and polytheistic religions, the primacy of an otherworldly orientation having been, in fact, a historical exception which was typical of the previous axial age. In this way, it can be seen as a religious adaptation to modernity.

If we return to the preceding model, we can see that, among the four principal effects that modernity has on religion — decline, adaptation and reinterpretation, conservative reaction, and innovation — only the first one necessarily means secularization; the second and the fourth terms contribute to secularization only insofar as they imply a breaking away from conservative religious authority, and the third actually works against secularization since it reinforces both religiosity and religious authority. We must stress that rationalization, individualization, and functional differentiation do not in themselves imply secularization, but they can lead to crossing these thresholds. It is certain that they favor crossing the first threshold by allowing for more autonomy, but this does not necessarily mean that they favor crossing the second, since they are themselves sources of religious adaptation, reaction and invention, as we have seen. This is true even in the case of science, which is the most rationalized area. Even functional differentiation is not in itself a factor in religion's loss of influence, since it does not necessarily prevent the economy from playing a dominant role, as was the case for religion in the Indo-European functional tripartition. It quite simply depends on the importance that people grant to religion. With this point made, let us return to the previously mentioned studies.

The Scope and Limits of Religious Functions According to WVS and ISSP

Using the WVS, Dobbelaere (1995) and Dobbelaere and Jagodzinski (1995) have performed an interesting statistical analysis insofar as it forms the first systematic attempt at an empirical confirmation of secularization and goes much farther than the work of Sabino Acquaviva (1979). However, because the data used were taken from the WVS, it concerns only Christianity, and furthermore, only with respect to rather traditional religious criteria. In fact, there are four principal religious trends at work in current Western religious evolution: (1) a decline in Christianity, (2) an internal redefinition of Christianity, (3) an expansion of parallel beliefs and of NRMs, (4) a shift toward relativism, probabilism, pragmatism, and subjectivism. From these trends, the analysis can hardly take into account any but the first one because this survey does not tap the three others, with the exception of the third one, and even then only on two non-Christian variables: reincarnation and the distinction between a "personal God" and "some sort of spirit or life force," agnosticism, and atheism. The use of the WVS leads the authors to overestimate religious decline and to bias the analysis of the relationship between religion and individualization. The ISSP somewhat corrects these drawbacks concerning the second trend (liberalism /tranditionalism, fundamentalism /secularism), the third one (good luck, fortune telling, astrology), and the fourth one in the case of probabilism (graduational rather than simply yes/no answers to the questions). However, neither of these studies asks questions pertaining to the influence of science or reason, nor do they evaluate the feeling of individual autonomy with respect to religious institutions, although in an indirect fashion the ISSP does ask a question about the power of the church and other religious organizations.

Nevertheless, the WVS does permit us to measure the importance attributed to religion and the relationships between religious variables and the variables concerning the other main spheres (economics, politics, work, family, education, ecology, civics). This will provide us with an indication of religion's functions at an individual level. In addition, the WVS presents several items concerning the problems about which "it is proper for churches to speak" (Third World problems, racial discrimination, euthanasia, disarmament, ecology and environmental issues, abortion, unemployment, extramarital affairs, homosexuality, and government policy, in the order of decreasing positive responses), which give an idea of the areas in which its external function is recognized, at least in terms of discourse. Other items ask whether the churches give answers to moral, social, family problems, which furnish an idea of the effectiveness of the churches' external function (Luhmann's "performance") in these areas. The ISSP asked six questions that permit us to identify attitudes that can be qualified as either fundamentalist or secularist according to whether or not a strong religious influence on society is desirable: daily school prayer, using God's law as the basis for right and wrong, banning antireligious books or films, attitudes toward the influence of religious leaders on government decisions, reserving public office for those who believe in God, and the power that the church and other religious organizations are thought to ought to have.

What are the results in the case of Western Europe (Lambert 1998)? With 19 percent responding that it is "very important" in life in general, religion comes in far behind the family (81 percent), work (53 percent), friends and acquaintances (43 percent), and leisure time (38 percent), but nonetheless ahead of politics (8 percent); 28 percent feel that religion is "quite important." On the other hand, in an almost symmetrical fashion, 21 percent say that it is "not at all important," and 31 percent that it is "not very important," moreover, 25 percent feel that they are nonreligious. The importance of the external functions of religion is intimately linked to the importance granted to religion (i.e., to the level of religiosity), but religion can be influential to the extent that its influence is accepted by the individual, something that is typical of an optional ("complementary" in Luhmann's terms) sphere. As it can be measured by the correlations, this influence concerns only the areas already mentioned (with moderate correlations: $r^2 = 0.2$ to 0.3). But the ecclesiastical stands are recognized by more than 50 percent when they concern "major causes" such as the Third World, disarmament, racial discrimination, and ecology; on the contrary, speaking out on private matters such as sexuality arouses feelings of reservation, and the issue of religious influence on government policy receives a clear refusal.

One-half of Europeans say that the churches offer answers to spiritual problems, while only one-third believe this to be true for moral, social, and family problems. In addition, for the six items taken into account by the ISSP, the proponents of a religious influence on society are fewer in number than those who are opposed to this influence, with the exception of daily school prayer; and those who are in favor of a religious influence on government policy or of banning nonbelievers from public office are particularly few in number (5 to 10 percent). Considering the extreme answers to these items (definitely yes /definitely not), we can observe a fundamentalist core of only about 11 percent and a secular focal area which is twice as large. We can therefore conclude that Christianity is felt to be socially relevant in several spheres, though essentially for only the most religious, except in the case of major causes and ethical issues. We must also add that, from the oldest to the youngest age groups, there is a noticeable decline in the perceived importance of religion (with the exception of the desire to see the churches speak out on "major causes"), and in the percentage of fundamentalists (6 percent, against 31 percent secularists).

The perceived social relevance of religion is highest in the most religious countries (Ireland, Italy, and Portugal) and lowest in France, the Netherlands, and the Scandinavian countries. All, however, accept the churches speaking out on "major causes," and all reject religious influence on government policy and on elections to public office — which is to say, they approve of the separation between church and state. On all of the previous points, the United States does not differ substantially from the most religious European countries, with the exception of the fact that Americans tend to have a greater interest in the churches' answers to moral, social, and family problems. This is probably due to a more adequate relationship between religious "supply" and "demand," given both a greater denominational diversity and a higher rate of religious mobility. Nonetheless, the level of biblical fundamentalism in the United States is especially high (32 percent), and fundamentalist attitudes outweigh secularist ones (18 percent against 15 percent), as is the case in Ireland, but in both cases, we observe the reverse among the young. In the former Eastern Bloc countries, there is in general a greater demand for religious "performance;" this is true even in Russia and East Germany, which have very low levels of religiosity, again showing respect for the separation between church and state, with the exception to some extent of Poland, where we also find the hightest levels of fundamentalism (about 30 percent). In all these countries, we observe the previous trends between the oldest and the youngest generations, albeit they are more moderate, and Poland is, once again, a partial exception.

What are the profiles of the fundamentalists and the secularists? The former are characterized by religious and moral traditionalism, a higher average age, a lower level of education, and a lower- or lower-middle-class status, so that it could be considered as a kind of "rear guard," but they are only slightly more conservative politically. The secularists show the opposite features. For instance, approximately 75 percent of fundamentalists think that it is wrong to engage in sex before marriage, while this is true for only 10 percent of the secularists (against a general average of 27 percent); about 60 percent of fundamentalists believe that the woman's place is in the home (general average: 25 percent); 40 percent feel that it is wrong to have an abortion if the fetus shows signs of serious birth defects (general average: 10 percent). As *the fundamentalists represent only one-third of those who grant great importance to religion* or show the firmest faith ("very close to God"), what is it that distinguishes them from the others? We can observe that they are characterized as having very strong traditional religious views and rigorous moral principles, as being older and more likely to be female, as having a lower level of education, and a greater likelihood of belonging to the more modest social classes and to the elderly housewives group.

One of the most important global effects of modernity on religion is the loss of religion's monopoly in the "symbolic field," which is now structured by both religious and secular systems (science, philosophies, ideologies, values). Even if these systems are not antireligious or are associated with religion, their very existence favors more autonomous attitudes vis-à-vis religion. In late modernity, landmarks in terms of values are given increasing importance (e.g., human rights) because they are the most universal and the best adapted to pluralism, although we need to keep in mind that these values are not separated from religion among the believers. We can observe that in the WVS some basic values are very widely shared. By doing a cluster analysis of the WVS data from Western and Eastern Europe without using religious or political variables, except salvation, but only using values, Szakolczai and Füstös (1996) have identified six main value types which they have called "Enlightenment rationalist," "materialist (post-communist)," "social democratic," "Christian," "Hedonist," and "traditional-disciplinary," which suggest that the first three are rather secular and that only one is predominantly religious. Unfortunately, they do not give the religious characteristics of these different value types.

The factor analyses of correspondences between religious variables always point to the existence of three different focal areas which we can call: (1) confessing Christianity according to Dietrich Bonhoeffer's definition (following Kerkofs 1988), which is to say the Christianity of faith in God; (2) cultural Christianity (i.e., a question of identity), meaning little personal involvement, rites of passage; and (3) secular humanism (Lambert 1996). It is significant that the notions of "personal God," "spirit, life force," and nonbelief in God are respectively linked to the three focal areas (agnosticism comes somewhere between the last two). It is also worth noting that the less people believe in God in a country, the less the God they believe in is a personal God, and the less God is important in their lives. Confessing Christianity is predominant in the United States, Ireland, Italy, and to a lesser extent in Portugal. Confessing Christianity and cultural Christianity are on equal footing in Canada, Spain, Greece, Luxembourg, and Germany. The majority of the French, Belgians, English, and Dutch are divided between cultural Christianity and secular humanism. The Scandinavian countries, where Christianity is more a civil religion, are largely dominated by cultural Christianity.

A general evaluation of secularization

It appears that the *first threshold* of secularization was largely crossed in the West with the coming of modernity, at three different levels.

(a) *The macro level.* States affirmed their autonomy in relation to religious institutions, even while they kept a civil religion (the United States) or a link with a particular denomination (Anglicanism in England, Lutheranism in Sweden). Political parties did the same, even when they kept a religious label (Christian-Democrat). Opposite attempts have failed politically (the Moral Majority). At the global level, the social bond rests first with democracy and human rights, and not with religion. In Europe, the current tendency is one of a weakening relationship between the state and the church in the countries that were most linked to a denomination, and of a strengthening relationship in the case of laïcity and, above all, in the case of the former communist countries. For instance, the Catholic church has been disestablished in Spain and Portugal; Sweden is ending the automatic affiliation of newborns with Lutheranism (when the parents did not express the desire for a different denomination). On the contrary, in France, the legitimacy of Catholic schools is no longer questioned, public schools are more open to religious culture, representatives from the main religions and denominations are members of the National Consultative Ethics Commitee (bioethics), not to mention Mitterrand's state funeral in Paris's Notre-Dame Cathedral; in the former communist countries, the churches cannot recover an authoritarian or monopolistic role, as Poland evidenced when the left won the elections. In any case, there is no clear relationship between the denominational systems and the religious states, with the most interesting example being that of the Scandinavian countries, which have very low levels of Christian religiosity (Lambert 1996).

(b) *The meso level.* With respect to schools and education, diverse situations exist. Sometimes schools follow a religious authority while nonetheless aligning their programs with national norms, sometimes they are autonomous. However, most often they dispense a religious education (except in the cases of laicity or laïc pillars). As for culture, in the general sense of the arts, intellectual life, and the media, we know that these sectors are for the most part autonomous with relation to religious institutions.

(c) *The individual level.* If we were to judge by the degree of autonomy that those who belong to a religion give themselves (according to the surveys), we can see that institutional secularization is strong on an individual level as well. This does not, however, prevent individuals from taking into account, in their own way, the positions of their religious authorities. Furthermore, we note a strong desire to desecularize society (Hervieu-Léger 1993) within fundamentalist, evangelical, Pentecostal, and charismatic groups, but as we have noted, their reach is, with the exception of Poland, rather limited.

What about the *second threshold*? Contrary to the preceding one, this threshold has been crossed only in a limited manner except, formerly, in the communist countries and, today, in certain spheres and among the youth of some countries, although it depends in part on the definition of the religious. Besides, the idea that religion would tend to disappear with modernization has declined, if not disappeared.

(a) *The macro level.* Only several states have removed all religious references from their constitutions (France, for example). On the contrary, Eastern European countries and Russia, which had largely crossed the threshold on a very hostile note, are returning either toward the first one after the collapse of Communism, or toward the more benevolent or neutral second one. We even can observe that religion has played an important role in rebuilding the civil society and the state in several countries, especially Poland (Casanova 1994).

(b) *The meso level.* Among the spheres of activity, only science and economics have clearly passed this threshold, but this does not necessarily mean that religion has been rejected in itself. Health and social services have more or less crossed this threshold according to the country and, as we know, only in the case of laicity or pillarization, as is the case with schools. Culture functions largely autonomously in relation to religion, knowing that religious culture has its proper place within the sphere of culture.

(c) *The individual level.* We have noted two opposite tendencies since the 1970s that differentiate the oldest from the youngest generations (Lambert 1993, 1996; Lambert and Voyé 1997): on one hand, an increase in the percentage of the nonreligious, and a decrease in the belief in God, less in the United States, more so in Europe (with a majority of nonreligious young in France, Great Britain, and Netherlands); on the other hand, a stability in belief in miracles and in an afterlife, a spread of NRMs, and above all, a growth in parallel beliefs, self-spirituality, loosely organized groups, "believing without belonging" (Davie 1995), such that approximately one-third of the nonreligious have in fact religious or parareligious beliefs. The balance depends upon the status we give to these parallel beliefs and new religious forms. It is the same in the former communist countries, where the return to religion is more limited than it first seemed to be and where the nonreligious remain a majority in Russia, the former East Germany, and Bulgaria, but where these parallel beliefs and new religious forms are spreading as well.

We can then conclude that, for the first threshold, there already exists a widespread secularization and it is *progressing.* For the second threshold, secularization is limited to some states, spheres, and subpopulations, noting that, on an individual level, it depends upon the status and importance of the parallel beliefs, the self-spirituality, the seeker spirituality, the loose networks, knowing that the spread of NRMs remains a very minor phenomenon, except if we include the New Age-type nebula. The problem is best illustrated by the case of Dutch youth (Janssen 1998), of whom, according to a 1991 national survey, only 39 percent belong to a religion, but 16 percent can be qualified as being influenced by New Age or Eastern religions, 18 percent are doubters, 16 percent are only praying, and a mere 8 percent are nonbelievers. Surprisingly, 82 percent pray at least sometimes and, among the nonchurchgoers, prayer is the most persistent religious element but only in a rather psychological and meditative way: to give strength, to accept the inevitable such as the death of a relative, as a release or as a time to ponder, in keeping with a primarily impersonal concept of the divine. Do these findings point to a stage of religious decomposition, to a minor form of religiosity (a vague backdrop, comforting beliefs), or to the seeds of possible reconfigurations? Are all of the parallel belief systems religious? If we keep our two criteria to define the religious (a superempirical reality and a symbolic relationship along with it), we will then exclude astrology and numerology for instance, but not the beliefs and practices of the Dutch youth, except a few of them.

Whatever the case might be, we are left to wonder whether or not we might be in the middle of an evolution toward a third threshold that we could define as "pluralistic secularization," in which religion has the same ascendancy upon society and life as any other movement or ideology, but can also play a role outside of its specific function and have an influence outside of the circle of believers as an ethical and cultural resource, as James Beckford stressed (1989) — as it is illustrated here in the case of "major causes." Once again, this seems possible only if religion can respect individual autonomy and democratic pluralism. We can also mention again Casanova's analysis, which illustrates this new public role of religion, but we would balance his stress on "deprivatization" with his own observations concerning the conditions for this role: the acceptance of pluralism and of functional differentiation. This new threshold would correspond to a step beyond the conflicts that were linked to the long and difficult redefinition of religion's place in modernity.

REFERENCES

Acquaviva, S. S. 1979. *The decline of the sacred in industrial society.* Oxford: Blackwell.

Barker, E. 1986. Religious movements: Cult and anti-cult since Jonestown. *Annual Review of Sociology* 12: 329-46.

Baubérot, J. 1990. *Vers un nouveau pacte laïque?* Paris: Seuil.

Beckford, J. 1984. Holistic imagery and ethics in new religious and healing movements. *Social Compass* 31: 259-72.

———. 1996. Postmodernity, high modernity, and new modernity: Three concepts in search of religion. In *Postmodernity, sociology, and religion,* edited by K. Flanagan and P. C. Jupp, 30-47. London: Macmillan.

Bellah, R. N. 1976. *Beyond belief: Essays on religion in a post-traditional world.* New York: Harper & Row.

Berger, P. 1967. *The sacred canopy.* New York: Doubleday.

———. 1994. *Religion and globalization.* London: Sage.

Campiche, R., et al. 1992. *Croire en Suisse(s).* Lausanne: L'Age d'homme.

Champion, F. 1993. La nébuleuse mystique-ésotérique. In *De l'émotion en religion,* edited by F. Champion and D. Hervieu-Léger, 18-69. Paris: Centurion.

Casanova, J. 1994. *Public religion in the modern world.* Chicago, IL: University of Chicago Press.

Davie, G. 1996. *Religion in Britain since 1945.* Oxford: Blackwell.

Dobbelaere, K. 1981. Secularization: A multi-dimensional concept. *Current Sociology* 29(2): 1-213.

———. 1995. Religion in Europe and North America. In *Values in western societies,* edited by R. de Moor, 1-29. Tilburg: Tilburg University Press.

Dobbelaere, K., and W. Jagodzinski. 1995. Secularization and church religiosity (chapter 4), Religious cognition's and beliefs (chapter 7), Religious and ethical pluralism (chapter 8). In *The impact of values,* edited by J. W. V. Deth and E. Scarbrough. Oxford: Oxford University Press.

Eisenstadt, S. 1986. *The origins and diversity of axial age civilizations.* Albany: State University of New York Press.

Ester, P., L. Halman, and R. de Moor. 1993. *The individualizing society: Value change in Europe and North America.* Tilburg: Tilburg University Press.

Flanagan, K., and P. C. Jupp. 1996. *Postmodernity, sociology, and religion.* London: Macmillan.

Giddens, A. 1991. *The consequences of modernity.* Cambridge, MA: Polity Press.

Heelas, P. 1996. De-traditionalisation of religion and self: The new age and postmodernity. In *Postmodernity, sociology, and religion*, edited by K. Flanagan and P. C. Jupp. London: Macmillan.

Hervieu-Léger, D. 1993. Present-day emotional renewals: the end of secularization or the end of religion? In *A future for religion? New paradigms for social analysis*, edited by W. H. Swatos, 129-148. London: Sage.

Hervieu-Léger, D., with F. Champion. 1986. *Vers un christianisme nouveau?* Paris: Cerf.

Hick, J. 1989. *An interpretation of religion.* New Haven, CT: Yale University Press.

Iannaconne, L. R. 1992. Religious markets and the economics of religion. *Social Compass* 39:123-31.

Janssen J. 1998. The Netherlands as an experimental garden of religiosity: Remnants and renewals. *Social Compass* 45: 101-13.

Jaspers, K. 1954. *Origine et sens de l'histoire.* Paris: Plon. (English ed. 1953. *The origin and goal of history.* New Haven, CT: Yale University Press.)

Kerkhofs, J. 1988. Between Christendom and Christianity. *Journal of Empirical Theology* 2: 88-101.

Kitagawa, J. M. 1967. Primitive, classical, and modern religions. In *The history of religion. Essays on problems of understanding*, edited by J. M. Kitagawa. Chicago, IL: University of Chicago Press.

Kurtz, L. 1995. *Gods in the global village: The world's religions in a sociological perspective.* London: Pine Forge Press.

Lambert, Y. 1985. *Dieu change en Bretagne.* Paris: Cerf.

———. 1993. Ages, générations et Christianisme, en France et en Europe. *Revue Française de Sociologie* 24: 525-55.

———. 1996. Denominational systems and religious states in the countries of Western Europe. *Research in the Social Scientific Study of Religion* 7: 127-43.

———. 1998. The scope and limits of religious functions according to the European value and ISSP surveys. In *On secularization: Homage to Karel Dobbelaere*, edited by J. Billiet and R. Laermans. Leuven: University Press of the Catholic University.

Lambert, Y., and L. Voyé. 1997. Les croyances des jeunes Européens. In *Cultures jeunes et religions en Europe*, edited by R. Campiche, 97-166. Paris: Cerf.

Luhmann, N. 1977 *Funktion der religion.* Frankfurt: Suhrkamp.

———. 1982. *The differentiation of society.* New York: Columbia University.

Martin, D. A. 1978. *A general theory of secularization.* Oxford: Blackwell.

Melton, J. G. 1998. Modern alternative religions in the west. In *A new handbook of living religions*, edited by J. R. Hinnels. Harmondworth, UK: Penguin.

Nakamura, H. 1986. *A comparative history of ideas.* London: Routledge.

Roof, W. C. 1993. *A generation of seekers.* San Francisco, CA: Harper.

Roof, W. C., J. W. Carroll, and D. A. Roozen, eds. 1995. *The post-war generation and establishment religion.* Boulder, CO: Westview Press.

Szakolczai, A., and L. Füstös. 1996. Value systems in axial moments: A comparative analysis of 24 European countries. *EUI Working Paper* N° 96/8. Florence: European University Institute.

Tschannen, O. 1992. *Les théories de la sécularisation.* Genève: Droz.

Walter, T. 1996. *The eclipse of eternity: A sociology of the afterlife.* London: Macmillan.

Wallis, R. 1984. *Elementary forms of new religious life.* London: Routledge.

Willaime, J.-P. 1995. *Sociologie des religions.* Paris: PUF.

Manuel Bachmann Die strukturalistische Artefakt- und
Kunstanalyse

ORBIS BIBLICUS ET ORIENTALIS

Im Auftrag des Biblischen Instituts
der Universität Freiburg-Schweiz,
des Ägyptologischen Seminars der Universität Basel,
des Instituts für Vorderasiatische Archäologie
und Altorientalische Sprachen der Universität Bern
und der Schweizerischen Gesellschaft
für Orientalische Altertumswissenschaft

herausgegeben von
Othmar Keel und Christoph Uehlinger

Zum Autor

Der Autor studierte von 1986 bis 1993 Philosophie, vorderorientalische
Archäologie und vergleichende Religionswissenschaft an der Universität
Basel. Seit 1993 ist er wissenschaftlicher Assistent und Lehrbeauftragter
für Philosophie an der Hochschule Luzern. Sein Hauptforschungsgebiet
betrifft Probleme der Philosophie der Logik. Bisherige Veröffentlichung:
Die paradoxale Struktur des Absoluten in Schellings Identitätssystem, in:
Philosophisches Jahrbuch 101 (1994), 76–97.

Orbis Biblicus et Orientalis   148

Manuel Bachmann

Die strukturalistische Artefakt- und Kunstanalyse

Exposition der Grundlagen
anhand der vorderorientalischen,
ägyptischen und
griechischen Kunst

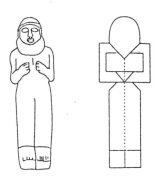

Universitätsverlag Freiburg Schweiz
Vandenhoeck & Ruprecht Göttingen

Die Deutsche Bibliothek – CIP-Einheitsaufnahme

Bachmann, Manuel:
Die strukturalistische Artefakt- und Kunstanalyse: Exposition
der Grundlagen anhand der vorderorientalischen, ägyptischen
und griechischen Kunst/Manuel Bachmann. – Freiburg,
Schweiz: Univ.-Verl.; Göttingen: Vandenhoeck und
Ruprecht, 1996
 (Orbis biblicus et orientalis; 148)
 ISBN 3-7278-1077-7 (Univ.-Verl.)
 ISBN 3-525-53784-0 (Vandenhoeck & Ruprecht)
NE: GT

Die Druckvorlagen wurden vom Verfasser
als reprofertige Dokumente zur Verfügung gestellt

© 1996 by Universitätsverlag Freiburg Schweiz
   Vandenhoeck & Ruprecht Göttingen

Paulusdruckerei Freiburg Schweiz

ISBN 3-7278-1077-7 (Editions Universitaires)
ISBN 3-525-53784-0 (Vandenhoeck & Ruprecht)

VORBEMERKUNG

Die vorliegende Untersuchung zum deutschen Strukturalismus ist von Herrn Prof. Dr. MARKUS WÄFLER angeregt worden.
Den Herren lic. phil. THOMAS HOFMEIER und lic. phil. CHRISTOPH SCHNEIDER danke ich für Hinweise, dem Herausgeber Herrn Prof. Dr. OTHMAR KEEL für die Aufnahme in die Reihe ORBIS BIBLICUS ET ORIENTALIS und schließlich dem Fonds zur Förderung der Geisteswissenschaften der FREIWILLIGEN AKADEMISCHEN GESELLSCHAFT in Basel für finanzielle Unterstützung.

Basel, im Frühjahr 1996   MANUEL BACHMANN

INHALTSVERZEICHNIS

§ 1 EINLEITUNG

Es ist eine Erkenntnis der neueren Philosophie, daß Wissenschaft die Struktureigenschaften der Gegenstände behandelt. Ein wissenschaftliches Theorieniveau ist erst dann erreicht, wenn die Aussagen so weit formal durchgebildet sind, daß sie einer reinen Strukturbeschreibung gleichkommen. In Formalwissenschaften wie Logik und Mathematik fällt die reine Strukturbeschreibung mit dem wissenschaftlichen Verfahren zusammen; in den Naturwissenschaften bildet sie das Resultat der zur Anwendung kommenden Verfahren. Wie deshalb jene Erkenntnis für die Gebiete der Formal- und Naturwissenschaften unbestreitbar sein dürfte, so hat sie umgekehrt in den Geisteswissenschaften keine Verbreitung gefunden. Indessen, daß sie auf diesem immer wieder vor den Ansprüchen strenger Wissenschaftlichkeit bewahrten Feld ebenso unverbrüchliche Geltung besitzt, erweist sich daran, daß auch die Gegenstände der Geisteswissenschaften allein mittels struktureller Bestimmung exakt beschrieben, unterschieden und eingeordnet werden können.

Diese Erkenntnis bildet den Ausgangspunkt einer Theorie, die angesichts ihres formalen Charakters für die meisten Disziplinen der vergleichenden Kulturwissenschaft fruchtbar zu machen wäre, hingegen lediglich in einer Teildisziplin entwickelt und zur Anwendung gebracht wurde – in der Archäologie. Von ihren Begründern FRIEDRICH MATZ (1890–1974), GUIDO KASCHNITZ VON WEINBERG (1890–1958) und BERNHARD SCHWEITZER (1892–1966) verschieden bezeichnet, namentlich als Formgeschichte, Formanalyse, Strukturanalyse, Strukturforschung oder Strukturwissenschaft, kann sie hinsichtlich ihres Ideals einer rein strukturellen Bestimmung kultureller Gegenstände einheitlich unter den Titel 'Strukturalismus' gestellt werden.

Strukturalismus ist nicht gleich Strukturalismus. Man muß wissen, daß zum französischen Strukturalismus, wie er in den ethnologischen Forschungen eines LÉVY-STRAUSS exemplarisch durchgeführt ist, inzwischen eine ganze Epoche der Archäologie geprägt hat und für dieselbe terminologisch geworden ist,[1] keinerlei Bezüge bestehen. Zwar versucht der französische Strukturalismus die Mechanismen kultureller Symbolsysteme ebenfalls formalisiert zu beschreiben, aber er stützt sich auf die Linguistik als Theoriebasis, während der hier gemeinte, deutsche Strukturalismus auf Mathematik und idealistische Philosophie zurückgreift. Dieser richtet sich auf die Erkenntnisziele der Archäologie und der Kunstgeschichte aus, genauer auf die Kunst- bzw. Artefaktanalyse, jener versteht sich als allgemeine Theorie vergleichender Kulturwissenschaft. Gerade für die Belange einer vergleichenden Kulturwissenschaft leistet der Strukturalismus STRAUSSscher Prägung indessen wenig, da er von der zweifelhaften Prämisse ausgeht, daß für alle Kulturen derselbe Rationalitätstypus gültig ist. Gegenüber dieser Voraussetzung zeichnet sich der deutsche Strukturalismus dadurch aus, daß er über ein Beschreibungssystem verfügt, das für die Berücksichtigung kultureller Andersartigkeit prinzipiell offen ist. Ausstrahlung gewann trotzdem nur das STRAUSSsche Theoriegebäude, von dem es bereits diverse Abarten und Neuformen gibt; jener Strukturalismus, den wir hier aufgreifen, ist über die deutsche Archäologie nicht weit hinausgekommen – nicht weiter als

---

[1] Zur Archäologie mit Wurzeln im französischen Strukturalismus vgl.: Ino Rossi (ed.): The Logic of culture. Advances in structural theory and methods, London 1982. – Ian Bapty und Tim Yates (ed.): Archaeology after structuralism. Post-structuralism and the practice of archaeology, London 1990.

bis zur Wiener Schule der Kunstgeschichte. Er hat aber auch hier keine Breitenwirkung erlangt, sondern ist mit dem Generationenwechsel nach der Zeit seiner Begründer verstaubt. Da bekanntlich die Felder der Wissenschaftsgeschichte und der Wissenschaftstheorie in der Archäologie nicht sonderlich gepflegt werden,[2] widerfuhr dem deutschen Strukturalismus nicht mehr als eine enzyklopädische Beachtung im Rahmen einer Geschichte der Archäologie. Die Behandlung des Themas im Handbuch der Archäologie[3] ist eine Selbstdarstellung, unternommen vom Strukturalisten SCHWEITZER. In der zweiten Auflage des Handbuchs[4] hat die Abhandlung schulmeisterliche Verbesserungen, Streichungen und abschwächende Schlußbemerkungen seitens des Herausgebers erlitten. Der Vorderasien-Band[5] des genannten Handbuchs begnügt sich mit einem Abriß von vier Seiten. In der Wissenschaftsgeschichte der Archäologie von WEGNER[6], die sich ausdrücklich unter den Gesichtspunkt der Methode stellt, wird die Epoche der Strukturforschung gänzlich unterschlagen. Ebenfalls enttäuscht die Cambridge Enzyklopädie der Archäologie.[7] Zwar ist jüngst die Altertumswissenschaft der 20er Jahre aufgerollt worden,[8] Anlaß genug, den Strukturalismus nicht nur beim Namen zu nennen: HOFTERS Äußerungen über KASCHNITZ bezeugen aber nicht geringe Inkompetenz, wenn sie dessen methodischen Standpunkt zwischen philosophischem Irrationalismus und vergleichender Stilforschung plazieren, ihn der kunst- und geschichtsphilosophischen Spekulation verdächtigen, ihm nicht klassifikatorische oder formale, sondern "ontologische" Absichten unterstellen und was der Mißverständnisse mehr sind.[9]

Das Schweigen der Gelehrten erscheint umso merkwürdiger, als die vom Strukturalismus thematisierten Rahmenprobleme, wie Kulturbegriff, Typologie, Probleme des Stilbegriffs und Mathematisierung der Methoden, durchaus in der gegenwärtigen Diskussion[10] gehandelt

[2] Bruce G. Trigger: A history of archaeological thought, Cambridge 1989 nennt für die Wissenschaftsgeschichte der Klassischen Archäologie nur wenige Namen, Schliemann, Curtius, Conze, mit welchen allein sich selbstverständlich keine Wissenschaftsgeschichte schreiben läßt. Die deutschen Schulen werden von den angelsächsischen durchgängig ignoriert. Vgl. Iain M. Mackenzie (ed.): Archaeological theory: Progress or posture ?, Aldershot etc. 1994. – Kenneth R. Dark: Theoretical archaeology, London 1995. – Peter J. Ucko (ed.): Theory in archaeology. A world perspective, London, New York 1995.

[3] Bernhard Schweitzer: Das Problem der Form in der Kunst des Altertums, in: Walter Otto (ed.): Handbuch der Archäologie, im Rahmen des Handbuchs der Altertumswissenschaft, München 1939, S. 363–399.

[4] Bernhard Schweitzer: Das Problem der Form in der Kunst des Altertums, ergänzt von Ulrich Hausmann, in: Ulrich Hausmann (ed.): Handbuch der Archäologie. Allgemeine Grundlagen der Archäologie. Begriff und Methode, Geschichte, Problem der Form, Schriftzeugnisse, München 1969, S. 163–203.

[5] Barthel Hrouda: Vorderasien I. Mesopotamien, Babylonien, Iran und Anatolien, München 1971, S. 307–310.

[6] Max Wegner: Geschichte der Archäologie unter dem Gesichtspunkt der Methode, in: Studium Generale, 17. Jg. (1964), S. 191–201.

[7] Andrew Sherratt (ed.): Die Cambridge Enzyklopädie der Archäologie, übersetzt von Claus Bruder u. a., München 1980.

[8] Helmut Flashar (ed.): Altertumswissenschaft in den 20er Jahren. Neue Fragen und Impulse, Stuttgart 1995.

[9] Mathias René Hofter: Die Entdeckung des Unklassischen: Guido Kaschnitz von Weinberg, in: Helmut Flashar (ed.): Altertumswissenschaft in den 20er Jahren. Neue Fragen und Impulse, Stuttgart 1995, S. 247–257.

[10] Zum Kulturbegriff: Rolf Hachmann (ed.): Studien zum Kulturbegriff in der Vor- und Frühgeschichtsforschung, Bonn 1987. – Marlies Wendowski: Archäologische Kultur und Ethnische Einheit. Möglichkeiten und Grenzen der Identifikation, Diss. Hamburg 1994, Frankfurt 1995. – Zur Typologie wirft Leo S. Klejn: Archaeological typology, übersetzt aus dem Russischen von Penelope Dole, Oxford 1982 alle einschlägigen Fragen auf wie: was ist ein Typus, was sind die Zuordnungskriterien, was ist eine archäologisch bestimmbare Kultur ? – In der Diskussion des Stilbegriffs werden Panofsky und Wölfflin in Margaret W. Conkey und Christine A. Hastorf (ed.): The uses of style in archaeology, Cambridge 1990 beiläufig erwähnt. – Zur Mathematisierung: Albertus Voorrips (ed.): Mathematics and information science in archaeology. A flexible framework, Bonn 1990. – Grundlagendiskussion wird betrieben in Lester Embree (ed.): Metaarchaeology. Reflections by archaeologists and philosophers, Dordrecht etc. 1992.

werden. Nicht weniger verwirrend ist, daß diejenigen, die strukturalistischer Artefaktanalyse erstaunlich nahe kommen, keinen Bezug zur strukturalistischen Schule erkennen lassen.[11] Um das Versäumte nachzuholen, gliedert sich vorliegende Untersuchung in zwei Teile, in einen wissenschaftshistorischen und einen wissenschaftstheoretischen Teil. Diese Aufteilung erfordert allerdings eine Präzisierung hinsichtlich der Frage, inwiefern der Strukturalismus Gegenstand sowohl einer wissenschaftshistorischen als auch einer wissenschaftstheoretischen Betrachtung sein muß.

Archäologische Forschung beschränkt sich nicht auf das Dokumentieren des zutage geförderten Materials, vielmehr muß sie imstande sein, das Material, insbesondere die Artefakte, hinsichtlich eines kulturgeschichtlichen Gesamtzusammenhangs auszudeuten.[12] Für eine solche Ausdeutung sind neben technischen auch hermeneutische Methoden erforderlich, nicht zuletzt in denjenigen Fällen, in denen es sich um sogenannte Kunstprodukte handelt. Hier setzt der Strukturalismus ein. Er versucht, für die Ausdeutung von Kunstprodukten die geeigneten methodischen Mittel bereitzustellen.

Nicht nur beiläufig ist anzumerken, daß der Ausdruck 'Kunst' oder 'Kunstprodukt' im weitesten Sinne zu verstehen ist und, da wir nicht wissen, was 'Kunst' in einem uns fremden Symbolsystem bedeuten soll, für alle Artefakte stehen muß. 'Artefakt' bezeichnet eine Gegenstandsklasse, die alle anthropogenen Objekte ein- und lediglich Naturprodukte ausschließt.

Indem der Strukturalismus eine Methode der Kunst- und Artefaktanalyse begründet, gehört er zum Methodenbestand der Archäologie. In diesem Bereich versucht er eine methodologische Absicherung der Disziplin, soweit sich diese kunstwissenschaftlicher Mittel bedient. Es handelt sich nicht um eine bloße Methode, die zur Anwendung kommt, ohne daß sie selbst reflektiert und eigens formuliert würde, vielmehr tritt der Strukturalismus ausdrücklich als eine Methodentheorie auf. Bedingung einer Methodentheorie ist, daß sie sich mehr auf theoretische Überlegungen abstützt als auf vorgeprägte Ergebnisse der Realienforschung. Anderenfalls verfehlte sie ihre Aufgabe, der Realienforschung gegenüber eine methodische Leitfunktion ausüben zu können. In dieser Hinsicht gehört der Strukturalismus in die archäologische Wissenschaftstheorie. Diese Stellung betrifft aber nur den systematischen Ort innerhalb einer Theorie der Archäologie. Denn inhaltlich betrachtet, das heißt, seiner konkreten Anwendung in der Forschung und seinen Resultaten nach, bildet der Strukturalismus einen Gegenstand der archäologischen Wissenschaftsgeschichte und muß im historischen Kontext abgehandelt werden. Zudem soll er einer wissenschaftstheoretischen Betrachtung hier hinsichtlich darauf unterzogen werden, daß er eine Theorie verkörpert, welche auf ihre Möglichkeiten und auf ihre Begründung hin diskutiert werden muß.

---

[11] So bei Dorothy K. Washburn: Style, perception and geometry, in: Christopher Carr und Jill E. Neitzel (ed.): Style, society, and person. Archaeological and ethnological perspectives, New York, London 1995, S. 101–122, die hinsichtlich ihrer Theorie und deren Anwendung als Strukturalistin bezeichnet werden muß.
[12] Zu diesem Problem liefert Merrilee H. Salmon: Philosophy and archaeology, New York etc. 1982 neopositivistische Wissenschaftstheorie.

ERSTER TEIL
WISSENSCHAFTSGESCHICHTE

§ 2 Ausgangslage

Wissenschaftsgeschichtlich gesehen reichen die Wurzeln des Strukturalismus in die Kunstwissenschaft des neunzehnten Jahrhunderts. Die dort unternommene Ausarbeitung kunstwissenschaftlicher Grundbegriffe wurde nach der Jahrhundertwende von der klassischen Archäologie aufgegriffen. Diese Aufnahme wird verständlich, sobald man die eigentümliche Forschungssituation jener Zeit betrachtet.

Bis tief ins neunzehnte Jahrhundert hinein waren von der griechischen Kunst nur diejenigen Stücke bekannt, welche die Römer geschätzt und deshalb in Form von Kopien überliefert hatten. Der Begriff von griechischer Kunst, den die Sammler seit der Renaissance in das neuzeitliche Bildungsgut einbrachten, hatte sich anhand willkürlich ausgezeichneter Exemplare ausgeprägt. Bezeichnend ist Goethes Begegnung in Rom mit einem Gipsabguß eines antiken Marmorkopfs, in welchem der Dichter in ekstatischer Schau die Essenz der griechischen Götter, "das erhabene, einzige Götterbild",[13] zu erblicken glaubte, später indessen sich jener Kopf als Portrait einer Sterblichen, einer römischen Frau, entpuppte.[14] Die griechische Kunst schlechthin war in dem vorgefundenen Stil des römischen Überlieferungsgutes ausgemacht. Exemplare der heute sogenannten archaischen Kunst waren nur vereinzelt zutage gekommen. Da sie der vorgenommenen Definition des Griechischen widersprachen, wurden sie nicht als Repräsentanten eines eigenen Stils, sondern als Mißbildungen verstanden, die der Korrektur durch das Klassische bedürfen. Dies ging so weit, daß an fragmentierte archaische Skulpturen sogar mit Hammer und Meißel Hand angelegt wurde, um sie in Richtung auf das klassische Ideal zu ergänzen. Auf die Weise wurde der berühmte dänische Bildhauer Thorvaldsen im Jahre 1816 an den 1811 gefundenen Giebelskulpturen des Aphaiatempels von Aegina tätig.[15]

Seine reductio ad absurdum erfuhr dieser dogmatische Stilbegriff erst durch die neue Fundlage im Ausgang des neunzehnten Jahrhunderts. Auf der athenischen Akropolis wurden im Perserschutt archaische Skulpturen entdeckt, desgleichen in den Ausgrabungen von Olympia. Ein riesiges archaisches Fundmaterial mußte nun bewältigt werden. Mit der Entdeckung der archaischen griechischen Kunst wurde bewußt, daß jener Stil, der bislang als feststehendes Merkmal griechischer Kunst galt, einem Werden und Vergehen unterworfen ist und damit gerade nicht paradigmatisch fixiert werden kann. Mit der Erkenntnis der Wandelbarkeit dessen, was man als Stil bezeichnete, wurde die bisherige Typologisierung über den Stilbegriff unmöglich. Das neu entdeckte archaische Material ergab, daß die über 'den griechischen Stil' definierte griechische Kunst gar nicht mehr zu erkennen war.

So tauchte zwangsläufig die Frage auf, was denn noch in der Kunstentwicklung als Substanz der Modifikationen, als Grundlage und Beharrendes der stetigen Stilveränderungen, aufgefaßt werden kann. Gerade auf diese Frage nach einer Substanz versuchten die Struk-

---

[13] Johann Wolfgang Goethe: Werke, Weimarer Ausgabe, Abt. 4, Bd. 38, Weimar 1906, S. 67.
[14] Gerhart Rodenwaldt: Goethes Besuch im Museum Maffeianum zu Verona, in: Winckelmannsprogramm der Archäologischen Gesellschaft zu Berlin, Bd. 102 (1942), S. 7.
[15] Zur Restauration der Aegiden durch Thorvaldsen äußerte sich zuletzt Raimund Wünsche: "Perikles" sucht "Pheidias". Ludwig I. und Thorvaldsen, in: Germanisches Nationalmuseum Nürnberg (ed.): Künstlerleben in Rom. Bertel Thorvaldsen (1770–1844). Der dänische Bildhauer und seine deutschen Freunde, Nürnberg 1991, S. 314 f.

turalisten mit dem Strukturbegriff eine Antwort zu geben. Rein historisch betrachtet ist der Strukturalismus als Reflex auf die besondere Forschungslage der damaligen Archäologie zu verstehen. Insbesondere die zwanziger Jahre des zwanzigsten Jahrhunderts markieren eine Zeit konzeptioneller Neuorientierung, eine Zeit, in der man sich mit archäologischen Arbeiten "Flugblätter eines neuen Sehens von Hand zu Hand"[16] reichte.

§ 3 Historische Entwicklung der Theorie

Für die Theoriebildung des Strukturalismus ist charakteristisch, daß er in der Archäologie keine Vorformen besitzt, sondern mit einer geschlossenen Ausarbeitung einsetzt. Das über Etappen auseinandergezogene Gedankengebäude, das ihm vorausgeht, wird in der Kunstwissenschaft entworfen.

Im neunzehnten Jahrhundert, nach dem Ausklingen der Philosophie HEGELs, übernimmt als philosophische Grundlagendisziplin aller Wissenschaften der Positivismus die Herrschaft. Die Realwissenschaften bauen von nun an auf der Begriffsbasis der Philosophie des "Gegebenen", der sinnlichen Daten. So auch die Kunstwissenschaft. Sie ist insofern positivistisch geprägt, als sie einen ihrer Grundbegriffe, den Begriff des Stils, in Abhängigkeit vom Handgreiflichen stellt, dem Material, den Verarbeitungstechniken und dem Zweck des Kunstwerks. Dies ist bei GOTTFRIED SEMPER (1803–1879), dem neben SCHINKEL bedeutendsten Architekten des 19. Jahrhunderts, in seinem Werk über Stil[17] breit ausgeführt. Nur das empirisch Verifizierbare kann Gegenstand der Kunstwissenschaft werden. Bei der Ausgrenzung der konkret bestimmbaren Faktoren Material, Technik und Zweck wird zwar die Existenz einer ideellen Komponente zugegeben, diese ideelle Komponente aber bleibt unbestimmt.

Von diesem Ausgangspunkt aus treten Vorläufertheorien des Strukturalismus auf. Vorläufer waren, neben Mit- und Nebenläufern, ALOIS RIEGL (1858–1905), HEINRICH WÖLFFLIN (1864–1945) und ERWIN PANOFSKY (1892–1968) mit ihren Theorien einer immanenten Gesetzlichkeit der Stilentwicklung. Es sind dies Theorien, die das Substanzproblem in der Stilforschung zu lösen versuchen. Sie alle haben mit dem Strukturalismus gemein, hierfür jene im positivistischen Stilbegriff nur diffus bezeichnete ideelle Komponente genauer zu bestimmen.

RIEGL ersetzt in seinem Werk über die spätrömische Kunstindustrie[18] das einstellige Ästhetikmodell des Positivismus, das von der materiellen Verfassung des Kunstwerks ausgeht, durch ein zweistelliges. In diesem Modell bildet das konkrete Kunstwerk nur eine Hinsicht, die als solche zur Stilbestimmung nicht hinreicht, sondern erst in einer zweiten Hinsicht, einer ideellen Größe, zu verstehen ist. Daß RIEGL, wie von KASCHNITZ nachdrücklich bemängelt, vom Positivismus beeinflußt bleibt, zeigt sich darin, daß er den formalen Begriffsrahmen der

---

[16] Karl Schefold: Neue Wege der Klassischen Archäologie nach dem ersten Weltkrieg, in: Helmut Flashar (ed.): Altertumswissenschaft in den 20er Jahren. Neue Fragen und Impulse, Stuttgart 1995, S. 183.

[17] Gottfried Semper: Der Stil in den technischen und tektonischen Künsten. Praktische Ästhetik. Ein Handbuch für Techniker, Künstler und Kunstfreunde, Bd. 1: Textile Kunst, Bd. 2: Keramik, Tektonik, Stereotomie, Metallotechnik, München 2. Aufl. 1878/79.

[18] Alois Riegl: Die spätrömische Kunstindustrie nach den Funden in Österreich-Ungarn, 1. Teil, Wien 1901, Neudruck Wien 1927.

Stiltypologie aus dem physiologischen Wahrnehmungsvorgang ableitet. Maßgebend für die in Frage stehenden Künste sind Sehsinn und Tastsinn. Die gesamte Kunst des Altertums wird entsprechend in drei Perioden unterteilt: in eine taktische oder haptisch-nahsichtige (ägyptische Kunst), in eine haptisch-optische oder normalsichtige (klassische griechische Kunst) und in eine optische oder fernsichtige (Kunst der späten römischen Kaiserzeit). Diese Begrifflichkeit erschöpft sich in einem Phänomenalismus, indem sie sich lediglich auf die unmittelbare, rein sinnliche Präsenz des Kunstwerks bezieht.

Darüber hinaus entwickelt RIEGL eine Theorie des "Kunstwollens". Dabei dürfte er weniger an die Lebensphilosophie eines BERGSON als vielmehr an die SCHOPENHAUERsche Kunstphilosophie angeknüpft haben, nach welcher Kunst die ideelle Vergegenständlichung eines zugrundeliegenden dynamischen Prinzips ist, das als Wille bezeichnet wird. RIEGL unterscheidet zwischen "äußerem Stilcharakter" und "Stilprinzip". Der Stilcharakter betrifft die eine Stelle seines Modells, die aus dem Wahrnehmungsvorgang abgeleiteten Formmöglichkeiten des Kunstwerks, wie es sich phänomenal darbietet. Das Stilprinzip dagegen bezieht sich auf die zweite Stelle im Modell des Kunstwerks, auf die ideelle Komponente, die komplementär zur ersteren steht. Das Stilprinzip zielt implizit über den phänomenalistischen Rahmen hinaus und bezieht sich auf eine basale Ebene, auf eine strukturelle Gesetzmäßigkeit des Kunstwerks, mit der das Kunstwollen greifbar wird. Dieses Kunstwollen darf allerdings nicht als ein bewußtes Wollen, als ein Wählen zwischen überblickten Möglichkeiten, mißverstanden werden. Es handelt sich vielmehr um einen ästhetischen Drang, der unbewußt determiniert ist.

Dies ist dahingehend zu verstehen, daß das Kunstwollen letztlich eine kulturkonstituierende Funktion besitzt. Es bezieht sich direkt auf den geistigen Gesamtkomplex einer Kultur; die Kunst selbst ist Produkt, Ausdruck und Definition dieses geistigen Komplexes, kurzum, die ausdrücklich gemachte Feststellung kultureller Identität. Mit dieser nicht mehr stiltheoretischen, sondern kunstphilosophischen These haben wir den Kern der Vorläufertheorien vor uns, den der Strukturalismus aufgreift. Mit HEINRICH WÖLFFLINS[19] kunstgeschichtlichen Grundbegriffen, die auf den Nachweis gesetzmäßiger Formensysteme führen, setzt sich an diesen Kern weiteres Fruchtfleisch an.

Mit der Rezension des Werkes von RIEGL, das einen "Wendepunkt, ja vielleicht sogar eine Revolution der historischen Betrachtung der bildenden Kunst"[20] darstelle, markiert KASCHNITZ das strukturalistische Programm, von der positivistischen Beschränkung auf den Wahrnehmungsvorgang zum Kunstwerk selbst vorzustoßen. Die Referenz auf die Substanz ist im Strukturbegriff kodiert, der die bisherigen Kategorien in mehreren Hinsichten ersetzt. Das Phänomenale des Kunstwerks bildet nicht mehr den einzigen Angelpunkt der Kunstbetrachtung, sondern es werden Bedingungen der Erscheinungsweise angepeilt. Zurückgegriffen wird hierbei auf RIEGLS Theorie des Kunstwollens. Nimmt man RIEGLS Theorie ernst, so muß jedes Kunstwerk in Zuordnung zu seiner kulturhistorischen Umgebung verstanden werden. KASCHNITZ bindet deshalb den Strukturbegriff an den Begriff kultureller Identität. Die Strukturanalysen in

---

[19] Heinrich Wölfflin: Kunstgeschichtliche Grundbegriffe. Das Problem der Stilentwicklung in der neueren Kunst, München 1915, 18. Aufl. Basel, Stuttgart 1991.

[20] Guido Kaschnitz von Weinberg: Rezension zu Alois Riegl, Spätrömische Kunstindustrie, in: Gnomon, Bd. 5 (1929), S. 195–213, S. 196.

seinem Vermächtnis, dem opus magnum et postumum Mittelmeerische Kunst[21] – das die Herausgeber kurioserweise als "Fragment" einführen –, weisen diese Bindung empirisch nach, und zwar in einer beispiellosen Gesamtsichtung des Materials, die von den Anfängen bis zur Spätantike reicht, einer Analyse der Strukturtypen der vorderasiatischen, ägyptischen, hethitischen, mykenischen, griechischen, etruskischen und römischen Kunst.

Man wird sich fragen dürfen, ob sich überhaupt ein angemessener Gesichtspunkt finden läßt, der einer derart breit ausgreifenden Synopse als Leitfaden dienen kann. Das Ansinnen der Theorie wäre allerdings mißverstanden, wenn man übersieht, daß für die Transzendierung des Einzelstücks – und nichts anderes kann eine nichttautologische Analyse sein – die Verkettung des Materials, vorzüglich in Form typologischer Zuordnungen, gefordert ist. Gelingen solche, dann liefern sie Anhaltspunkte, den ersten oder letzten Schritt historischer Bestimmung vorzunehmen, nämlich Kulturkreise zu ziehen, kulturelle "Identitäten" auszumachen und deren interne Entwicklungen anhand ihrer Prinzipien nachzuvollziehen. Hier greift der Strukturbegriff, der als Raumstruktur definiert ist. Die Raumrelationen des zur Ausdeutung anstehenden Artefakts dienen als Leitkategorie der Strukturanalyse. Methodisch setzt diese beim Einzelstück an, dessen Erscheinungsbedingungen nun als seine in ihm abgebildeten Raumverhältnisse bestimmt sind.

"Zu den wichtigsten methodischen Grundlagen der Strukturforschung rechnen wir daher das Ausgehen vom Existentiellen des Kunstwerks. Dazu gehört in erster Linie die objektive Feststellung des Verhältnisses, in dem der Formungswille zu Körper und Raum als Kategorien unserer sinnlichen Wahrnehmung und Medien der Formgestaltung steht. Die Bedeutung dieses Verhältnisses wurde von der kunstgeschichtlichen Forschung zwar immer wieder betont, doch beschränkt sich diese im wesentlichen auf die Aufstellung abstrakter Theorien. Zum Unterschied von diesen Theorien geht die Strukturforschung von der Untersuchung des tatsächlich gegebenen historischen Materials aus, die bisher nur in einzelnen Fällen durchgeführt wurde, und sucht erst auf Grund dieser objektiven Feststellungen zu einer Deutung der metaphysischen Wurzeln und Ausdrucksgehalte des schöpferischen Wesens vorzudringen, die schon in diesen allgemeinsten Voraussetzungen der Formbildung enthalten sein müssen."[22]

KASCHNITZ arbeitet zwar mit Begriffen wie 'Gravitation', 'Masse', 'Kraft', 'Energie', letztlich aber hat er immer räumliche Beziehungen im Auge und sucht für sie lediglich bildhafte Ausdrücke. Alle von ihm verwendeten Termini beziehen sich auf das räumliche Koordinatensystem der Anschauung, in dessen Gitter die Materie dargestellt wird. Die Raumrelationen werden dabei nicht auf Sehformen im Sinne des physiologischen Wahrnehmungsvorgangs

---

[21] Guido Kaschnitz von Weinberg: Mittelmeerische Kunst. Eine Darstellung ihrer Strukturen, hrsg. von Peter H. von Blanckenhagen und Helga von Heintze, Berlin 1965 [Ausgewählte Schriften Bd. 3]. – Zeitlebens publizierte oder vom Autor zur Publikation bestimmte Strukturforschungen sind: Guido Kaschnitz von Weinberg: Die Grundlagen der antiken Kunst, Bd. 1: Die mittelmeerischen Grundlagen der antiken Kunst, Frankfurt 1944, Bd. 2: Die eurasischen Grundlagen der antiken Kunst, Frankfurt 1961. – Guido Kaschnitz von Weinberg: Italien mit Sardinien, Sizilien und Malta, in: Reinhard Herbig (ed.): Handbuch der Archäologie, im Rahmen des Handbuchs der Altertumswissenschaft. Die Denkmäler. Jüngere Steinzeit und Bronzezeit in Europa und einigen angrenzenden Gebieten bis um 1000 v. Chr., München 1950, S. 311–397.

[22] Guido Kaschnitz von Weinberg: Mittelmeerische Kunst. Eine Darstellung ihrer Strukturen, hrsg. von Peter H. von Blanckenhagen und Helga von Heintze, Berlin 1965 [Ausgewählte Schriften Bd. 3], S. 15.

zurückgeführt, sondern auf eine "Funktion der metaphysischen Vorstellungskraft".[23] Damit ist der innere Blick gemeint, die Wirklichkeitswahrnehmung in ihrer Totalität, die Perspektive der kulturellen Identität, die Raumperspektive als "symbolische Form".[24]

Diese Gleichung zwischen Perspektive und symbolischer Form stellt der Kunsthistoriker PANOFSKY[25] auf, der RIEGLs Theorie des Kunstwollens weiterbearbeitet, jedoch Perspektive und Raumanschauung im Hinblick auf den mathematischen Raum trennt, wie ihn die Renaissance mit der mathematisch durchkonstruierten Perspektive ausbildete; die Beziehung des mathematischen zum anschaulichen, zu Typen gestaltbaren Raum, wie ihn der Strukturalismus versteht, wird zum erörterten Problem. PANOFSKY bleibt dabei grundsätzlich im Horizont der Theorie RIEGLs befangen, geht doch auf letzteren das Mißverständnis zurück, die Perspektive der Renaissancekunst als Entdeckung des Raumes schlechthin einzuschätzen und den antiken Kulturen, um sie kunstgeschichtlich zu charakterisieren, die Kenntnis des Raumes als künstlerischen Gegenstandes abzusprechen. Gewicht bei PANOFSKY aber behält – womit er als waschechter Strukturalist in Erinnerung bleibt – die als räumliche Durchsicht auf die Welt gefaßte unverbrüchliche Verbindung von Raumanschauung und Weltvorstellung.[26]

Alle diese neuen Ideen keimen auch in der Philosophie, bei OSWALD SPENGLER (1880–1936). Auf dem Fundament von Raumbegriff und Mathematik errichtet er das Gebäude einer umfassenden Kulturmorphologie. In seinem nach wie vor imposanten Hauptwerk, dem Untergang des Abendlandes[27], wird dem vieldeutigen Ausdruck 'Kultur' über den Symbolbegriff und diesem über den Raumbegriff ein Weg zu einem präzisen Verständnis gebahnt: "Symbole, als etwas Verwirklichtes, gehören zum Bereich des Ausgedehnten. Sie sind geworden, nicht werdend – auch wenn sie ein Werden bezeichnen –, mithin starr begrenzt und den Gesetzen des Raumes unterworfen. Es gibt nur sinnlich-räumliche Symbole. Schon das Wort Form bezeichnet etwas Ausgedehntes im Ausgedehnten ..."[28] Und an anderer Stelle heißt es: "Die Art der Ausgedehntheit soll von nun an das Ursymbol einer Kultur genannt werden. Die gesamte Formensprache ihrer Wirklichkeit, ihre Physiognomie im Unterschiede von der jeder anderen Kultur und vor allem von der beinahe physiognomielosen Umwelt des primitiven Menschen ist aus ihr abzuleiten; denn die Deutung der Tiefe [des Raumes] erhebt sich nun zur Tat, zum gestaltenden Ausdruck in Werken, zur Umgestaltung des Wirklichen, die nicht mehr wie bei Tieren einer Not des Lebens dient, sondern ein Sinnbild des Lebens aufrichten soll, das sich aller Elemente der Ausdehnung, der Stoffe, Linien, Farben, Töne, Bewegungen bedient, und oft noch nach Jahrhunderten, indem es im Weltbild späterer Wesen auftaucht

---

23 Siehe die gesamte Einleitung bei Guido Kaschnitz von Weinberg: Mittelmeerische Kunst. Eine Darstellung ihrer Strukturen, hrsg. von Peter H. von Blanckenhagen und Helga von Heintze, Berlin 1965 [Ausgewählte Schriften Bd. 3], S. 1–21. .

24 Guido Kaschnitz von Weinberg: Mittelmeerische Kunst. Eine Darstellung ihrer Strukturen, hrsg. von Peter H. von Blanckenhagen und Helga von Heintze, Berlin 1965 [Ausgewählte Schriften Bd. 3], S. 18 ff.

25 Erwin Panofsky: Die Perspektive als symbolische Form, in: Vorträge der Bibliothek Warburg 1924/25, Leipzig, Berlin 1927, S. 258–330. Der Begriff der symbolischen Form stammt entweder von Panofsky selbst oder aber von einem anderen berühmten Benutzer der Bibliothek Warburg, von Ernst Cassirer.

26 Vgl. Erwin Panofsky: Die Perspektive als symbolische Form, in: Vorträge der Bibliothek Warburg 1924/25, Leipzig, Berlin 1927, S. 270.

27 Oswald Spengler: Der Untergang des Abendlandes. Umrisse einer Morphologie der Weltgeschichte, München 1927–31, ungekürzte Sonderausg. in 1 Bd., München 1979.

28 Oswald Spengler: Der Untergang des Abendlandes. Umrisse einer Morphologie der Weltgeschichte, München 1927–31, ungekürzte Sonderausg. in 1 Bd., München 1979, S. 214.

und seinen Zauber übt, von der Art zeugt, wie seine Urheber die Welt verstanden haben."[29] In diesen gedrängten Worten sind die wichtigsten Gedanken des Strukturalismus ausgesprochen.

In der Kunstwissenschaft führt der Weg von PANOFSKY weiter zu HANS SEDLMAYR (1896-1984), der ausgiebig den Strukturbegriff benutzt, seine Untersuchungen als Strukturanalyse bezeichnet[30] und direkt auf den harten Kern der Theorie zurückgreift. Verlust der Mitte[31] – der Titel seiner wichtigsten Abhandlung, an der sich die Geister noch heute scheiden – bezeichnet die Strukturformel für die europäische Kunst der Neuzeit und der Gegenwart. Sie transzendiert alle Binnenunterscheidungen bezüglich Epoche und Stil, um rein mathematisch, in bezug auf den Raum und seine Relationen, gleichsam das konstitutionelle Zentrum einer stilistisch nur mühsam zu überblickenden Entwicklung zu treffen. Das konstitutionelle Zentrum ist zugleich das metaphysische, das geistige Zentrum des Kunstwerks, dessen ideeller Hintergrund, der ausschließlich topologisch gewonnen wird, das heißt, streng nur über eine Raumlehre. Das Schlußverfahren vom Sichtbaren auf das Geistige, auf die Bedeutung, auf die im Artefakt indizierte Idee, ist mathematisch fundiert. Die "Methode der kritischen Formen", wie SEDLMAYR sein Verfahren nennt, reinigt die Kunstinterpretation von der Schöngeisterei.

Die Methode der kritischen Formen "beruht im wesentlichen auf folgender Überlegung: Unter den Formen, in denen eine Epoche sich im Felde der Kunst verkörpert, sind radikal neue immer selten ... Und weil radikale neue Formen so selten sind, liegt es nahe, sie als bloße Absonderlichkeiten zu nehmen, ... als Entgleisungen oder Absurditäten ... Es ist vielmehr geradezu zum heuristischen Prinzip zu machen, daß sich in solchen absonderlichen Formen Eigentümlichkeiten enthüllen, die in gemäßigter und deshalb weniger auffallender Weise auch sonst das Schaffen einer Zeit bestimmen, dessen Eigenart in ihnen gleichsam auf die Spitze getrieben wird."[32] Was die Anwendung dieser Methode auf die neuzeitliche Kunst des Abendlandes hergibt, ist bestechend. SEDLMAYR gelangt, durch Analyse der jeweils kritischen Formen, zu einer Mathematisierung der Kunstepochen. Ihm gelingt die Abbildung der Kunstgeschichte auf ein cartesisches Koordinatensystem. Auf diese Grundlage, die ihm die Bestimmung der Raumrelationen liefert, stützt sich er sich, wenn er schließlich zur Formulierung eines Entwicklungsprinzips der abendländischen Kunst seit 1760 ansetzt, eines Entwicklungsprinzips, das dem Titel seiner Untersuchung eine primär geometrische, gravitationstheoretische und hierauf bezogene anthropologische Bedeutung zuweist und weniger (was unbestrittenermaßen auch anklingt) eine theologische, metaphysische: "Verlust der Erdbasis"[33] – eine Formel, die auf allen Ebenen des sichtbaren Artefakts wie der geistigen Einordnung des Menschen in die Welt aufgeschlüsselt wird.

[29] Oswald Spengler: Der Untergang des Abendlandes. Umrisse einer Morphologie der Weltgeschichte, München 1927–31, ungekürzte Sonderausg. in 1 Bd., München 1979, S. 226.

[30] Hans Sedlmayr: Kunst und Wahrheit. Zur Theorie und Methode der Kunstgeschichte, Hamburg 1955.

[31] Hans Sedlmayr: Verlust der Mitte. Die bildende Kunst des 19. und 20. Jahrhunderts als Symptom und Symbol der Zeit, Salzburg 1948, 10. Aufl. 1983.

[32] Hans Sedlmayr: Verlust der Mitte. Die bildende Kunst des 19. und 20. Jahrhunderts als Symptom und Symbol der Zeit, Salzburg 1948, 10. Aufl. 1983, S. 9.

[33] Vgl. Hans Sedlmayr: Verlust der Mitte. Die bildende Kunst des 19. und 20. Jahrhunderts als Symptom und Symbol der Zeit, Salzburg 1948, 10. Aufl. 1983, bes. S. 87.

Im Schatten SEDLMAYRS steht WERNER HAGER, der die Theorie aufmerksam aufnimmt. Unter Berufung auf RIEGL und SCHWEITZER versteht er eine abendländische Kunstgeschichte sinnvoll nur als eine Geschichte ihrer Raumkonzeptionen; für alle Künste, selbst für Dichtung und Musik, ist eine Analyse der in ihnen ausgedrückten Raumvorstellungen einzufordern. Der Raum wird schlechthin zur "Stätte des Kunstwerks".[34]

Mit dem Begriff der Raumstruktur als Grundkategorie der Artefaktanalyse zieht der Strukturalismus die in der Kunstwissenschaft vorgezeichnete Theorielinie aus und verselbständigt sich zu einer spezifisch archäologischen Kunsttheorie. Die Eigenständigkeit des Strukturalismus gegenüber PANOFSKYS Kunsttheorie, die den Raumbegriff in der Kunst auf die mathematische Perspektive der Renaissance einschränkt, wird bei MATZ deutlich, der durchgängig vom anschaulichen Raum ausgeht. In seinem Standardwerk über die frühkretischen Siegel[35], die KASCHNITZ' Untersuchungen noch vorausgeht, demonstriert er, wie die Raumanschauung sich als Strukturform vom Ornament bis zur Architektur bestätigt. Hier wird ebenfalls das gesamte anstehende Material – Siegel, Keramik und Plastik – des vorderasiatischen, ägyptischen, hethitischen und kretischen Kulturkreises herangezogen und die jeweils entsprechende Raumstruktur herausgearbeitet. Eine Vertiefung hinsichtlich des Griechischen erfahren die Untersuchungen in MATZ' Geschichte der griechischen Kunst.[36]

Neben diesen drei groß angelegten Untersuchungen stehen eine Reihe kleinerer Arbeiten zur griechisch-archaischen, ägyptischen und vorderasiatischen Kunst, insbesondere von KASCHNITZ[37], daneben auch von MATZ[38]. Eine Pionierleistung stellen SCHWEITZERS Beobachtungen zum geometrischen Stil dar.[39] Als Strukturalisten zu erkennen sind aber auch GERHARD KRAHMER (1890-1931), VALENTIN KURT MÜLLER und, wenngleich verschleiert, ERNST LANGLOTZ[40].

KRAHMER arbeitet mit der überaus fruchtbaren Unterscheidung zwischen hypotaktischem und parataktischem Raum, zwischen dynamischer Unterordnung der Teile unter ein Raumganzes gegenüber derer statischer Gleichordnung. Bezogen auf die Plastik ergeben sich, legt man diese zwei verschiedenen Raumstrukturierungen zugrunde, zwei entsprechend unterschiedliche Auffassungen des menschlichen Körpers. Einmal als "Organismus, der durch sich in

---

34 Werner Hager: Über Raumbildung in der Architektur und in den darstellenden Künsten, in: Studium Generale, 10. Jg. (1957), S. 632 (Zitat eines Ausspruches von H. Focillon).

35 Friedrich Matz: Die frühkretischen Siegel. Eine Untersuchung über das Werden des minoischen Stils, Berlin, Leipzig 1928.

36 Friedrich Matz: Geschichte der griechischen Kunst, Bd. 1: Die geometrische und die früharchaische Form, Frankfurt 1950.

37 Gesammelt zugänglich in Guido Kaschnitz von Weinberg: Kleine Schriften zur Struktur, hrsg. von Helga von Heintze, Berlin 1965 [Ausgewählte Schriften Bd. 1].

38 Weitere wichtige Arbeiten sind: Friedrich Matz: Die Ägäis, in: Reinhard Herbig (ed.): Handbuch der Archäologie, im Rahmen des Handbuchs der Altertumswissenschaft. Die Denkmäler. Jüngere Steinzeit und Bronzezeit in Europa und einigen angrenzenden Gebieten bis um 1000 v. Chr., München 1950, S. 179–308. – Friedrich Matz: Torsion. Eine formenkundliche Untersuchung zur aigaischen Vorgeschichte, in: Akademie der Wissenschaften und Literatur in Mainz, Abhandlungen der Geistes- und Sozialwissenschaftlichen Klasse, Jg. 1951, Nr. 12, S. 991–1015. – Friedrich Matz: Bemerkungen zur römischen Komposition, in: Akademie der Wissenschaften und Literatur in Mainz, Abhandlungen der Geistes- und Sozialwissenschaftlichen Klasse, Jg. 1952, Nr. 8, S. 625–647. – Friedrich Matz: Kreta und frühes Griechenland. Prolegomena zur griechischen Kunstgeschichte, Baden-Baden 1962, 2. Aufl. 1964.

39 Bernhard Schweitzer: Untersuchungen zur Chronologie und Geschichte der geometrischen Stile in Griechenland II, in: Mitteilungen des Deutschen Archäologischen Instituts, Athenische Abteilung, Bd. 43 (1918), S. 1–152.

40 Ernst Langlotz: Frühgriechische Bildhauerschulen, Nürnberg 1927, bes. S. 13.

allen seinen Partien bestimmt ist, insofern alle seine Bewegungskomplexe aufeinander Bezug nehmen, ineinander wirken und gleichsam von einem Punkt aus regiert, um einen Kern versammelt und ihm untergeordnet erscheinen", andererseits, "indem wir von den einzelnen Körperteilen ausgehen", "ein jeder dieser Teile in seiner ihm besonders eigentümlichen, charakteristischen Form gesehen" wird und das Aufbauprinzip "einen erzählenden Charakter [erhält], indem es die Teile beschreibt und aneinanderfügt ... ohne Bewußtsein des einheitlich bewegenden Zentrums".[41] Hypotaxe und Parataxe sind als Kategorien insbesondere für die strukturalistische Analyse der Plastik fundamental, und zwar für die Bestimmung der hypotaktischen Raumstruktur des Griechischen in Abgrenzung vom parataktisch geleiteten Ägyptischen und Vorderasiatischen.

Parallel zu KRAHMER geht MÜLLER vor, der die Typenbildung der gesamten Plastik im ägäischen Raum, in Vorderasien, Kleinasien und Griechenland vom Neolithikum bis in die griechisch-archaische Zeit verfolgt. Mit seiner Habilitationsschrift[42] fügt er der strukturalistischen Bibliothek eine vierte Monumentalsichtung des Materials ein.

Alle diese Arbeiten sind, abgesehen von einem Strukturvergleich zwischen griechischer und ägyptischer Plastik von KASCHNITZ,[43] Produkte aus der Zeit zwischen 1920 und 1940. Erwähnung verdient noch NIKOLAUS HIMMELMANN-WILDSCHÜTZ, der 1964 eine Untersuchung[44] vorlegt, in der die Struktur der griechisch-geometrischen Plastik aus ihrem Verhältnis zum Raum bestimmt wird.

Mit dem Raumbegriff als definiens der Struktur des Kunstwerks nehmen die Strukturalisten unausgesprochen auf ältere Kunsttheorien Bezug.[45] Neben jener von ERNST TROSS, der mit der Relation zwischen "Raumwert und Funktionswert"[46] arbeitet und sich bereits in seiner Dissertation von 1913 als gleichsam vorzeitiger Strukturalist gebärdet, sind diejenigen von ADOLF VON HILDEBRAND (1847–1921) und HEINRICH ALFRED SCHMID zu nennen, bezüglich deren eine exemplarisch verfahrende Untersuchung wie die von BRINCKMANN[47] als mustergültige Anwendung auftritt. HILDEBRAND[48] erörtert den kunstgeschichtlichen Formbegriff und bestimmt den Raum als allgemeinstes Verhältnis sowohl des Kunstwerks zur Natur als auch des Be-

---

[41] Gerhard Krahmer: Figur und Raum in der ägyptischen und griechisch-archaischen Kunst, in: 28. Hallesches Winckelmannsprogramm, Halle 1931, S. 5, 7 ff. – Vgl. die für die Methode sehr bezeichnende, postum publizierte Untersuchung von Gerhard Krahmer: Hellenistische Köpfe, vorgelegt von H. Tiersch, in: Nachrichten von der Gesellschaft der Wissenschaften zu Göttingen, Göttingen 1936 [Altertumswissenschaft NF, Bd. 1, Nr. 10], S. 217–255.

[42] Valentin Müller: Frühe Plastik in Griechenland und Vorderasien. Ihre Typenbildung von der neolithischen bis in die griechisch-archaische Zeit (rund 3000 bis 600 v. Chr.), Augsburg 1929. – Frühere Arbeiten: Valentin Müller: Die monumentale Architektur der Chatti von Bogazköi, in: Mitteilungen des Deutschen Archäologischen Instituts, Athenische Abteilung, Bd. 42 (1917), S. 99–203. – Valentin Müller: Die Raumdarstellung der altorientalischen Kunst, in: Archiv für Orientforschung, Bd. 5 (1928), S. 199–206.

[43] Aus dem Jahre 1946, wiederabgedruckt in: Guido Kaschnitz von Weinberg: Kleine Schriften zur Struktur, hrsg. von Helga von Heintze, Berlin 1965 [Ausgewählte Schriften Bd. 1], S. 146–155; siehe dort weitere spätere Aufsätze.

[44] Nikolaus Himmelmann-Wildschütz: Bemerkungen zur geometrischen Plastik, Berlin 1964.

[45] Zur Kategorie des Raumes in der älteren Kunstwissenschaft siehe Hans Jantzen: Über den kunstgeschichtlichen Raumbegriff, in: Sitzungsberichte der Bayerischen Akademie der Wissenschaften. Philosophisch-historische Abteilung, Jg. 1938, Heft 5. Jantzen geht bis auf Leonardo zurück.

[46] Ernst Tross: Studien zur Raumentwicklung in Plastik und Malerei, Diss. Giessen 1913, S. 7.

[47] Albert E. Brinckmann: Plastik und Raum als Grundformen künstlerischer Gestaltung, München 1922.

[48] Adolf Hildebrand: Das Problem der Form in der bildenden Kunst, Straßburg 1893.

schauers zum Kunstwerk. Auf ihn geht der terminus technicus "Raumwert der Erscheinung"[49] (des Objekts oder des Kunstwerks) zurück, aus dem Raumwert ist die "Form" des Kunstwerks abzuleiten. Diese Raumästhetik wird bei SCHMID[50] gleichsam vom Subjekt auf das Objekt verlagert. Form bedeutet nach SCHMID einen gesetzmäßigen Aufbau des Kunstwerks, der sich daraus ergibt, wie im Kunstwerk der Raum erscheint. SCHMID hat deshalb den Raumbegriff ausdrücklich als objektives Kriterium und den Raumwert als Träger der Stilentwicklung in die Kunsttheorie eingebracht.

§ 4 THEORETISCHE DARSTELLUNGEN

Die Strukturalisten haben gelegentlich ihre Theorie unabhängig von der Materialforschung dargestellt. So erläutert KASCHNITZ den Begriff der Struktur in einem Lexikonartikel[51], MATZ im Studium Generale[52] anläßlich einer Rückschau auf die ausgebliebene Aufnahme in der Archäologie. Die frühesten theoretischen Reflexionen stellt SCHWEITZER auf wenigen Seiten und beinahe unauffindbar inmitten seiner nicht kurzen Untersuchung über die geometrischen Stile an.[53] In den genannten Darstellungen wird allerdings exemplifizierend verfahren; als Theorieexposition können nur drei Texte gelten. Zum ersten derjenige, den SCHWEITZER im Handbuch der Archäologie über das Problem der Form in der Kunst des Altertums liefert,[54] zum zweiten derjenige, den MATZ in seiner Geschichte der griechischen Kunst[55] zur methodischen Orientierung gibt. Zum dritten ist SCHWEITZERs nicht gehaltene Leipziger Rektoratsrede zu nennen.[56] Hinzu kommen knappe Bemerkungen über Struktur und Form von WILHELM KRAIKER[57] und die bündige, mit dem Gütesiegel zu versehende Einführung von HAGER.[58]

[49] Adolf Hildebrand: Das Problem der Form in der bildenden Kunst, Straßburg 1893, S. 39.

[50] Heinrich A. Schmid: Ueber objektive Kriterien der Kunstgeschichte. Zugleich eine Recension, in: Repertorium für Kunstwissenschaft, Bd. 19 (1896), Sonderabdruck 1896, S. 269–284.

[51] Guido Kaschnitz von Weinberg: Ricerca di struttura, in: Ranuccio Bianchi Bandinelli (ed.): Enciclopedia dell'arte antica classica e orientale, Bd. 8, Rom 1966, S. 519–521; übersetzt in: Guido Kaschnitz von Weinberg: Kleine Schriften zur Struktur, hrsg. von Helga von Heintze, Berlin 1965 [Ausgewählte Schriften Bd. 1], S. 198-202.

[52] Friedrich Matz: Strukturforschung und Archäologie, in: Studium Generale, 17. Jg. (1964), S. 203–219.

[53] Bernhard Schweitzer: Untersuchungen zur Chronologie und Geschichte der geometrischen Stile in Griechenland II, in: Mitteilungen des Deutschen Archäologischen Instituts, Athenische Abteilung, Bd. 43 (1918), S. 115–121. Zur besseren Plazierung gesondert abgedruckt unter dem Titel: Die Begriffe des Plastischen und Malerischen als Grundformen der Anschauung, in: Zeitschrift für Ästhetik und allgemeine Kunstwissenschaft, Bd. 13 (1918), S. 259–269.

[54] Bernhard Schweitzer: Das Problem der Form in der Kunst des Altertums, in: Walter Otto (ed.): Handbuch der Archäologie, im Rahmen des Handbuchs der Altertumswissenschaft, München 1939, S. 363–399.

[55] Friedrich Matz: Geschichte der griechischen Kunst, Bd. 1: Die geometrische und früharchaische Form, Frankfurt 1950, darin: Kunstgeschichte und Strukturforschung. Zur methodischen Orientierung, S. 1–36.

[56] Bernhard Schweitzer: Vom Sinn der Perspektive, Tübingen 1953 [Die Gestalt. Abhandlungen zu einer allgemeinen Morphologie, Heft 24].

[57] Wilhelm Kraiker: Struktur und Form, in: Wilhelm Kraiker (ed.): Archaische Plastik der Griechen, Darmstadt 1976, S. 261–266. Vgl. seine umständliche Kritik an den Resultaten von Krahmer, Matz und Kaschnitz, in Wilhelm Kraiker: Theorien zur archaischen Plastik, in: Wilhelm Kraiker (ed.): Archaische Plastik der Griechen, Darmstadt 1976, S. 235–260.

[58] Werner Hager: Über Raumbildung in der Architektur und in den darstellenden Künsten, in: Studium Generale, 10. Jg. (1957), S. 630–645.

Als theoretische Position SCHWEITZERS läßt sich Folgendes festmachen. Die Kunstwissenschaft hat von der Notwendigkeit auszugehen, Kategorien der Kunstbetrachtung kriteriologisch festzulegen. Als Kriterium gilt SCHWEITZER der Begriffsumfang möglicher Kategorien. Diese müssen die Vielfalt der historisch gewachsenen Stil- und Formtypen in der Funktion allgemeiner Bezugspunkte, schließlich eines letzten Bezugspunktes, übergreifen. Als solche Inbegriffe der Stil- und Formtypen gelten ihm gleichwertig Raum und Zeit, wobei er es offen läßt, inwiefern Zeit sich auf Kunst beziehen und in Kunst dargestellt werden kann.[59] Als letztes Bezugssystem der Strukturanalyse postuliert er ein undefiniert bleibendes Absolutes, das er auch als "letzten Existenzgrund" bezeichnet, zu welchem der Künstler oder die Kunst einer Kultur sich verhalte. Raum- und Zeitauffassung gelten ihm als Repräsentationen des Verhältnisses zu jenem Absoluten. In diesem Punkt spielt er den Metaphysiker unter den Strukturalisten, der Sache nach meint er aber nichts anderes als den engen Zusammenhang zwischen Kunst und dem geistigen Gesamtkomplex, der die Identität einer Kultur ausmacht.

Zu seiner Auffassung gelangt er über eine "transzendental-psychologische Betrachtungsweise".[60] Unter objektiven Kriterien versteht er näherhin "Kategorien des künstlerischen Schauens"[61]. Sie erlauben es, Plastik und Malerei gleichsam aus sich selbst heraus zu deuten: "Das Bestreben der vollkörperlichen Bildwerdung geht auf allseitige Begrenzung im unbegrenzten, dreidimensionalen Raum, die malerische Wiedergabe will Darstellung einer unbegrenzten Vielheit in der begrenzten, zweidimensionalen Fläche. Jede Skulptur, jedes Flächenbild ist ein je nach dem durch eine Reihe geschichtlicher und psychologischer Voraussetzungen bestimmten Vorstellungswunsch oder Vorstellungsvermögen des Schöpfers mehr oder weniger weit geführter Lösungsversuch der in diesen beiden Begriffspaaren ruhenden Gegensätze. Beide Grundformen des künstlerischen Denkens sind eine Bemeisterung des Unendlichen durch Abgrenzung, beide kennen den Raum als Voraussetzung der Erscheinung, ihr Unterschied besteht in der entgegengesetzten Stellung zum äußeren Raum."[62]

MATZ präzisiert die Methode, indem er klarstellt, daß es nicht um eine logische Systematik von Typen geht, wie sie die Kunstwissenschaftler des neunzehnten Jahrhunderts mit dem Programm verfolgten, ein Entwicklungsgesetz der Formtypen ausfindig zu machen. Es geht allein um eine geschichtliche – zeitliche und örtliche – Zuordnung der auszumachenden Strukturtypen, die nur konstatiert und nicht gemäß einer hypothetischen logischen Gesetzmäßigkeit konstruiert werden können. In diesem Sinne äußert sich auch MÜLLER in einer methodischen Vorbemerkung. Das Einzelstück wird nicht "nach seinem Einzelwert und seiner nur ihm gehörigen Eigenart behandelt, sondern nach dem, was es an Wesenhaftem bietet, wofür es repräsentativ ist. So heben sich eine Anzahl von Gemeinsamkeiten aus einer Grup-

---

[59] So spricht auch Kaschnitz mit Goethe von der Zeitlosigkeit der ägyptischen Kunst. Diese Beurteilung beruft sich auf die Mumifikation, die Pyramide und das Schweben der Gestalten, welche alle auf Dauer, auf Unveränderlichkeit und Unvergänglichkeit angelegt sind. Jedoch ist die Anlage auf Dauer nicht zwingend Negation von Zeit, sondern kann nicht weniger als Bejahung der Zeit in Form einer unendlichen Ausdehnung in der Zeit verstanden werden.

[60] Bernhard Schweitzer: Untersuchungen zur Chronologie und Geschichte der geometrischen Stile in Griechenland II, in: Mitteilungen des Deutschen Archäologischen Instituts, Athenische Abteilung, Bd. 43 (1918), S. 121.

[61] Bernhard Schweitzer: Untersuchungen zur Chronologie und Geschichte der geometrischen Stile in Griechenland II, in: Mitteilungen des Deutschen Archäologischen Instituts, Athenische Abteilung, Bd. 43 (1918), S. 117.

[62] Bernhard Schweitzer: Untersuchungen zur Chronologie und Geschichte der geometrischen Stile in Griechenland II, in: Mitteilungen des Deutschen Archäologischen Instituts, Athenische Abteilung, Bd. 43 (1918), S. 118.

pe von Werken heraus; sie haben ihren Grund in einem gemeinsamen Formprinzip, das alle Einzelformen der betreffenden Werke bedingt und von einheitlicher Art ist. Indem es selbst nun individueller Art und an Ort und Zeit gebunden ist, grenzt es sich gegen andere ab. Dadurch stellt sich die Kunst ... nicht als ein loser Haufen von Werken dar, die mit minimalen Unterschieden zunächst sich aneinanderreihend, schließlich doch zu ganz verschiedenen und am Ende zusammenhangslosen Formen kommen, sondern als ein System von einerseits getrennten, andererseits in der Verwandtschaft sich abstufenden und aufeinanderwirkenden Formprinzipien."[63]

Um solche Affinitätssysteme rekonstruieren zu können, orientiert MATZ den Strukturbegriff auf den herkömmlichen Stilbegriff. Struktur ist komplementär zum Stil zu verstehen. So handelt es sich nicht um eine Substitution des Stilbegriffs durch den Strukturbegriff, der Stilforschung durch die Strukturforschung, sondern um eine Vertiefung der Analyse, die mit der Stilforschung als erster Stufe einsetzt, welche zwar notwendig ist, jedoch erst auf einer zweiten Stufe, eben in der Strukturbestimmung des Kunstwerks, ihre zureichende Begründung findet. Die Strukturforschung steht zur Stilforschung in einem Fundierungsverhältnis.

Den Strukturbegriff stützt MATZ auf den Verhältnisbegriff. Das Artefakt baut sich aus Verhältnisbeziehungen auf, aus denen es seine Form, seine Gestalt, seine Erscheinungsweise gewinnt. Die strukturalistische Analyse zielt exakt auf diese inneren Beziehungen des Artefakts, die in seinen Raumrelationen verkörpert sind. Plausibel wird das im Hinblick auf die Erscheinungsform des Kunstwerks, die primär eine räumliche ist. Demzufolge ist der Struktur- oder Formbegriff auf den Raumbegriff zurückzuführen. Der Zeitbegriff, der bei SCHWEITZER noch eine Rolle spielt, wird fallengelassen, weil er sich nicht an der Erscheinungsform des Kunstwerks festmachen läßt.

§ 5 ERGEBNISSE

In der Anwendung ihrer Methode sind die Strukturalisten zu eindeutigen Ergebnissen gelangt. Eine Sichtung des Materials zeigt, daß die Verknüpfung von Raumkonzeption und kultureller Identität hält, was sie verspricht. Seinen Niederschlag findet dieser Zusammenhang in allen Epochen der kulturellen Entwicklung, deutlich greifbar bereits im kupfersteinzeitlichen Übergangsfeld zu den sogenannten Hochkulturen.

Im Paläolithikum existieren weder Raumkonzeptionen noch Kulturunterschiede. Die bezüglich des Fundortes und der zeitlichen Einordnung auseinanderliegenden Artefakte des altsteinzeitlichen Menschen lassen von ihrer Erscheinungsform keinerlei Rückschlüsse auf voneinander typologisch abgrenzbare Kulturkreise zu. Ein Faustkeil gleicht dem anderen aufs Haar. Die paläolithischen Figuren schweben schwerelos, gezeichnete Figuren stehen, wenn überhaupt in Zusammenhängen, so noch nicht in räumlichen.

---

63   Valentin Müller: Frühe Plastik in Griechenland und Vorderasien. Ihre Typenbildung von der neolithischen bis in die griechisch-archaische Zeit (rund 3000 bis 600 v. Chr.), Augsburg 1929, S. 2.

Abb. 1: Weibliche Figur, sogenannte Venus von Willendorf, aus Willendorf, Niederösterreich, jungpaläolithische
Kulturgruppe: Gravettien, um 23 000 v. Chr.

Betrachten wir die berühmte Venus von Willendorf (Abb. 1)! Nicht nur infolge ihrer wulstigen Körperformen, denen ein ebenso mächtiger Kopf entwächst, scheint sie auf den ersten Blick gar nicht stehen zu können, vielmehr sind ihre Stummelfüße, gerade dadurch, daß sie sich in der Fortführung zu dicken Schenkeln aufblasen, schlechterdings nicht imstande, der Figur auf einer Fläche einen Stand zu bieten. Überdies muß es fraglich bleiben, ob für ihren Schöpfer die Figur überhaupt eine bevorzugte, "richtige" Stellung besaß; sie könnte auch liegen, oder aber, bedenkt man ihre kugelige Gesamtform, jegliche vertikale oder horizontale Stellung einnehmen. Dies ist untrügliches Anzeichen dafür, daß sie gar nicht für ein definiertes Dimensionssystem geformt wurde.

Ähnliches gilt für die Höhlenmalerei – auch wenn von Spezialisten immer wieder versichert wird, sie bezeuge räumliche Ordnung, Horizont, Perspektive usw. Verweilt man vor einer solchen Malerei (Abb. 2), dann fällt auf, daß es prinzipiell unmöglich ist, die Raumrelation nur einer einzigen Figur zu einer anderen exakt zu entscheiden: Welches Tier steht hinter dem anderen, welches berührt welches, welche Distanzen sind zu denken, wo ist oben, wo ist unten, liegen alle Figuren auf dem Boden, sind es bloß zur Zählung oder zur katalogmäßigen Erfassung addierte Einzelfiguren? Wo befindet sich der Betrachter bzw. der Zeichner, links unten, rechts unten, dort, wohin die Tiere blicken, oder steht er in einem Bezug zur dargestellten Menschenfigur? Die Fragen können deswegen nicht beantwortet werden, weil sie ein in sich ausgeprägtes kategoriales Raumsystem voraussetzen, das in der Darstellung offensichtlich noch gar nicht verfügbar ist.

Abb. 2: Rinder und menschliche Figuren, steinzeitliche Felsmalerei, ʿAin Dūʿa, Südost-Libyen

Für die Schärfung des analytischen Blicks auf Artefakte ist die Einsicht in die hier manifeste Gesetzmäßigkeit gleichsam das methodische Propädeutikum. Raumstrukturen entstehen erst mit Ausbildung einer Standlinie, einem Stehvermögen der Figuren. Denn von Raumbewußtsein kann erst gesprochen werden, wenn zumindest der Richtungsgegensatz zwischen oben und unten ausdifferenziert und als absolutes Bezugssystem festgelegt ist. Und dieses läßt sich allein über die Standlinie bestimmen, welche die Gravitationsverhältnisse des Körpers berücksichtigt. Erst die Erfindung der sowohl bei Figuren wie der Venus von Willendorf als auch der Höhlenmalerei fehlenden Standlinie bedeutet Bewußtwerdung und Bewältigung der Gravitationsverhältnisse.

Im Neolithikum entwickeln sich erste spezifische Raumstrukturen, indem Fläche und Gravitationslinie zueinander in Beziehung gesetzt werden. Durch die Ausbildung zusammenhängender Ornamentsysteme und eingerahmter Flächen zeigt sich eine Abstraktion auf die Fläche, welche in den steinzeitlichen Höhlenzeichnungen noch nicht vorhanden ist, weil die Fläche dort an einzelne Figuren gebunden bleibt und keinen Flächenzusammenhang ergibt. Ornamentsysteme und eingerahmte Flächen ergeben aber darüber hinaus noch keine Abstraktion auf einen zusammenhängenden Raum. Diese Abstraktion wird erst mit der Erkenntnis der Schwerkraftwirkung geleistet, und zwar dadurch, daß die mit der Schwerkraft gegebene dritte Dimension mit der Fläche über die Erfindung des rechten Winkels verbunden wird. Hieraus entwickeln sich die beiden Grundstrukturen der altorientalischen Raumvorstellung:

KALKSTEINTEMPEL DER SCHICHT V

Abb. 3: Kalksteintempel von Eanna, Uruk

1. der orthogonale Koordinatenraum
2. der sphärische Raum.

Diese beiden Strukturen des Orthogonalen und des Sphärischen sind an sich Gegensätze. Das Fundamentalcharakteristikum der mesopotamischen Raumauffassung bildet aber gerade die Verbindung orthogonaler und sphärischer Strukturen.

In der Schrift, in der Glyptik, im Relief und in der Plastik läßt sich der orthogonale Koordinatenraum nachweisen. Auf gesellschaftlicher Ebene entspricht er der Konstituierung einer einheitlichen politischen Macht, indem Orthogonalität das Gravitative, Dauernde assoziiert. Die frühsumerische Monumentalarchitektur in Uruk (Abb. 3) folgt in Planung und Aufbau, in der

Abb. 4: Sogenanntes Wappensiegel: Siegel des Ibni–
šarrum, Diener des Šar–kali–šarri, Mitte 3. Jts.

Gesamtform wie in den Einzelheiten vollständig der orthogonalen Raumstruktur. Dabei sind Symmetrie und Axialität dominant. Bei den Rollsiegeln wird im Bild Orthogonalität realisiert, indem das Bild die Koordinatenordnung der Ebene übernimmt. Die Figuren stehen in einer wohldefinierten Reihenordnung. Die wappenartigen Tierdarstellungen, die auf Siegeln seit Uruk IV bezeugt sind, haben zum zentralen Strukturmerkmal die Symmetrie, die die orthogonale Ordnung nur noch bekräftigt (Abb. 4). Das Siegel selbst prägt durch Abrollung nichts anderes als einen orthogonalen Koordinatenraum in die undifferenzierte Fläche des Materials. Dasselbe Phänomen zeigt sich in der Entwicklung der Schrift. Die Schriftzeichen werden

Abb. 5: Schale aus Sāmarrā'   Abb. 6: Abdruck eines Stempelsiegels, althethitisch

in Form der erst allmählich auftretenden Zeilenschreibung fest mit der Fläche verbunden und gewinnen eindeutige Relationen zueinander, indem sie nach den Koordinatenachsen der Fläche ausgerichtet werden. Nicht weniger ist das Relief von einer orthogonalen Ordnung beherrscht, die mit der Verflachung aller Strukturen in die Alternative von Nebeneinander und Übereinander gar nicht deutlicher ausgedrückt werden kann. Und dieselbe Struktur wiederholt sich in der Plastik. Hier werden mit der Masse des Materials die orthogonalen Raumachsen verbunden. So entsteht die blockartige Form der mesopotamischen Plastik, wie sie am ausgeprägtesten frühsumerische Figuren verkörpern (Abb. 23 a).

Abb. 7: Abdruck eines Rollsiegels, Urukzeit

Die orthogonale Struktur wird nun von sphärischen Strukturen überlagert. In der Dekoration der Keramik ist der Kreis die Grundstruktur, die sich aus der Betonung von Zentrum und umlaufender Peripherie ergibt. Diese Betonung von Zentrum und Peripherie findet sich bereits in der Ḥalaf- und der Sāmarrā'-Keramik (Abb. 5, vgl. auch Abb. 31 a). Sie kehrt wieder bei den Stempelsiegeln, die Figuren zentrums- und nicht achsialsymmetrisch anordnen (Abb. 6). Die sphärische Grundstruktur dokumentiert sich aber selbst bei den orthogonal abdruckenden Rollsiegeln, namentlich in der Zylinderform des Siegels einerseits und in den unendlichen in sich zurücklaufenden Figurenbändern andererseits. Letztere, die unendlichen Figurenbänder, wie sie das urukzeitliche Rollsiegel in Abb. 7 darstellt, sind insofern in sich zurücklaufend, als die Abrollung mit einer Drehung die bruchlose Entsprechung zwischen linkem und rechtem Bildrand ergibt. Infolgedessen besitzt das Muster in der Horizontalen keine Grenze, vielmehr ist es selbstbezüglich: es reproduziert die Unendlichkeit des Kreises in seinem Gegensatz, im Linearen. Umgekehrt heißt das den Betrachter, das Lineare letztlich immer als Abrollung des Kreises zu lesen, als Funktion desselben.

Alle genannten Formen können als vorderorientalische Rundkomposition zum Typus zusammengefaßt werden. Denn die sphärische Raumauffassung, die von der Rundkomposition vorausgesetzt wird, bekundet sich nicht nur in der Ornamentik als ausgezogener oder angedeuteter Kreis, sondern weiter in der Plastik als Zylinder, Kegel und Kugel: Die Statue (vgl. Abb. 33 a und 33 c) muß als lediglich vorübergehende Unterbrechung einer zylindrischen Grundform gelten, die sich in Ellipsoid des Sockels und im Kreis der Kopfbedeckung wiederherstellt, überdies gekrümmt ist und in der Fortführung wahrscheinlich als kreisförmig geschlossener Schlauch gedacht ist; der Schriftkegel – eine unzweckmäßigere Schreibunterlage gibt es nicht – ist belegt (Abb. 8); angeblich soll sogar eine eiförmig ausgefallene vorderorientalische Nachbildung eines ägyptischen Würfelhockers (für diesen vgl. Abb. 17) existieren, des Inbegriffs der Herrschaft der Würfelform, die sich im epigonalen Stück unerbittlich der Kugel beugen muß. In der architektonischen Innengestaltung der Räume begeg-

Abb. 8: Schriftkegel der Könige Enmetena und Irikagina

net der rundumlaufende Fries, der die Ecken der orthogonalen Raumgliederung übergeht und einer Projektion des sphärisch-unendlichen Figurenbandes auf die orthogonale Linearität des Gebäuderaumes gleichkommt. Man denke an die Darstellungen im Palast von Nimrūd, wo Prozessionen von einem Eingang aus links und rechts ohne Rücksicht auf Ecken und Unterbrechungen der Wände kontinuierlich rundumlaufen und sich zum Kreis schließen. Was die Ignorierung der Ecken angeht, so sind dieselben mit Bäumen dekoriert, deren Zweige auf die Seitenwände übergreifen (Abb. 9). Alle diese architektonischen Eigenheiten deuten jeden rechteckigen Raum zum Zylinder um. Als weiteres Beispiel für die Zylinderform sei der Schwarze Obelisk Salmanassars III. genannt. Hier bilden die Bilder trotz der eckigen Form und der Vertikalstreifen an den Kanten einen um die vier Seiten herumlaufenden Fries. Verstärkt noch findet sich dasselbe Prinzip auf dem Obelisken Aššurnaṣirpals aus Nimrūd, auf dem die Pferde mit ihren Köpfen um die Ecken herum blicken (Abb. 10).

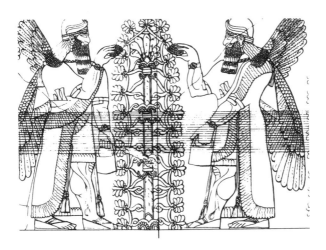

Abb. 9: Palmendarstellung in einer Raumecke: NW–Palast von Nimrūd

Abb. 10: Weißer Obelisk Aššurnaṣirpals aus Nimrūd (Ausschnitt)

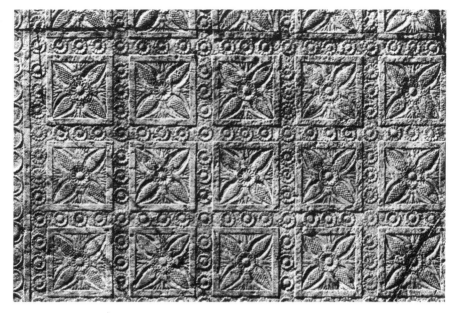

Abb. 11: Türschwelle, aus Ninua, 'Irāq, neuassyrisch

Für die direkte Verbindung von orthogonalem Koordinatenraum mit sphärischen Strukturen steht die Türschwelle aus dem N-Palast in Ninua (Abb. 11). Daß der vorderorientalischen Raumauffassung die paradoxe Verbindung von Orthogonalem und Sphärischem möglich ist, gründet offensichtlich darin, daß der mesopotamische Mensch hier gar keinen Widerspruch empfindet, vielmehr einen folgerichtigen Übergang. Grundlagen der Rundkomposition sind konzentrische Kreise und Wirbel, in denen die vertikale Achse der orthogonalen Raumordnung in den Radius und die horizontale Achse in die Umlauflinie des Kreises transformiert sind. Damit kann die sphärische Raumstruktur als Ausdeutung des orthogonalen Koordinatenraumes verstanden werden. Die Koordinaten des orthogonalen Raumes sind parallel und treffen sich im Unendlichen. Im sphärischen Raum dagegen treffen sie sich im Zentrum, von dem sie strahlenförmig ausgehen oder um das sie kreisen. Die sphärische Raumstruktur veranschaulicht in der Weise die Unendlichkeit des orthogonalen Raumes und deutet denselben als eine unendliche Kugel.

Diese Interpretation des gleichzeitigen Auftretens von orthogonaler und sphärischer Raumstruktur hat KASCHNITZ geliefert. Trifft sie zu und zieht man seinen Schluß weiter, so bedeutet die sphärische Raumstruktur letztlich nichts geringeres, als daß der vorderorientalischen Raumauffassung ein nichteuklidischer, RIEMANNscher Raum zugrunde liegt. In der Geometrie, die im Abendland im neunzehnten Jahrhundert von RIEMANN entwickelt wurde, ist der Begriff der Geraden als einer unendlichen Linie ersetzt durch den Begriff der kürzesten Verbindung in einem unendlichen gekrümmten Raum. Dabei versteht sich von selbst, daß die sphärische Raumvorstellung des Vorderorientalen noch keine Abstraktion auf den mathematischen Begriff des gekrümmten Raumes darstellt, vielmehr gerade im Anschaulichen verbleibt. Wem trotz solcher Einschränkungen die vorgeführte Strukturbestimmung zu spekulativ erscheint, der werfe ein Auge auf den Kudurru aus der Zeit Meli–šipaks (Abb. 12) und die Raumordnung der auf solchen Steinen dargestellten Figuren (Abb. 13): die Geraden, sofern sie überhaupt noch vorkommen, fungieren als kürzeste Verbindung zweier Punkte in einem sphärisch gekrümmten Raum.

Abb. 12: Kudurru aus der Zeit Meli–šipaks

Abb. 13: Kudurru aus der Zeit Marduk–apla–iddinas I., Susa

Abb. 14: Transport einer Statue, Zeichnung nach Reliefs aus Ninua, ʿIrāq, neuassyrisch

Abb. 15: Transport einer Statue, Szene im Grab des ḏḥwtjhtp, al–Barša, 12. Dynastie

Ist die sphärische Raumanschauung eine Eigentümlichkeit, welche den vorderasiatischen Kulturkreis von den anderen umliegenden Kulturen entscheidend abhebt, so lassen sich auch deren Raumkonzeptionen auszeichnen. In Ägypten – um zuerst den schärfsten Gegensatz zum Vorderasiatischen zur Sprache zu bringen – herrscht eine stereometrische Grundstruktur, die über den orthogonalen Koordinatenraum nicht hinausgeht. Was sich gegenüber der konzentrisch-sphärischen Raumauffassung des Vorderorientalischen verändert, führen Abb. 14 und 15 vor Augen, die beide dasselbe Motiv, den Transport einer Statue, präsentieren. Während das vorderorientalische Bild (Abb. 14) die Figuren kreisförmig auffächert, zwängt sie das ägyptische (Abb. 15) in orthogonale Register. Selbst die Landschaft mit ihren natürlich krummen Formen wird auf einer ägyptischen Landkarte rechtwinklig gerastert (Abb. 16). Und die Pyramide ersetzt die vorderorientalische Sphäre durch den Kristall. Treu diesem Leitbild hegen die Ägypter eine Vorliebe für glatte Platten, sauber behauene Prismen und riesige Würfel. Die Strukturen in der Plastik und in der Architektur folgen dem orthogonalen Koordinatenraum, indem dieser als Gerüst der Formen immer hinzugedacht werden kann.

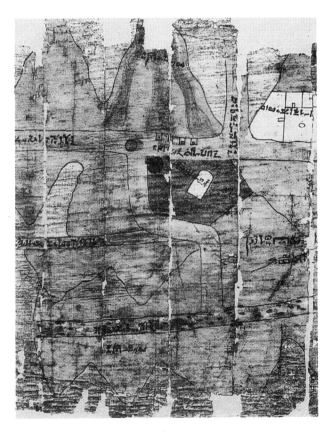

Abb. 16: Ägyptische Landkarte, Papyus (Turin), Neues Reich

Nicht umsonst werden die Statuen des Typs von Abb. 17 als Würfelhocker bezeichnet. Die Pyramide macht vom orthogonalen Koordinatenraum keine Ausnahme. Sie verkörpert nichts anderes als die Unterwerfung desselben unter die Gesetze der Schwerkraft. Letztlich zeigt

Abb. 17: Würfelhocker aus Karnak, um 1250 v. Chr.

sich die Dominanz des orthogonalen Koordinatenraumes darin, daß auch dort, wo Kugeln und Zylinder auftreten, sie stereometrisch abgeplattet werden. Das bestätigen auch die Strukturen in den Ornamenten der Keramik, die keine Zentralsymmetrie kennen wie die mesopotamische, sondern aus rechtwinklig zueinander stehenden Elementen Achsen-symmetrien bilden (Abb. 18). Noch auffälliger ist die Schale in Abb. 19, deren Verzierung trotz der runden Form des Materials optisch einen Kubus vortäuscht. Es trifft die Funktions-formel der ägyptischen Raumauffassung, von einer Quadratur des Kreises zu sprechen.
Für die kretische Kunst dagegen gilt das Prinzip der Torsion. Insbesondere die Keramik zeigt augenfällig die eigentümlichen Strukturen tordierter Meridiansysteme. Typisch hierfür ist ge-rade die Verbildlichung dieser Struktur über die Seepferdchen- und Tintenfisch-Verzierungen (Abb. 20 b). Analysiert man diese Ornamentik auf ihre Strukturrelationen, so tritt neben der Verdrehung die Eigenschaft der Selbstähnlichkeit als herrschender Wesenszug hervor. Bei-de zusammen ergeben potenzierte Spiralstrukturen (Abb. 20 a), die an visualisierte Julia-Mengen der fraktalen Geometrie erinnern.

Die griechische Raumauffassung begreift den Raum unter dem Gesichtspunkt organischer Bewegungsfunktionen. Die organische Raumstruktur zeigt sich augenfällig in der Plastik. Die Bewegungsfunktionen des dargestellten Körpers werden in Beziehung zur Schwerkraft dargestellt, also so, wie der Körper sich im Raumsystem bewegt, was zur Hypotaxe im Aufbau führt, in welcher die Einzelteile der Skulptur einer einheitlichen Bewegungsfunktion unterge-

Abb. 18: Ägyptische Keramikdekoration, Naqada I - Kultur, 1. Hälfte des 4. Jts. v. Chr.

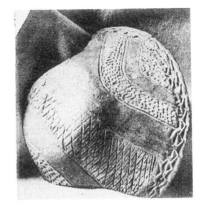

Abb. 19: Schale aus Dandara, Beginn Altes Reich

Abb. 20 a: Minoische Schale aus Phaistos, Kreta, um 1800 v. Chr.

Abb. 20 b: Minoisches Gefäß aus Palaikastro, Kreta, um 1500 v. Chr.

Abb. 21: Diskobol Lancelotti (antike Kopie)

ordnet sind. Paradebeispiel hierfür ist der Diskuswerfer (Abb. 21). Das hypotaktische Prinzip wirkt auch in der Architektur nach, die den Raum als Gliederstruktur, als ein System der Gelenke mit Bezug auf die Schwerkraft ordnet. Exemplarisch realisiert ist das Prinzip in der Säule, die sich verjüngt und, mit Basis und Kapitell ausgestattet, Proportionen besitzt, die die wirkenden Gravitations- und Trägerkräfte zum Ausdruck bringen (Abb. 22).

§ 6 Kritische Positionen

Die Theorie, wie sie bei Kaschnitz, Schweitzer und Matz ihre Darstellung und Durchführung gefunden hat, konnte sich in der Forschung nicht durchsetzen. Soweit sie überhaupt beachtet wurde, sah sie sich vor allem mit nachstehenden Einwänden konfrontiert.
Der lockerste Einwand, der zugleich so tief wie möglich zu treffen versuchte, lautet, das ganze strukturalistische Verfahren sei zu allgemein und rein spekulativ (Bianchi Bandinelli, Levi, Schefold, Wace). Dieser Vorwurf, der, sofern er zuträfe, die strukturalistischen Bemühungen um eine gegenstandsbezogene Kunstbetrachtung zunichte machte, läßt sich in drei Teilthesen aufgliedern.
Zum ersten wird beanstandet, der Abstraktion auf eine Struktur entfalle die Besonderheit des einzelnen Werkes. Der erste Einwand geht also dahin, der Strukturbegriff verunmögliche aufgrund seiner Allgemeinheit die Spezifikation, wie sie die Vielfalt der Objekte verlangt.
Zum zweiten wird bezweifelt, daß sich allein mit Raumkategorien die Kunst ganzer Epochen und ausgedehnter Kulturkreise hinreichend begreifen lasse. Der zweite Einwand kehrt sich

Abb. 22: Delphi (Marmaria), Rekonstruktion der Front des Schatzhauses von Marseille und Glieder seines Aufbaus

somit stillschweigend gegen den ersten: der Begriff der Raumstruktur sei nicht allgemein genug, um die Komplexität der Objekte zu umgreifen. Zum dritten wird der Theorie die empirische Anwendbarkeit in der Feldforschung abgesprochen. Dies geschieht mit der Begründung, daß die Theorie nicht in der Realienforschung ihren Ursprung habe, sondern im Horizont kunsttheoretischer, raumtheoretischer und kulturphilosophischer Überlegungen. Der dritte Einwand behauptet also, der formale Rahmen lasse sich nicht auf das empirische Material anwenden.

Da sich erster und zweiter Einwand in ihrem Widerspruch zueinander gegenseitig neutralisieren, ist ungewiß, was der dritte genau genommen noch besagen will. In der wissenschaftstheoretischen Betrachtung wird sich erweisen, daß alle zusammen jeder Grundlage entbehren. Überdies wäre es den Aufwand wert, Stiltheorien daraufhin zu befragen, inwiefern sie den Kriterien des Übergreifens, der Besonderung und der Feldtauglichkeit nachkommen. Zu vermuten steht, daß sie im Lichte solcher zugespitzter Entscheidungsgründe ihren Anspruch, Leittheorien mit Exklusivitätsanspruch gegenüber strukturalistischen Ansätzen zu bilden, aufgeben müßten.

Die ausgebliebene Nachwirkung ist umso mehr zu beklagen, als auch eine der kritischen Stimmen, OTTO J. BRENDEL, zur Feststellung gelangt, "das methodologische Instrumentarium", das der Strukturalismus biete, werde sich "als das wertvollste Element seiner Theorie erweisen".[64] Dem ist in der Tat zuzustimmen. Das bedeutet, die Rezeption der Theorie, besonders

[64] Otto J. Brendel: Was ist römische Kunst?, mit einem Vorwort von Eberhard Thomas, aus dem Amerikanischen von Helga Willinghöfer, Köln 1990, S. 113.

ihres methodologischen Instrumentariums, steht in krassem Gegensatz zu ihren sachlichen Möglichkeiten. MATZ wird also Recht behalten, wenn er die allenthalben kritischen Positionen zum Strukturalismus als "mehr oder weniger ausgesprochene Berufung auf die durch Überlieferung und Konvention sanktionierte Unangreifbarkeit des eigenen Standortes"[65] zurückweist.

---

[65] Friedrich Matz: Strukturforschung und Archäologie, in: Studium Generale, 17. Jg. (1964), S. 217.

ZWEITER TEIL

DIE THEORETISCHEN GRUNDLAGEN

§ 7 Die Aufgabe einer systematischen Entwicklung des Strukturbegriffs

Die wissenschaftstheoretische Betrachtung des Strukturalismus stellt sich die Aufgabe, die Theorie nach Maßgabe der Logik der Sache zu exponieren. Eine solche Exposition ist schon deshalb ein Desiderat, weil eine systematische Entwicklung der Methode in den Beiträgen der Strukturalisten ausgeblieben ist. Dies dürfte der Grund dafür sein, weshalb Kaschnitz' und Schweitzers Werke unter Begriffswucherungen leiden, die einerseits den bei Matz exakt auf Raumrelationen festgelegten Strukturbegriff aufweichen, andererseits den Strukturbegriff mit solchen Begriffen zu definieren versuchen, die die Definition des Strukturbegriffs bereits zur Voraussetzung haben. Die fehlende Systematik wirkt sich aus in mangelnder Präzision und in Zirkularität, was die Definition von Struktur betrifft. Als Beispiel sei Kaschnitz' Strukturdefinition in seiner Mittelmeerischen Kunst vorgeführt. Dort lautet die Grunddefinition, Struktur sei "Prinzip der inneren Organisation der Form"[66]. Sie ergeht sich in einem Zirkel, denn Struktur als Grundsachverhalt ist in der Abstraktion auf Prinzip, Organisation und Form schon vorausgesetzt. Letztere Begriffe bezeichnen bereits das rein Strukturelle gegenüber dem Stil, dem Inhalt, der Materie und der ästhetischen Wirkung.

Bereichert wird die Definition mit Umschreibungen des Verfahrens wie "Beschränkung auf den objektiven Charakter des Kunstwerks" oder "formwissenschaftliche Deutung", die das "Existentielle" und den "symbolischen Wert" freilegen.[67] Zusammengefaßt werden alle diese Begriffe unter dem Oberbegriff "formale Elemente des Kunstwerks".[68] Es handelt sich aber auch hier nur um eine zirkuläre Erweiterung mit übrigens, für sich genommen, ziemlich unscharfen Vorstellungen. Objektivität des Kunstwerks kann nichts anderes meinen als das Strukturelle am Kunstwerk im Gegensatz zu seiner ästhetischen Wirkung. Genauso klärt die verlangte formwissenschaftliche Deutung den Strukturbegriff auch nicht weiter auf, geht sie doch zuallererst von ihm aus und bezieht sich auf ihn als ihren Gegenstand. Wird der Gegenstand seinerseits mit dem Begriff des Existentiellen in Verbindung gebracht, dann kann sinnvoll nichts anderes darunter als wiederum die Struktur verstanden werden, weil außer der reinen Materie nur diese substantiell existiert. Schließlich beziehen sich alle diese Begriffe tatsächlich auf die formalen Elemente am Kunstwerk, um deren Aufklärung es gerade ginge.

Mit dem eingebrachten Vorbehalt an der Strukturdefinition soll diese selbst aber nicht ad absurdum geführt werden. Im übrigen ist mit dem Begriff der Raumstruktur der Strukturbegriff bereits zureichend präzisiert. Vielmehr sei deutlich gemacht, daß der Strukturbegriff im Strukturalismus, wie er betrieben wurde, den Status eines reinen Operationsbegriffs besitzt, das heißt, eines Grundbegriffs, den man dadurch zu definieren versucht, daß er angewandt wird. In der Operationalisierung erweist sich dann seine Brauchbarkeit. Diese Operationalisierung ist in der Strukturforschung denn auch geleistet worden.

---

[66] Guido Kaschnitz von Weinberg: Mittelmeerische Kunst. Eine Darstellung ihrer Strukturen, hrsg. von Peter H. von Blanckenhagen und Helga von Heintze, Berlin 1965 [Ausgewählte Schriften Bd. 3], S. 17.

[67] Guido Kaschnitz von Weinberg: Mittelmeerische Kunst. Eine Darstellung ihrer Strukturen, hrsg. von Peter H. von Blanckenhagen und Helga von Heintze, Berlin 1965 [Ausgewählte Schriften Bd. 3], S. 17.

[68] Guido Kaschnitz von Weinberg: Mittelmeerische Kunst. Eine Darstellung ihrer Strukturen, hrsg. von Peter H. von Blanckenhagen und Helga von Heintze, Berlin 1965 [Ausgewählte Schriften Bd. 3], S. 17.

Sucht man bei den Strukturalisten dagegen nach metatheoretischen Reflexionen, so haben zwar insbesondere KASCHNITZ, SCHWEITZER und MATZ die Theorieansätze formuliert, indessen nicht eigentlich die Grundlagen namhaft gemacht. Die nun folgenden Ausführungen haben die Aufgabe, die Grundlagen zu erarbeiten. Hierzu wird von den konkreten Resultaten abgesehen und die Methode isoliert. Wenn die Grundlagen des Ansatzes zur Sprache kommen, so geht es um eine wissenschaftstheoretische Prämissenexplikation, die über Plausibilität und Tragfähigkeit des Strukturalismus als Methode befinden muß.

A. DIE KRITERIEN DER METHODE

§ 8 TRAGWEITE DER THEORIE

Die strukturalistische Methode erstreckt sich über vier Ansatzpunkte, die aufeinander aufbauen und die Tragweite der Theorie überschaubar machen:

1. In den Blick genommen wird Kunst als Spiegel jenes ideellen Komplexes, den wir in überaus ausgefranster Bedeutung Kultur nennen. Das erklärte Ziel der Strukturforschung ist die kulturspezifische Zuordnung von Kunst.
2. Sollen die Kunstprodukte selbst die Bezugspunkte für ihre Zuordnung zu einem bestimmten Kulturkreis liefern, so muß ein taugliches Begriffsinstrumentarium zur Verfügung stehen, das Kunst auf einen kulturspezifischen Gehalt hin auszudeuten vermag. Im methodischen Idealfall sollte ein Stück allein aufgrund seiner formalen Eigenschaften kulturspezifisch gesondert und identifiziert werden können.
3. Zu diesem Zweck unternimmt es der Strukturalismus, die Kunstbetrachtung als eine objektive Wissenschaft zu begründen. Denn allein für den Fall, daß es gelingt, Artefakte und Kunstprodukte nicht nach subjektiven, beliebigen und willkürlichen, sondern nach überprüfbar gegenstandsbezogenen Gesichtspunkten zu beurteilen, werden Kunstformen zu archäologisch verwertbaren Indizien.
4. Eine kulturspezifische Identifizierung bedeutet, daß ein im Gegenstand selbst verankertes Klassifikationsprinzip der Kunstformen erforderlich ist, das eine eindeutige räumlich-zeitliche Zuordnung der verschiedenen Kunstformen ermöglicht.

Überblickt man diese vier Punkte, so kommen sie darin überein, als theoretisches Ziel die Unterordnung der verschiedenen Kunstformen unter einheitliche Gesichtspunkte anzugeben und Kunstwissenschaft auf Klassifikation festzulegen.

Hinsichtlich dieses Anforderungsrahmens wird die methodologische Leistung der Theorie sichtbar. Sie leistet folgendes:

1. Eine exakte Problemstellung der Kunstwissenschaft, nämlich Klassifikation,
2. mit dem Prinzip der Struktur die Angabe eines Klassifikationsprinzips,
3. mit dem Strukturbegriff die Festlegung des Gegenstandes, der untersucht werden soll,
4. mit dem Begriff der Raumrelation die Bereitstellung eines Begriffsrahmens, mit welchem der Gegenstand analysiert werden soll.

Indem hier eine klare Problemstellung formuliert, das Prinzip der Problemlösung angegeben, der Gegenstand der Kunstbetrachtung exakt festgelegt und der Begriffsrahmen der Strukturanalyse bereitgestellt wird, erfüllt diese Theorie alle Aufgaben, die einer wissenschaftlichen Methodentheorie zu stellen sind.

§ 9 DIE KRITERIEN OBJEKTIVER KATEGORIEN

Der letztgenannte Punkt, welcher die Operationsbegriffe der Strukturanalyse betrifft, macht deutlich, worauf sich unsere Überlegungen zu beziehen haben. In Frage steht das kategoriale Bezugssystem, stehen die Gesichtspunkte einer wissenschaftlichen Kunstbetrachtung. Hierzu können die möglichen Kategorien in zwei Klassen geteilt werden, einerseits in jene der ästhetischen, andererseits in jene der formalen Kategorien. Zwar kennt die klassische Archäologie noch eine dritte Klasse, jene der Kategorien des Numinosen; doch diese, auch wenn sie mit dem "religiösen Ernst"[69] eines BUSCHOR und anderer an das Objekt herangetragen werden, um in ihm einen "Sinn"[70] zu ergründen, überdies in einer "Sprache der Verantwortung vor der Würde des Kunstwerks"[71], gleichsam als hermeneutischer Priester, enden im Nebulösen – die Unterteilung der griechischen Plastik in die Epochen der "Ahnungswelt", der "Wirklichkeitswelt", der "hohen Schicksalswelt" usw.[72] mag als Beispiel dienen, welche Irrwege tatsächlich beschritten wurden. Zwecks Vermeidung solcher sind die Kategorien allesamt daran zu messen, inwieweit sie Anspruch auf Objektivität erheben können, inwiefern sie Gegenstandskategorien im Vollsinne des Wortes sind.

Zu den ästhetischen gehören Kategorien wie 'schön' oder 'häßlich'. Solche sind für eine wissenschaftliche Kunstanalyse untauglich, da sie insofern subjektiv bleiben, als sie den zu bestimmenden Gegenstand in ein vorgängig aufgestelltes axiologisches System einordnen. Ein Urteil, auch wenn es SCHEFOLD fällt, wie: "Neolithische Vasen aus Mittelgriechenland gehören zur schönsten Keramik, die es überhaupt gibt",[73] macht nicht nur den Strukturalisten ratlos. Ähnliches gilt für ästhetische Entwicklungskategorien, insbesondere für das immer wieder bemühte Dekadenz-Schema, das übrigens schon bei römischen Autoren wie PLINIUS und VITRUV auftritt, die über einen angeblichen Verfall der Kunst klagen. Zwar sind im Schema von Frühform – Blüte – Verfall Idealvorstellungen im Spiel, Begriffe des Eigentlichen, das getroffen oder verfehlt wird, und diese Begriffe transzendieren die Einschätzungen erster Stufe von schöner oder diesbezüglich defizienter Kunst hin auf ein axiologisches System

---

[69] So die lobende Einschätzung von Buschors Arbeitshaltung durch Karl Schefold: Neue Wege der Klassischen Archäologie nach dem ersten Weltkrieg, in: Helmut Flashar (ed.): Altertumswissenschaft in den 20er Jahren. Neue Fragen und Impulse, Stuttgart 1995, S. 186.

[70] Ernst Buschor: Vom Sinn der griechischen Standbilder, Berlin 1942 [Veröffentlichung des archäologischen Instituts des Deutschen Reiches], 2., um ein Nachwort erweiterte Aufl. Berlin 1977.

[71] Karl Schefold: Neue Wege der Klassischen Archäologie nach dem ersten Weltkrieg, in: Helmut Flashar (ed.): Altertumswissenschaft in den 20er Jahren. Neue Fragen und Impulse, Stuttgart 1995, S. 191.

[72] Ernst Buschor: Vom Sinn der griechischen Standbilder, Berlin 1942 [Veröffentlichung des archäologischen Instituts des Deutschen Reiches], 2., um ein Nachwort erweiterte Aufl. Berlin 1977, S. 9, 10, 15, 20, 24, 29.

[73] Karl Schefold: Neue Wege der Klassischen Archäologie nach dem ersten Weltkrieg, in: Helmut Flashar (ed.): Altertumswissenschaft in den 20er Jahren. Neue Fragen und Impulse, Stuttgart 1995, S. 185.

zweiter Stufe, welches das Kunstwerk an der Realisierung einer höheren Entelechie mißt. Indes, die Art und Weise, wie diese ausgemacht wird, übersteigt nicht das subjektiv gefertigte Vorurteil, das sich im wesentlichen aus dem bloßen Befinden speist. Ästhetische Kategorien beziehen sich auf das Verhältnis zwischen Kunstwerk und dessen Betrachter, namentlich auf die Wirkung, die ein Kunstwerk auf den Betrachter ausübt. Welches Prädikat unter dem Gesichtspunkt des Schönen ein Artefakt verdient, berührt dieses in seiner Eigentümlichkeit überhaupt nicht. Auch objektiv anmutende ästhetische Kategorien wie 'malerisch', 'plastisch', 'optisch', 'haptisch' beschränken sich auf das Verhältnis zwischen Kunstwerk und Betrachter und können deshalb nicht als objektive Kategorien des zu analysierenden Gegenstandes selbst gelten. So kommen für eine objektive Kunstbetrachtung nur formale Kategorien in Frage.

Die grundlegende formale Kategorie der Kunstgeschichte, selbst einer jeden archäologischen Bestandesaufnahme, ist der Stil. Jedoch bleibt rätselhaft, wie sich Stilbestimmungen objektiv begründen. Sie lassen sich lediglich willkürlich oder nach dem Vorbild der eigenen mitgebrachten kulturellen Prägung zuordnen. Und auch wenn dem Stil ein objektiver Bezug auf das Artefakt zuzugestehen wäre, so taugt er nicht als Klassifikationsbegriff verschiedener Kunstformen, weil er in deren Diversität und Entwicklungsdynamik aufgeht. Man denke an die Verwirrung, welche die Unterscheidung von Stilen in den Chronologien bewirkt hat: Um verschiedene Stile zeitlich zu verorten, wurden ganze historische Epochen erfunden. Überspitzt gesagt, haben wir so viele Stile, wie wir Artefakte haben – nach einem Modell vorgefertigte Massenware selbstverständlich ausgenommen. Dies findet seinen Grund darin, daß für eine objektive Kunstbetrachtung nur Verhältnisbegriffe (Relationsbegriffe) in Frage kommen, die sich auf gewisse Konstanten des zu analysierenden Gegenstandes beziehen. In der Funktion zwischen Artefakt und Interpretation bezeichnet Stil die abhängige Variable. Um vom untauglichen Stilbegriff wegzukommen, ist zu fragen, welche Anforderungen solche formalen Kategorien zu erfüllen haben, welche die ursprüngliche Gegebenheit des Kunstwerks nicht mehr nach bestimmten Voraussetzungen verstellen. Kriteriologisch definiert werden kann hierzu folgendes. Kategorien erreichen dann Objektivität, wenn sie zwei Bezugspunkte anpeilen:

1. das konkrete Kunstwerk selbst
2. eine allgemeine Konstante.

Zum ersten müssen die Kategorien im Kunstwerk selbst verankert sein. Das können solche sein, die auf ein Aufbauprinzip ausgehen, das die Darstellung beherrscht. Struktur, verstanden als "Prinzip der inneren Organisation der Form" im Gegensatz zum Stil, welcher nur den Modus der Struktur bezeichnet, gewährleistet den geforderten Gegenstandsbezug. Die Struktur liegt in der Tiefenebene der Darstellung, liegt gleichsam hinter dem Stil. Erst an einer bestimmten Darstellungsstruktur kann sich ein Stil ausformen, der damit in ein Abhängigkeitsverhältnis zu den inneren Strukturprinzipien gerät. Die Eigenheit der Struktur ihrerseits wird dabei vom Stil nicht berührt; der Stil bleibt der Struktur äußerlich, so daß jederzeit vom Stil auf die Struktur abstrahiert werden kann. Dieses Verhältnis zwischen einem konstanten Prinzip, der Struktur, und variablen, abstrahierbaren Eigenschaften, dem Stil, demonstriert Abb. 23 a–c, die drei verschiedene vorderorientalische Statuenstile (frühsumerisch, späthethitisch und neuassyrisch) vorführt. Sie liegen nicht nur geographisch, sondern auch zeitlich auseinander und besitzen dennoch exakt dieselbe Struktur.

Abb. 23: Die Differenz von Stil und Struktur: variabler Stil bei konstanter Struktur

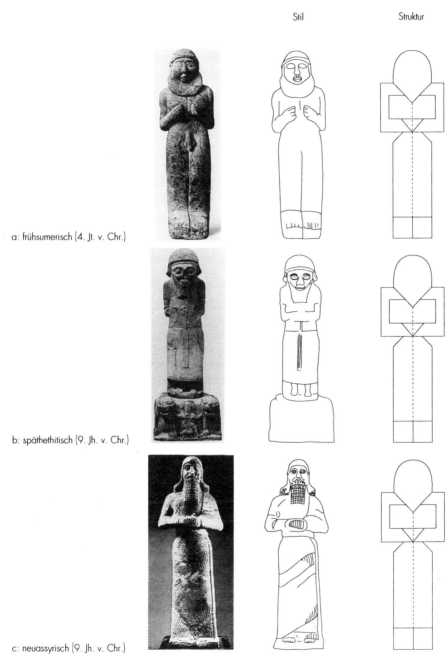

Stil   Struktur

a: frühsumerisch (4. Jt. v. Chr.)

b: späthethitisch (9. Jh. v. Chr.)

c: neuassyrisch (9. Jh. v. Chr.)

Mit der Struktur sind keine Formen der Ausgestaltung bezeichnet, die gegenüber dem Dargestellten eine sekundäre Stellung einnähmen, sondern die Faktoren des Aufbaus der Darstellung. Unter dem Strukturbegriff als Aufbauprinzip des Kunstwerks sind nichts anderes als die internen Konstruktionsbeziehungen zusammengefaßt, die letztlich in diejenige Beziehung münden, in der das Kunstwerk zu sich selbst steht. Damit entfallen die als Maßstab der Stilvergleiche angesetzten Kategorien wie 'Natur' oder 'Realität' – Kategorien, die zu der berüchtigten Definition des "Classischen" bei GERHART RODENWALDT (1886–1945) als bestimmter Ausformung in der Relation 'Ähnlichkeit mit der Natur – Abweichung von der Natur', 'Nachahmung – Stilisierung' führten.[74] Der Strukturbegriff bezieht sich objektiv auf das Kunstwerk als solches, frei von objektexternen Voraussetzungen.

Zum zweiten bedarf es des Bezugs auf eine Konstante, welche die Vielfalt möglicher Strukturtypen übergreift. Es muß dies eine Strukturkonstante sein, die einen bestimmten Strukturtyp in einen allgemeinen Rahmen einzuordnen und nach den Vorgaben dieses Rahmens zu beurteilen ermöglicht. Die Strukturkonstante muß demnach so beschaffen sein, daß sie a) Klassifikationen von Strukturtypen erlaubt und b) auch die vom Betrachter immer schon mitgebrachten Voraussetzungen einbezieht.

Allein der Bezug auf eine solche Konstante erlaubt, den im Kunstwerk zur Darstellung gebrachten Strukturtyp als kulturspezifischen anzusprechen und als Merkmal einer bestimmten Kultur zu identifizieren. Denn mit der besagten Konstante läßt sich das im einzelnen Kunstprodukt Dargestellte auf ein Beziehungssystem abbilden, dem einerseits das Dargestellte untersteht und in dem es spezifisch verkörpert ist, und das andererseits auch für den Betrachter verfügbar ist. In der Weise wird das Charakteristische einer Darstellungsstruktur objektiv erkennbar.

Vorerst haben wir mit dem Strukturbegriff lediglich den Platzhalter für die beiden genannten Kriterien. Jene Struktur, welche beide Bezugspunkte abdeckt, also sowohl das Aufbauprinzip im Kunstwerk selbst trifft als auch eine Kultur- und Strukturtypen übergreifende Konstante, ist nun – wir haben es wiederholt gehört – der Raum, genauer, die Raumvorstellung bzw. Raumanschauung. Es ist dies deshalb der Raum, weil die Strukturen, die sich im Kunstwerk herausheben lassen, allesamt räumlich sind und räumliche Verhältnisse wiedergeben.

§ 10 DIE KRITERIEN DER RAUMKATEGORIE

Es gilt zu prüfen, ob und inwiefern die Kategorie des Raumes die beiden genannten Anforderungen erfüllt. Auf den Raum bezogen, können wir die zwei Kriterien für Objektivität folgendermaßen reformulieren:

1. Um sich auf das konkrete Kunstwerk zu beziehen, muß der Raum einer anschaulichen Darstellung, einer Versinnlichung zugänglich sein. Dies bedeutet, es muß möglich sein,

---

[74] Gerhart Rodenwaldt: Zur begrifflichen und geschichtlichen Bedeutung des Klassischen in der bildenden Kunst. Eine kunstgeschichtsphilosophische Studie, in: Zeitschrift für Ästhetik und allgemeine Kunstwissenschaft, Bd. 11 (1916), S. 113–131. Vgl. dazu Adolf H. Borbein: Die Klassik-Diskussion in der Klassischen Archäologie, in: Helmut Flashar (ed.): Altertumswissenschaft in den 20er Jahren. Neue Fragen und Impulse, Stuttgart 1995, S. 214.

nicht bloß räumliche Gegenstände in einer beliebigen Form abzubilden, sondern den Raum selbst als Form des Abgebildeten darzustellen. In der Hinsicht muß der Raum eine Darstellungsform, ein Medium für künstlerischen Ausdruck bilden.

2. Um eine Strukturkonstante abgeben zu können, welche die individuellen Ausdrucksformen übergreift, sollte eine Beziehung nachweisbar sein zwischen Raum einerseits und kulturspezifischer Selbst- und Weltwahrnehmung innerhalb einer Kultur andererseits. Der Raum sollte sich nicht nur als eine Darstellungsform, sondern auch als eine Auffassungsform entpuppen, eine Auffassungsform von Welt, in welcher das geistige Universum einer bestimmten Kultur sich spiegelt.

B. Der Bezug auf das Kunstwerk

§ 11 Spezifizierung der Raumkategorie auf den Anschauungsraum

Bevor dieser kriteriologischen Absteckung des Raumbegriffs nachgegangen werden kann, muß zuerst entschieden werden, um welchen Raumbegriff es sich genauer handeln kann. Es sind drei Raumbegriffe zu unterscheiden:
1. Realraum bzw. physikalischer Raum
2. mathematischer Raum
3. Anschauungsraum

Keine Rolle spielen kann in unserem Zusammenhang der Realraum bzw. physikalische Raum, weil gewisse seiner kategorialen Eigenheiten den beiden genannten Kriterien zu genügen verhindern. Diese Eigenheiten sind Einzigkeit, Substratcharakter, Homogenität, Stetigkeit, Unbegrenztheit, Größenlosigkeit, Maßlosigkeit. Ein Raum mit diesen Eigenschaften ist keiner Versinnlichung fähig, er ist nicht anschaulich darstellbar, weil es keine Gestalt gäbe, die ihn repräsentieren könnte. Der Realraum ist kein Strukturraum. Und auch dem zweiten Kriterium tut er nicht Genüge. Als ein Dimensionssystem der realen Welt fällt er nicht zusammen mit Vorstellungen und Auffassungsformen von der Welt, vielmehr unterscheidet er sich von letzteren prinzipiell.

Auch der mathematische Raum entfällt als möglicher Kandidat. Dies mag auf den ersten Blick erstaunen, ist doch der mathematische Raum von seiner Seinsweise her ein idealer Raum, also ein im Geiste konstruierbarer und intuitiv zugänglicher Raum. Angesichts seiner Konstruktivität gibt es ihn nicht bloß als einen einzigen, einheitlichen, sondern als mannigfaltigen: den euklidischen Raum, den positiv oder negativ gekrümmten Raum, den vieldimensionalen Raum usw. Insofern, als der mathematische Raum eine die Vielheit möglicher Raumformen umfassende Konstante bildet, welche zugleich auch eine Form verschiedener möglicher Raumkonstruktionen ist, genügt er dem zweiten Kriterium. Dem ersten nun aber nicht. Der mathematische Raum ist ähnlich wie der Realraum homogen, stetig, unbegrenzt, größen- und maßlos. Zudem kann er vier- oder n-dimensional sein und das Anschauliche sprengen. Von der Möglichkeit einer Versinnlichung kann dann nicht mehr die Rede sein. Denn auch die geometrischen Konstruktionen, die bildlich darstellbar sind, betreffen nur indirekt die

Struktur des mathematischen Raumes, weil sie innerhalb desselben als ihres externen Bezugssystems konstruiert werden und mit ihm nicht zusammenfallen.

Unter Berufung auf KANTs Raumtheorie, auf die transzendentale Ästhetik, setzt der Strukturalismus den Anschauungsraum als gesuchte Struktur ein. Nach KANT ist der Raum – genauso wie die Zeit – eine Form der Anschauung, das heißt, eine Form des Subjekts, in welcher Gegenstände vorgestellt werden. Ist die Zeit die Form der inneren Anschauung, so der Raum spezifisch Form der äußeren Anschauung. Der Raum ist die, wie es in KANTs Kritik der reinen Vernunft heißt, "Form aller Erscheinungen äußerer Sinne, d.i. die subjective Bedingung der Sinnlichkeit, unter der allein uns äußere Anschauung möglich ist"[75]. Demnach ist der Raum neben der Zeit die Form, in der jeglicher mögliche Erkenntnisgegenstand wahrgenommen wird. MATZ definiert den strukturellen Raumbegriff in diesem Sinne als die "innere Einheit ... der Erscheinungen".[76]

Daß der Raum eine subjektive Anschauungs- und Vorstellungsform bildet, ergibt sich aus seiner erfahrungsunabhängigen Gegebenheit, seiner Apriorizität. Es ist möglich, alle Gegenstände im Raum wegzudenken, hingegen den Raum als solchen wegzudenken, ist unmöglich. Selbst die aller räumlichen Gegenständen entledigte Vorstellung von Zeit ist immer auch eine räumliche in Form einer linearen Ausdehnung.

Dergestalt kann der Raum, weil er in jeder Erfahrung immer schon vorausgesetzt ist, unmöglich aus der Erfahrung gewonnen sein. Vielmehr ermöglicht er erst die Erfahrung als eine ihrer formalen Bedingungen. So erweist er sich als eine innere Wahrnehmungsform des erkennenden und vorstellenden Bewußtseins. Der erfahrungsunabhängige Bedingungsstatus des Raumes ist es also, welcher darauf deutet, daß dieser eine Wahrnehmungsform des Bewußtseins ist.

Daß er in dieser Stellung einer Bewußtseinsform aber nicht aufgeht und somit der Realraum nicht auf den Anschauungsraum reduziert werden kann, wie dies idealistische Raumtheorien versuchen, beweist der reine Formcharakter, den der Anschauungsraum besitzt. Formcharakter bedeutet, daß im Anschauungsraum kein Gegenstand, kein Ding, keine Welt existiert, sondern bloß unter der Form des Raumes vorgestellt wird, während der Realraum Gegenstände aufnimmt und deren Realdimension ist, in welchem sie existieren. Zwischen dem realen Dimensionssystem, in welchem Dinge existieren, und der Vorstellungsform des Bewußtseins, in welcher Dinge räumlich wahrgenommen werden, muß unterschieden werden.

Deutlich wird diese Sachlage auch daran, daß Stufen des Anschauungsraumes voneinander gesondert werden können. Sie entsprechen den verschiedenen Bewußtseinsstufen, wie sie mit Erleben, Vorstellung und begrifflichem Denken gegeben sind.

Raum ist eine Form des äußeren Erlebens, da alle äußeren Dinge und Prozesse räumlich wahrgenommen werden; ebenso ist er eine Form der Vorstellung, weil jegliche Vorstellung, sei es Erinnerung, sei es Phantasie, sich aus räumlichen Bildern aufbaut; und schließlich ist er eine Form auch des begrifflichen Denkens, indem selbst die abstrakten Begriffe überwiegend auf Vorstellungen räumlicher Beziehungen beruhen.

---

[75] Immanuel Kant: Kritik der reinen Vernunft, A 41, in: Immanuel Kant: Gesammelte Schriften, Akademie-Ausgabe, Abt. 1, Bd. 4, Berlin 1911, S. 33.

[76] Friedrich Matz: Geschichte der griechischen Kunst, Bd. 1: Die geometrische und früharchaische Form, Frankfurt 1950, S. 18.

Genannte Bewußtseinsstufen lassen sich in Wahrnehmungs- und Vorstellungsraum einerseits und Erfahrungs- und Denkraum andererseits aufgliedern. Im Wahrnehmungs- und Vorstellungsraum sind der Erlebnisraum und der Phantasieraum des natürlichen Alltagsbewußtseins einbegriffen, im Erfahrungs- und Denkraum das erkennende und wissenschaftliche Raumbewußtsein.

Die Trennung der genannten drei Raumbegriffe ist eine ontologische, die das wissenschaftliche Raumbewußtsein vollzieht. In der konkreten Raumerfahrung des natürlichen Bewußtseins indessen überlagern sich alle drei Raumarten. Denn der Anschauungsraum ist 1. genuin auf den Realraum bezogen, indem das räumlich anschauende und objektgerichtete Subjekt den Realraum zu erkennen versucht, und 2. an und für sich durchweg mathematisierbar, da nichts hindert, den Anschauungsraum geometrisch abzubilden. Die Möglichkeit geometrischer Abbildung und Mathematisierung des Anschauungsraumes ist denn auch die Voraussetzung für eine Beziehung sowohl zwischen Anschauungsraum und räumlichen Erscheinungsformen des Kunstwerks als auch zwischen Kunstwerk und den Operationsmitteln der strukturalistischen Analyse. Gleichwohl ist die Unterscheidung zwischen Anschauungsraum und mathematischem Raum unverzichtbar, weil die mathematische Abbildung des Anschauungsraumes – beispielsweise die Abbildung eines RIEMANNschen Raumes in den sphärischen Strukturen der vorderorientalischen Kunst – immer im Anschaulichen verbleibt. Sobald auf den reinen RIEMANNschen Raum abstrahiert wird, ist nicht mehr auf den Anschauungsraum Bezug genommen, sondern auf den reinen mathematischen Raum. Erst im mathematischen Raum wird seine Abbildung in Form mathematischer Funktionen möglich, welche ihrerseits räumlich nicht mehr anschaulich sind. Wird der Anschauungsraum nicht mehr in anschaulichen Strukturen abgebildet, sondern in reinen Funktionen, so ist der Anschauungsraum bereits in den mathematischen Raum transformiert. Gerade diese Transformierbarkeit beweist trotz der grundlegenden ontologischen Differenz von Anschauungsraum und mathematischem Raum die enge Beziehung beider Raumarten aufeinander.

Mit der Überlegung, daß der Raum eine erfahrungsunabhängige Form, damit eine Form des erfahrenden Bewußtseins ist, ist erst einmal plausibel gemacht, weshalb zum Realraum und dem mathematischen Raum tatsächlich ein Anschauungsraum hinzukommen muß. Es gilt nun zu prüfen, inwiefern der Anschauungsraum die besagten Kriterien erfüllt – einerseits die Versinnlichungsfähigkeit und andererseits eine genuine Beziehung auf die Selbst- und Weltwahrnehmung.

§ 12 DIE VERSINNLICHUNG DES ANSCHAUUNGSRAUMES

a. Die Eigenschaften des Anschauungsraumes

Um das erste Kriterium zu überprüfen, die Möglichkeit einer Versinnlichung des Anschauungsraumes, muß der Anschauungsraum auf seine Eigenschaften hin untersucht werden. Der Anschauungsraum ist kein homogenes Dimensionssystem, sondern ein Strukturraum. Als Strukturraum unterscheidet er sich grundsätzlich sowohl vom Realraum wie vom mathematischen Raum. Seine Strukturiertheit besteht in folgenden sechs Eigenschaften.

1. Der Anschauungsraum ist kein unendlicher Raum, sondern besitzt verschwimmende Grenzen, die sich mit der Verschiebung des Anschauungsfeldes mitverschieben. Er ist immer

nur im Ausschnitt gegeben. Damit besitzt er Größe und – davon abzuleiten – auch ein Maß des Großen und Kleinen. Dieses Maß liegt in der Reichweite des jeweiligen Horizontes, die Maßverhältnisse und Proportionen vorgibt. Aufgefaßt werden diese nicht nur quantitativ, sondern auch qualitativ, man denke beispielsweise an den Goldenen Schnitt.

2. Der Anschauungsraum ist nur bedingt stetig. Wohl zeigt er eine Kontinuität in der Möglichkeit, den Blick über verschiedene Gegenstände im Raum hinweggleiten zu lassen. Indessen kann sich der einheitliche Gesamtraum in mehrere Teilräume aufspalten, beispielsweise in bruchstückhaft erinnerte oder unzusammenhängend phantasierte Räume, die jeweils in ihren Teilen unverbunden nebeneinander stehen bleiben. So entsteht die Diskontinuität des Anschauungsraumes in Form einer Vielheit nebeneinander existierender Räume.

3. Der Anschauungsraum ist perspektivisch. Das bedeutet, er ist abhängig von einem wahrnehmenden Standpunkt, von der Einnahme eines Gesichtspunktes, einer Perspektive eben. Dabei werden alle Gegenstände im Raum auf einen bestimmten Blickpunkt bezogen, was geometrisch ihre Verzeichnung und Verzerrung zur Folge hat. Ein entferntes großes Objekt erscheint nicht größer als ein kleines Objekt in der Nähe, Parallelen laufen zusammen, rechte Winkel bei schräger Sicht deformieren sich. Die perspektivische Verzerrung wird nun aber nicht als solche wahrgenommen, sondern sofort und automatisch ausgeglichen. Infolgedessen wird die Perspektive nicht mitgesehen, sondern bleibt unbewußt. Exakt dieser Sachverhalt ist der Grund dafür, daß das perspektivisch Gesehene nicht ohne Anstrengung gezeichnet werden kann und letztlich an der Entwicklung eines Perspektivenbewußtseins hängt.

4. Der Anschauungsraum ist zwar ebenso wie der Realraum ein System von drei Dimensionen, jedoch können die Dimensionen auf- und ineinander überführt werden. Die Anschauung kann sich auf die Fläche oder die Linie beschränken und von der Lage im Raum absehen. Deshalb können dreidimensionale Lage- und Ausdehnungsverhältnisse auf ein zweidimensionales Flächensystem abgebildet werden. Zweidimensionale Flächensysteme, beispielsweise Zeichnungen, können wieder reobjektiviert werden, das heißt, in ihre urbildlichen Raumverhältnisse zurückübersetzt werden. Dies ist die Leistung der Raumanschauung – Mehrdimensionales um eine Dimension zu reduzieren und dabei jederzeit die ursprünglichen Verhältnisse in der Vorstellung reproduzieren zu können.

5. Der Anschauungsraum ist deshalb nicht homogen wie der Realraum oder der mathematische Raum, weil die Perspektive gerade Raumdeformierung und damit Heterogenisierung bedeutet. Der Anschauungsraum ist ein Anschauungsfeld, das von einem Gesichtspunkt ausgeht und auf denselben zentriert ist. Dieses Anschauungsfeld ergibt eine Art Ordnungssystem, in welchem die Gegenstände im Raum auf den Gesichtspunkt orientiert werden. Die Heterogenität des Anschauungsraumes bedeutet somit, daß er ein Stellen- und Lagesystem darstellt, daß er ein natürliches Koordinatensystem besitzt, in welchem die verschiedenen Orte nicht gleichwertig sind, sondern nach den Vorzügen der Perspektive abgestuft erscheinen. Im natürlichen Sehen ist die ganze Horizontalebene vorherrschend, desgleichen das in der direkten Front Liegende, das den übrigen Raum verdrängt. Links und rechts, oben und unten, vorn und hinten sowie die vier Himmelsrichtungen sind absolute Richtungsgegensätze.

6. Umgekehrt ist es der Anschauung möglich, durch Perspektivenwechsel beliebige Raumstellen anzupeilen und bestimmte Lageverhältnisse hervorzuheben. So kann die Raumanschauung natürlich, punktuell, holistisch oder sphärisch usw. sein. In diesen Anschauungsmöglichkeiten offenbart sich der Anschauungsraum als eine Veränderliche, als ein Stellen- und Lagesystem, das nach euklidischer oder exotischer Geometrie modelliert werden kann.

b. Die Repräsentation des Anschauungsraumes im Kunstwerk

Die angegebenen Eigenschaften, welche den Anschauungsraum als einen Strukturraum bestätigen, ermöglichen nun eine Versinnlichung, eine konkrete Darstellung und Vergegenständlichung, eine Repräsentation des Raumes im Kunstwerk.

Jegliches Kunstwerk verkörpert – in bezug auf das Dimensionssystem, in dem es steht, das es aufnimmt und mit der eigenen Ausgedehntheit von neuem erschafft – einen bestimmten Ausschnitt, einen Horizont mit eigenen Grenzen und festgelegten Größen- und Maßverhältnissen. Nicht selten kombiniert es verschiedene Teilräume zu einem komplexen Gesamtraum; zumindest ist es ein Gebilde, das ganz bestimmte räumliche Diskontinuitäten setzt. Es verlangt die Perspektive eines Betrachters und ist zugleich selbst eine bestimmte fixierte Perspektive. Es leistet eine Abbildung mehrdimensionaler Verhältnisse in ein gleichdimensionales oder zweidimensionales Raumsystem. Es ist ein Stellen- und Lagesystem, in welchem es seiner Struktur nach völlig aufgeht und von welchem es eine bestimmte Modellierung liefert.

Damit decken sich die Eigenschaften des Anschauungsraumes mit den Grundsachverhalten der Verzierung und Darstellung, sei es der Flächenkunst, sei es der Plastik, sei es der Architektur. Das Kunstwerk erreicht der Anschauungsraum über seinen Ausschnittscharakter und seine Horizontbildung. Weiter stimmt er mit dem Perspektivischen der Kunst sowie mit ihrer Abbildfunktion von Dimensionssystemen überein. Mit dem sich ausgerichteten Stellen- und Lagecharakter, der in der Raumstruktur des Kunstwerks seine Ausprägung erhält, besitzt jedes Bild, jede Plastik, jedes Bauwerk, jedes Ornament einen räumlichen Wert, der den anschaulichen Strukturraum spiegelt.

"Dies geschieht, indem die Ordnung der Koexistenz der Substanzen, als welche Leibniz den Raum definiert, in das seinerseits selbstgesetzliche Ordnungsgefüge des Kunstwerks übertragen wird. Die Ordnung, in der die gegenständlichen Elemente im Aufbau des Kunstwerks zueinander gestellt sind, tritt als seine Raumordnung, als seine Raumqualität in Erscheinung. Als Teil eines anschaulichen Ganzen nimmt dieses Räumliche notwendig ebenfalls anschaulichen Charakter an. Es wird sichtbar als der Innenraum eines Gebäudes, als Zwischen- und Umraum der Glieder einer Figur, als Tiefe bedeutende Fläche zwischen den Gegenständen eines Bildes; es ist faktisch vorhanden und der Gestaltung mit unterworfen und wird dadurch selbst zum künstlerischen Gegenstande, der mit einem gegenständlich gemeinten Worte bezeichnet werden darf."[77]

---

77 Werner Hager: Über Raumbildung in der Architektur und in den darstellenden Künsten, in: Studium Generale, 10. Jg. (1957), S. 631.

Abb. 24: Löwe aus Šaiḫ Saʿd, aramäisch, um 1000 v. Chr.

Obwohl zur Exemplifizierung des Sachverhalts letztlich jedes Artefakt herbeigezogen werden könnte, sei pars pro toto ein einfaches Beispiel für die direkte Abbildung des Anschauungsraumes im Kunstwerk gegeben. Der in Abb. 24 sichtbare Portallöwe läßt deutlich seine, von der Seite augenfällige Überlänge erkennen, die für den vor der Portalfront stehenden Betrachter die perspektivische Verkürzung des Anschauungsraumes genau so ausgleicht, daß der Löwe in angemessener Länge erscheint.

c. Die Erscheinungsformen der Raumstruktur im Artefakt

An den durchgespielten Punkten ist demonstriert, daß sich in der Raumstruktur des Artefakts das auf ganz bestimmte Weise modellierte Stellen- und Lagesystem des Anschauungsraumes ausbildet. Die Erscheinungsformen der Raumstruktur des Artefakts sind nun anzugeben.

MATZ erklärt den strukturalistischen Raumbegriff hinsichtlich seiner Repräsentation im Kunstwerk zum "sinnlichen Medium der Erscheinungen"[78] und unterscheidet diesbezüglich sechs Erscheinungsformen des Raumes, die er in zwei Gruppen unterteilt, einerseits in konkret-anschauliche Formen und andererseits in Grenzformen, die vom Anschaulichen ins Abstrakte übergehen. Die erste Gruppe bezeichnet einen Raum ersten Grades, die zweite einen Raum zweiten Grades.

Raum ersten Grades:
1. Zierform
2. Figur
3. Körper und körperräumlicher Komplex

Raum zweiten Grades:
1. Funktionsraum
2. Bildraum
3. Existenzraum

Der Raum ersten Grades ist der Raum, den das Kunstwerk selbst verkörpert, seine eigene räumliche Form, die es darstellt. Der Raum zweiten Grades bildet sich erst auf der Basis des

---

[78] Friedrich Matz: Geschichte der griechischen Kunst, Bd. 1: Die geometrische und früharchaische Form, Frankfurt 1950, S. 15 f.

Raumes ersten Grades aus. Er ist das Dimensionssystem, das vom Raum ersten Grades aufgebaut wird. So erscheint die Räumlichkeit des Kunstwerks auf zwei Stufen.
Abb. 25 a–c veranschaulichen den Raum ersten und den Raum zweiten Grades für die Zierform: das Ornament der Schale besitzt eine zweidimensionale bildliche Struktur, die einen bestimmten Funktionsraum in Gestalt ihrer Drehungsverhältnisse vorgibt. Abb. 26 a–c

Abb. 25: Die Erscheinungsformen des Raumes: Funktionsraum

Schale   Raum ersten Grades: Raum zweiten Grades:
Zierform und Körper   Funktionsraum

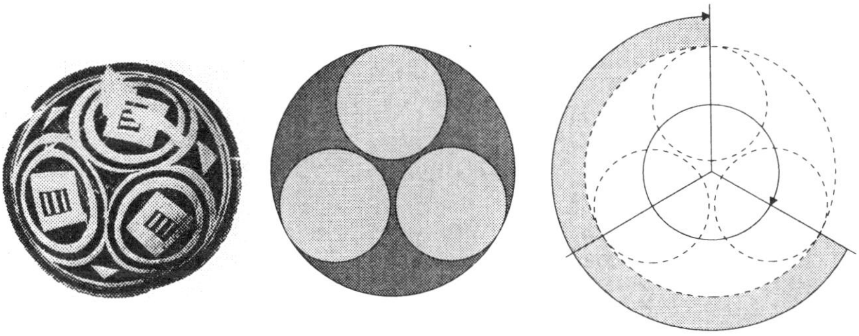

Abb. 26: Die Erscheinungsformen des Raumes: Funktionsraum

Gefäß   Raum ersten Grades: Raum zweiten Grades:
Zierform und Körper   Funktionsraum

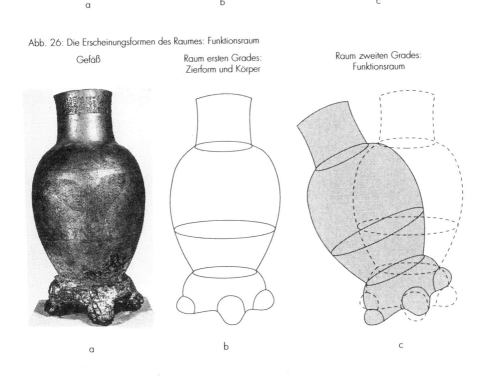

a   b   c

und Abb. 27 a–c zeigen dasselbe für den Körper: sowohl die Vase mit Standfuß wie das Gewicht in Löwenform besitzen einen über die anschaubare Körperform hinausgehenden Funktionsraum. Im ersten Fall ergibt sich dieser aus den Steh- bzw. Kippeigenschaften des

Abb. 27: Die Erscheinungsformen des Raumes: Funktionsraum

a: Gewicht

b: Raum ersten Grades: Form des Gewichts

c: Raum zweiten Grades: Funktionsraum

Körpers, im zweiten Fall aus dem Raum des Griffes und dem Unterraum der Fläche, die mit dem Gewicht des Objekts wiegt bwz. lastet. Abb. 28 a–c geben den Bildraum eines Reliefs, der sich aus der zweidimensionalen Anordnung der Figuren im Raum ersten Grades

Abb. 28: Die Erscheinungsformen des Raumes: Bildraum

a: Relief

b: Raum ersten Grades: Schema des Reliefs

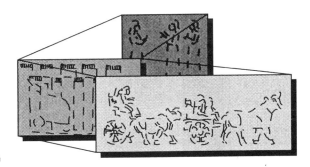

c: Raum zweiten Grades: Bildraum

(Abb. 28 b) als dreidimensional zu denkender Aufbau verschiedener Bildebenen ableiten läßt (Abb. 28 c). Abb. 29 a–c führen Raum ersten und zweiten Grades für den Körper einer Statue vor, bei welcher der Funktionsraum im Dimensionssystem des umliegenden Raumes

Abb. 29: Die Erscheinungsformen des Raumes: Funktionsraum/Existenzraum

| Statue | Raum ersten Grades:
Form der Statue | Raum zweiten Grades:
Funktionsraum/Existenzraum |

a   b   c

besteht, in demjenigen Raum, in welchem die Statue den Betrachter durch ihre Haltung und ihren Blick positioniert. Der Funktionsraum der Statue ist zugleich der Existenzraum des Betrachters. Abb. 30 a–c präzisiert, was Existenzraum bedeutet: Abb. 30 a zeigt den archäologischen Aufnahmeplan von Gebäuderesten, Abb. 30 b deren Grundriß und Abb. 30 c den Raum, den das Gebäude mit seinen Wänden und Durchgängen aufbaut, so daß er räumliche Wesen leibhaftig aufzunehmen und deren "räumliche Existenz" zu strukturieren vermag, zumal er Bildräume und Funktionsräume einbefaßt.

Die Strukturanalyse erfährt über die Bestimmung von Funktionsraum, Bildraum und Existenzraum eine systematische Vertiefung hinsichtlich des komplexen Raumsystems ihres Gegen-

Abb. 30: Die Erscheinungsformen des Raumes: Existenzraum

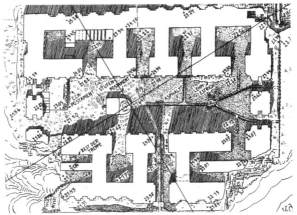

a: Aufnahmeplan

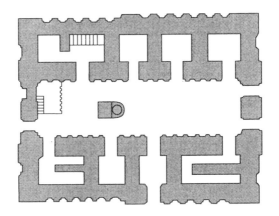

b: Raum ersten Grades: Grundriß

c: Raum zweiten Grades: Existenzraum

standes, wobei man nicht übersehen darf, daß hiermit erst die objektiven Erscheinungsformen des Raumes bestimmt sind und noch nicht deren Struktur. Was MATZ bei der Aufstellung von Formen der Raumerscheinung denn auch nicht mehr reflektiert, ist das Problem, wie die Struktur aus den Erscheinungsformen des Raumes isoliert werden kann. Welches Verfahren macht die Strukturen sichtbar?

Die Frage kann ebenfalls raumtheoretisch beantwortet werden. Zu isolieren ist die Struktur durch eine fundamentale Eigenschaft räumlicher Objekte – nämlich durch deren Rotationsfähigkeit. Alles räumlich Ausgedehnte kann im Raum rotieren, woraus ein neuer Körper entsteht, der Rotationskörper. Dieser ist es, der den vom Körper eingenommenen Raum, wie letzterer als solcher strukturiert ist, sichtbar macht. Denn die Rotationsmöglichkeiten ergeben die Achsenverhältnisse und damit den räumlichen Aufbau des betreffenden Körpers. Mit der Rotation ist ein Prinzip gefunden, durch das die Isolierung der Struktur methodisch exakt gesichert wird. Dieses Prinzip funktioniert im Fall einer Identität von Objekt und Rotationskörper, einer monoachsialen Raumstruktur, gleichsam sich selbst augenscheinlich bestätigend, aber es versagt auch nicht vor einer zusammengesetzten (polyachsialen) Raumstruktur,

Abb. 31a–b: Die Raumstruktur aufgrund der Rotationsachsen: 1. Identität von Objekt und Rotationskörper (monoachsiale Raumstruktur)

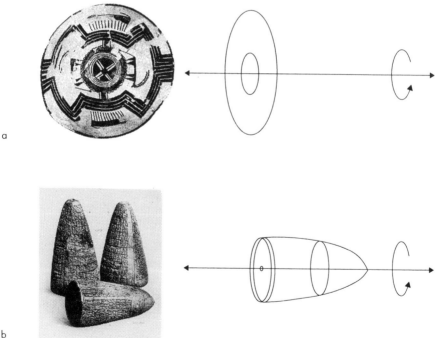

a

b

im Gegenteil, eine solche wird erst nach Auswertung der Rotationsverhältnisse in ihrem Aufbau durchschaubar. Betrachten wir zur Veranschaulichung ausgesuchte Beispiele!

Abb. 31a zeigt eine Schale, deren Verzierung die für ihre Raumstruktur signifikante Rotationsachse geometrisch markiert: Sie trifft sich mit dem Fluchtpunkt der Musterung, dem Gleichgewichtspunkt der Schale und dem Sehpunkt des Betrachters. Man muß also sagen, daß das Ornament die Identität von Objekt und Rotationskörper direkt kodiert, indem der Funktionsraum – das Dreh- und Standverhalten des Objekts –, der Bildraum – der Raum der Figuren und Linien der Verzierung – sowie der Existenzraum – hier die Position des Betrachters in der Achse des Zentrums – zusammenfallen. Ähnlich verhält es sich mit den Schriftkegeln von Abb. 31b: Sie verjüngen sich parallel zur signifikanten Rotationsachse, die ihrem Funktionsraum entspricht, dem Lesen der Schriftzeilen durch Drehung des Kegels. Dasselbe gilt für den Keulenkopf von Abb. 31c, dessen Rotationsachse, durch den Bildraum seines Reliefs vorgegeben, funktional auf die Achse des Keulenstieles ausgerichtet ist. Nicht anders auch das Rollsiegel von Abb. 31d, dessen Schnurloch mit der Rotationsachse des Bild- wie des Funktionsraumes, dem Drehverhalten bei der Abrollung des Siegels, übereinstimmt.

Abb. 31c–d: Die Raumstruktur aufgrund der Rotationsachsen: 1. Identität von Objekt und Rotationskörper (monoachsiale Raumstruktur)

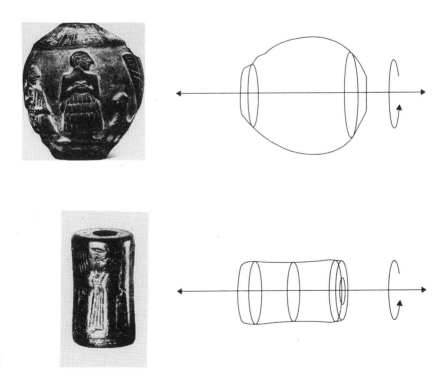

Eine polyachsiale Raumstruktur zeigt das Relief von Abb. 32 a, sichtbar gemacht über die Rotationsachsen (Abb. 32 b), die sich innerhalb des Bildraumes sinnvoll denken lassen. Deutlicher noch sind die Rotationsachsen in der Skulptur vorgezeichnet, wie sie in Abb. 33 a–d paradigmatisch vorgeführt ist und den parataktischen Aufbau, das Klotzige der vorderorientalischen Plastik im Gefüge der voneinander durch eigene Rotationsachsen isolierbaren Teile sehen läßt.

Daß Struktur in jener Beziehung verkörpert ist, in der das Kunstwerk zu sich selbst steht – ein ohne die vorgeführten Beispiele vor Augen nicht auf Anhieb nachvollziehbarer Gedanke, der uns früher schon begegnete ʹ–, dies ist im Rotationsprinzip geometrisch begründet. In Gestalt der Rotation bezeichnet Struktur die räumliche Selbstbeziehung des Kunstwerks, seine Identität, seine Eigenständigkeit, sein Unterscheidungskriterium zu anderem usw. Hierin bestätigt sich unüberbietbar die Objektivität der Strukturkategorie.

Abb. 32: Die Raumstruktur aufgrund der Rotationsachsen: 2. 1. Polyachsiale Raumstruktur: Fläche

a

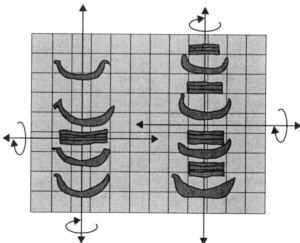

b

Abb. 33: Die Raumstruktur aufgrund der Rotationsachsen: 2. 2. Polyachsiale Raumstruktur: Körper

a – b

c – d

C. Der Bezug auf eine Strukturkonstante

§ 13 Die Apperzeption als doppelter Bezugspunkt

Leistet das Kunstwerk die Veranschaulichung des selbst nicht anschaubaren Anschauungsraumes und wird so zum Medium, in welchem sich der Anschauungsraum versinnlicht, so
muß nun weiter geklärt werden, inwiefern diese Versinnlichung einen Bezug auf eine Konstante besitzt, welche mögliche Typen der Raumstruktur übergreift und einen jeweiligen
Typus als kulturspezifischen einzuordnen ermöglicht. Hierzu muß nachgewiesen werden,
daß der Anschauungsraum eine Form der Selbst- und Weltwahrnehmung ist, die sich ihrerseits kulturspezifisch ausprägt.
Dies geschieht in zwei Gedankenschritten. Zum ersten ist der Zusammenhang zwischen
Selbst- und Weltwahrnehmung einerseits und Raumanschauung andererseits herzustellen.
Zum zweiten muß angegeben werden, wie Selbst- und Weltwahrnehmung, die vorerst
immer nur die eines konkreten Individuums sind, eine kulturelle Konstante zu bilden vermö-
gen, wie die subjektive Raumanschauung eine Kultur einheitlich prägen kann. Wenn wir
das Phänomen, das mit Selbst- und Weltwahrnehmung angesprochen ist, mit dem Terminus
'Apperzeption' bezeichnen, geht es um die Fragen, inwiefern 1. der Anschauungsraum eine
Apperzeptionsfunktion erfüllt und 2. die Apperzeption kulturell determiniert ist.

§ 14 Die Apperzeptionsfunktion des Anschauungsraumes

Die Überlegung, die den Zusammenhang von Apperzeption und Raumvorstellung nahe-
bringt, verlangt keine weitschweifenden Ausführungen. Ichbewußtsein wie überhaupt jede
Form von Daseinsbewußtsein, und sei sie noch so keimhaft, geht mit einem Bewußtsein von
einem dem Subjekt äußerlichen Gegenstand einher. Jedes Ichbewußtsein gründet in der
Unterscheidung von Innen und Außen, beispielsweise von inneren Vorstellungen und äußeren Ereignissen, Gegenständen, Sachverhalten usw. Selbstwahrnehmung ist also immer schon
gekoppelt mit Weltwahrnehmung.
Die Unterscheidung von Innen und Außen basiert aber bereits auf der Raumvorstellung, denn
sie bezeichnet ein quasiräumliches Verhältnis, nämlich das Verhältnis der eigenen Innerlich-
keit zu einem Raum. Dieser Raum ist nichts anderes als das Dimensionssystem, in welchem
alle äußeren Gegenstände wahrgenommen und vorgestellt werden.
So ist die Selbstwahrnehmung an die Art und Weise gebunden, wie der Raum wahrgenommen wird. Und dieser Satz gilt angesichts der Interdependenz von Selbstwahrnehmung und
räumlichem Dimensionssystem auch in seiner Umkehrung: Die Art und Weise, wie Raum
wahrgenommen wird, dependiert von der Selbstwahrnehmung.
In beiden Fällen aber offenbart sich die Raumvorstellung als mit der Selbst- und Weltwahrnehmung unlöslich verbunden. Das bedeutet, daß die Struktur des Anschauungsraumes
Rückschlüsse auf das Selbstbewußtsein erlaubt, das räumliche Verhältnisse anschaut und
strukturiert. Die hier angestellte Überlegung wird denn auch Matz vorgeschwebt haben,

wenn er sagt, daß die Auffassung des Raumes letzten Endes nichts anderes sei als Ausdruck, Spiegel oder Symbol des Weltverständnisses in einem jeweils ganz bestimmten Sinne.[79] Einsicht in diesen verborgenen Zusammenhang besitzt bereits die Sprache im Wort 'Weltanschauung' – Welt, ein Begriff, der nur in bezug auf einen Beobachter, auf ein Subjekt, mithin auf ein Selbstbewußtsein Sinn macht, ist eine 'Schau'; anschaubar aber ist allein das Räumliche, nicht das Zeitliche, nicht das Begriffliche, dieselben werden es erst in einer sinnlichen Übersetzung in das Räumliche.[80]

Damit sind wir an einem Punkt angelangt, der auf unser Problem ein neues Licht wirft. Erst jetzt kann der Bedeutungshintergrund des Kunstwerks genauer bestimmt werden. Nach den vorangegangenen Überlegungen, die den Anschauungsraum als eine Funktion der Apperzeption auswiesen, vereinigt das Kunstwerk in seiner Raumstruktur zwei Ebenen: die Ebene des Sinnlich-Konkreten mit der Ebene des Geistigen. Das Kunstwerk leistet die Veranschaulichung der selbst nicht anschaulichen Raumanschauung, die ihrerseits Ausdruck von Selbst- und Weltauffassung ist. Treffend spricht HAGER von der Weltvorstellung, die in der künstlerischen Raumordnung ihr geistiges Gegenbild findet: "Die künstlerische Behandlung des Raumes in ihren wechselnden Formen, seine mehr oder weniger aufmerksame Beachtung ist also abhängig von der jeweils herrschenden Weltvorstellung. Unter den welterbauenden Mitteln der Kunst ist die Raumordnung eines der vornehmsten und wirksamsten. Sie hat die Macht, Wirklichkeit zu interpretieren, durch Interpretation in ihrer Bedeutung zu erschließen und durch diese Erschließung erst zu erschaffen als geistiges Gegenbild zur Tageswirklichkeit."[81] Diese Funktion mündet folgerichtig in ihre Interpretation als "Objektivierung des Ichgefühles und seines Gegensatzes zur Umwelt" (SCHWEITZER)[82], ist doch das Artefakt, als die Grenzziehung im unendlichen Raum genommen, Identifikation des Zentrums, abgebildete Konstitution des Selbst, die Grenze zwischen Ich und Nicht-Ich, und was für Ausdrücke mehr noch für dieses Wechselverhältnis zwischen Vergegenständlichung und Raumbewußtsein eingesetzt werden könnten.

Es dürfte deutlich geworden sein, daß der Strukturbegriff in dieser Fassung keine statische Instanz einnimmt, die hinter der geschichtlichen Entwicklungsdynamik läge wie die Kategorien 'Natur' oder 'Wirklichkeit' oder metaphysische Kategorien mit der Unterstellung eines absoluten Geistes, der die stehende Finalursache kultureller Formen bildete. Im Gebrauch der Raumkategorie ist der verhandelte Strukturbegriff als eine Funktion der Apperzeption

---

[79] Friedrich Matz: Geschichte der griechischen Kunst, Bd. 1: Die geometrische und früharchaische Form, Frankfurt 1950, S. 25. Angesichts dieses Gedankens einer ursprünglichen Verbundenheit von Selbst- und Weltwahrnehmung einerseits und Raumanschauung andererseits dürfte Matz daselbst der Irrtum unterlaufen sein, in bezug auf Kant vom Raum als Form der "inneren Anschauung" zu sprechen (S. 17), während Kant gegenüber der Zeit den Raum als Form der Anschauung äußerer Dinge abgrenzt (vgl. Immanuel Kant: Kritik der reinen Vernunft, in: Immanuel Kant: Gesammelte Schriften, Akademie-Ausgabe, Abt. 1, Bd. 4, Berlin 1911, S. 37). Sachlich ist diese Verwechslung dem strukturalistischen Theoriegebäude allerdings nicht abträglich, weil sich laut Kant Zeit- und Raumanschauung überlagern.

[80] Daß auch die Zeit, die anschaulich vorgestellt wird – man denke an den "Zahn der Zeit" und ähnliches –, einer Übersetzung in das Räumliche bedarf, um faßbar ins Bewußtsein treten zu können, beweist die Uhr, welche Zeit als eine Funktion von Zifferblatt und Zeiger, als eine räumliche Beziehung, darstellt.

[81] Werner Hager: Über Raumbildung in der Architektur und in den darstellenden Künsten, in: Studium Generale, 10. Jg. (1957), S. 632.

[82] Bernhard Schweitzer: Untersuchungen zur Chronologie und Geschichte der geometrischen Stile in Griechenland II, in: Mitteilungen des Deutschen Archäologischen Instituts, Athenische Abteilung, Bd. 43 (1918), S. 119.

bestimmt. Mit diesem funktionalen Strukturbegriff ist der Gegenstand der Artefakt- und Kunstanalyse in die Primärursachen der Entwicklungsdynamik zurückverlegt, sofern man zuge-
steht, daß geistig-kulturelle Entwicklung ihr Prinzip in apperzeptiven Funktionen findet, in der
ideellen Entwicklung des Selbstbewußtseins, aus der die Symbolsysteme ursprünglich entstehen. Der Begriff der Raumstruktur ist also eine durchaus dynamische Kategorie, die der
Prozessualität und Relativität geschichtlicher Entwicklung in keiner Weise widerspricht.

§ 15 APPERZEPTION UND OBJEKTIVER GEIST

Zum zweiten geht es weiter darum zu klären, inwiefern die Apperzeption, also der Zusammenhang von Selbst- und Weltwahrnehmung, nicht individuell, sondern kulturell determiniert
ist. Wie kann der Raum als Anschauungsform des individuellen Subjekts überdies Spiegel
der Welt- und Selbstwahrnehmung eines bestimmten Kulturkreises sein? Die Frage ist iden-
tisch mit jener nach der Existenz von kulturspezifischen Konstanten überhaupt.
Gesetzt, kulturspezifische Konstanten existierten, dann befänden sie sich auf einer dem
individuellen Subjekt übergeordneten Ebene. Der erste Theoretiker dieses Gebiets, HEGEL,
nennt – im Gegensatz zum "subjektiven Geist", der Ebene des Individuums – die Ebene
solcher Konstanten "objektiven Geist".[83] Es bietet sich an, diese Terminologie zu überneh-
men, weil der Strukturalismus, wenngleich ihm selbst nicht ganz durchsichtig, eine spezifische und empirisch angewandte Weiterentwicklung der HEGELschen Theorie eines objektiven Geistes ist. Laut HEGEL ist Kunst als eine bestimmte Form der Selbstobjektivierung und
Selbstbetrachtung des Geistigen zu lesen, das objektiv existiert: in den Institutionen des
Individuums und der Gemeinschaft.[84]
Unabhängig von HEGEL gilt es zu entscheiden, ob kulturspezifische Konstanten existieren.
Der Nachweis hierzu kann bereits in zwei Punkten geleistet werden, von denen der erste
von einem phänomenologischen, das heißt, ausschließlich beschreibenden Standpunkt ar-
gumentiert, der zweite von einem logisch-transzendentalen, der auf die Funktionsfaktoren
der geistigen Existenz des Individuums hinweist.
Zum ersten ist es phänomenologisch evident, daß das Individuum nicht isoliert existiert,
sondern immer schon in allgemeine geistige Vorgaben seiner Kultur eingebunden ist: durch
Anpassung, Erziehung und Bildung über Sprache, Sitte, Wertschätzungen, Wissen und
weltanschauliche Vorstellungen.
Zum zweiten kann man von einem logisch-transzendentalen Gesichtspunkt aus argumentie-
ren, daß der subjektive Geist des Indivduums allgemeine begriffliche Strukturen voraussetzt,

---

[83] Vgl. Georg Wilhelm Friedrich Hegel: Enzyklopädie der philosophischen Wissenschaften im Grundrisse (1830),
hrsg. von Friedhelm Nicolin und Otto Pöggeler, 7. Aufl. Hamburg 1969, Nachdruck Hamburg 1975, §§ 483–
552.
[84] Insofern ist Hegels Theorie des objektiven Geistes eine Spezifizierung der Kantischen Apperzeptionstheorie, so
wie die gesamte Hegelsche Philosophie als deren Spezifizierung und Konkretisierung gelesen werden muß. Zu
bemerken ist noch, daß im engeren Rahmen der Hegelschen Ästhetik die Kunst keine Erscheinung mehr des
objektiven, sondern des absoluten Geistes ist. Sie ist dies aber nur, weil in ihr der objektive Geist sich selbst
betrachtet. Die Selbstbeziehung ihrerseits ist eine absolute Struktur. Deshalb wird der objektive Geist zum absoluten Geist, indem er sich in der Kunst, in gesteigerter Form in der Religion und schließlich in der seiner Natur allein
adäquaten Form, der Philosophie, auf sich selbst bezieht.

Abb. 34: Stele des Narām-Sîn, Susa, altakkadisch

um sich mitzuteilen, sei es anderen, sei es erst einmal sich selbst. Die mit den begrifflichen Strukturen vorgegebene Gesetzmäßigkeit gewährleistet ein Regelbewußtsein, das in den Stand versetzt zu denken und zu sprechen. Und sollte die Annahme logisch-begrifflicher Ermöglichungsbedingungen von Denken und Sprache geleugnet werden, so ist es schlicht unbestreitbar, daß bereits das Sprachsystem der Muttersprache eine für das Individuum prägende Konstante darstellt, deren Mächtigkeit der wesentliche Faktor für die Ausbildung einer kulturellen Identität ist. Unter allen Umständen ist WEISGERBER Recht zu geben, der die Muttersprache als für das Individuum wirkungsmächtigste Kulturkonstante in Anschlag bringt. Kein Mensch entgeht dem "Gesetz der Sprachgemeinschaft".[85]

---

[85] Leo Weisgerber: Die Sprache unter den Kräften des menschlichen Daseins, Düsseldorf 1949, S. 10.

Mit diesen der Übersicht halber nur kurz gefaßten Überlegungen ist entschieden, daß von der Existenz überindividueller Konstanten ausgegangen werden muß, und es dürfte unbestreitbar sein, daß jede Kultur, soweit sie als eine Einheit zu greifen ist, ihre je eigenen und für sie bezeichnenden Konstanten ausbildet. In der individuellen Apperzeption werden sich also zu einem guten Teil immer auch die kulturspezifischen Konstanten niederschlagen. Auf die strukturalistische Raumtheorie bezogen heißt das, daß der Raum in genau der Hinsicht, in welcher er eine Form der Apperzeption ist, auch Ausdruck der kulturspezifisch determinierten Konstanten der Selbst- und Weltwahrnehmung ist.

Man wird vielleicht einwenden wollen, das Theorem kulturspezifischer Raumstrukturen werde durch den Umstand widerlegt, daß sich allenthalben Gegenbeispiele finden, die sich nicht der vorgenommenen Strukturbestimmung gemäß einordnen lassen. Eines der schlagendsten Beispiele im Alten Orient ist wohl die Naram-Sîn-Stele (Abb. 34), in deren Bildaufbau sich weder Orthogonalität noch Sphärisches ausmachen lassen, dagegen das schiefe Achsenkreuz, das sich erst wieder in der hellenistischen Kunst findet. Indessen, die Ausnahme bestätigt insofern die Regel, als es sich hier um eine Singularität handelt, die sich in der altorientalischen Kunst nie mehr wiederholt und nichts auch nur Ähnliches hat. Der Sachverhalt aber, daß mit dieser Stele eine neue Raumstruktur auftritt, die keine Vorformen besitzt und nicht mehr weitergeführt wird, beweist, wie stark die orthogonal-sphärische Raumstruktur auf den Altorientalen wirkt. Daß ein Übersteigen dieser auf eine andere Raumkonzeption nur singulär auftritt, um sofort wieder vergessen zu werden, bestätigt direkt, daß die Raumauffassung eine kulturspezifisch determinierte Konstante bildet, deren Wirkungsmacht sich zu entziehen nur ausnahmsweise gelingt.

D. Die Vermittlung kultureller Eigenbegrifflichkeit

§ 16 Die Universalität des Raumes als Struktur

Damit stoßen wir auf das letzte Problem, welches der Strukturalismus aufwirft. Wenn von kulturspezifischen Konstanten auszugehen ist, welche gerade die Eigentümlichkeit, ja Eigenbegrifflichkeit einer bestimmten Kultur begründen, so ist zu fragen, wie es möglich ist, solche Konstanten auszumachen und zu bestimmen angesichts der Verschiedenheit der eigenen kulturellen Prämissen, die der Betrachter mitbringt. Wenn gerade von kulturspezifischer Eigenbegrifflichkeit ausgegangen werden muß, wie ist dann die Anwendung der dem Beobachter eigenen Begriffe auf den fremden Begriffsrahmen zu rechtfertigen? Anders gefragt: Was erlaubt, von einer kulturspezifischen Raumstruktur zu sprechen, wenn diese sich von der kulturell geprägten Raumanschauung des strukturalistischen Theoretikers genuin unterscheidet?

Mit dem in dieser Frage aufgeworfenen Sachverhalt steht und fällt die Möglichkeit von vergleichender Kulturwissenschaft, wie auch immer sie betrieben werden soll, ob archäologisch, philologisch, ethnologisch, philosophisch. Der Sachverhalt erfordert somit, Raumstruktur nicht bloß als kulturell determinierte, kulturspezifische Konstante auszuweisen, sondern ihr einen Bezug auf eine Konstante höherer Stufe zu sichern. Die Feststellung einer Verschiedenheit von Raumstrukturen und insbesondere die Typologisierung der Raumstrukturen in verschiedene Strukturtypen setzt eine überzeitliche und überkulturelle Konstante, ein historisch und kulturell universales Bezugssystem voraus.

Für dieses Problem verkörpert die strukturalistische Raumtheorie die Lösung. Der Raum, der eine Anschauungsform von Selbst- und Weltwahrnehmung überhaupt bildet, zeichnet sich gerade darin aus, sich sowohl in seiner Struktur kulturspezifisch auszubilden, als auch ein letztes, unhintergehbares Bezugssystem im kulturell vermittelten Wahrnehmungsprozeß zu liefern. Raum als Struktur ist historisch universal.

§ 17 RAUM ALS SPEZIFIKATIONS- UND VERBINDUNGSPRINZIP

Zu der historisch-kulturellen Universalität in keinerlei Widerspruch stehend, ist Raum nichts Monolithisches, Gleichförmiges, kein starrer Oberbegriff, von dem kein Weg zu den verschiedenen konkreten Kulturtypen führte. Es gibt mehrere, auch streng mathematisch faßbare Arten einer dreidimensionalen Ausgedehntheit. Es war die große Entdeckung des Mathematikers GAUSS zu sehen, daß diese Arten sämtlich a priori gewiß sind ohne die Möglichkeit, eine von ihnen als die eigentliche Form der Anschauung herauszuheben. Der Raum ist gleichsam der Stoff, aus dem sich jede Kultur ihr eigenes, unverwechselbares Symbolsystem schafft, eben deshalb, weil er der Modifikation, der verschiedenartigsten Ausprägung zugänglich ist. Raum ist ein kulturtypologisches Spezifikationsprinzip im ergänzenden Gegensinne zu der Tatsache, daß er aufgrund seiner Universalität in der Fremdheit der Symbolsysteme zueinander ein methodisch einwandfrei aufweisbares Verbindungsprinzip bildet. Die methodentheoretische Tragweite des Strukturalismus ist erst auf der nun erreichten Stufe der hermeneutischen Problemexplikation ausgelotet. Wird die Raumstruktur als Kategorie archäologischer Kunstbetrachtung eingesetzt, so wird gerade diejenige Kategorie zur Anwendung gebracht, welche zum einen allein den Bezug zum Gegenstand objektiv besitzt und zum anderen zugleich die strukturelle Disposition, die eigene Begriffsprämisse, mit welcher die so begründete Kunstwissenschaft an ihren Gegenstand herantritt, einbegreift. Ersteres, daß sich die Kategorie der Raumstruktur objektiv auf das Kunstwerk bezieht, hat sich darin bestätigt, daß das Kunstwerk selbst ein Phänomen des Anschauungsraumes ist und seine Form in jeder Hinsicht aus Beziehungen des Anschauungsraumes gewinnt. Letzteres, das Einbegriffensein der Prämissen der Betrachtung, bestätigt sich darin, daß die Kunstbetrachtung selbst, das heißt, das methodische Vorgehen als solches, in erster Linie Raumanschauung ist, nämlich Anschauung der mit dem Kunstwerk gegebenen Räumlichkeit.

Daß dabei nicht die vom Betrachter mitgebrachte Raumanschauung Maßstab der Analyse ist, geht daraus hervor, daß die Kategorie der Raumstruktur gerade die Vielfalt möglicher Raumanschauungen impliziert. Die Eigenbegrifflichkeit einer Kultur wird damit in der Strukturanalyse vollauf berücksichtigt oder kommt überhaupt erst in den Blick. Dennoch fungiert dieser Strukturbegriff als übergeordnetes Bezugssystem, indem er sich nicht nur auf den Gegenstand, sondern auch auf den methodischen Standpunkt der Analyse bezieht. Die Raumstruktur fungiert also einerseits als Spezifikationsprinzip wie auch andererseits als Verbindungs- und Vergleichsprinzip der Betrachtung im nun präzisierten Sinne, daß alle Stationen der Interpretationsrelation gedeckt sind: das Objekt, dessen Beschreibung sowie ihre Prämissen. Von daher dürfte die Feststellung nicht mehr verwegen erscheinen, daß allein mit der strukturalistischen Methode eine Klassifikation verschiedener Kunstformen durchführbar wird. Bestätigt sieht sich eine solche Einschätzung im Umstand, daß die strukturalistische Raumanalyse einer Mathematisierung der Kunstbetrachtung gleichkommt. Diese Mathematisierung ermöglicht, in der Beschreibung von Kunstformen Präzision und Eindeutigkeit zu erreichen. Deshalb ist sie – um ein in der Altertumswissenschaft berühmt gewordenes Wort von WILAMOWITZ aufzugreifen – das Blut, das die Schatten der Überlieferung reden macht.

§ 18 AUSBLICK: KULTUR ALS ENDOGENES PHÄNOMEN

Im Hinblick auf den Alten Orient, auf die ältesten Hochkulturen der Menschheit, kurz vor deren Erscheinen sich erstmals die menschliche Raumanschauung zu diversifizieren begann, legt das strukturalistische Kategoriensystem eine Antwort auf eine alte, wiewohl bis heute nur unbefriedigend behandelte Frage nahe: Wie kann das Phänomen, daß Hochkulturen aus der einfachen Welt des neolithischen Menschen wie aus dem Nichts entstehen, angemessen beurteilt werden, und zwar in Absehung von den empirisch-konkreten Voraussetzungen, welche der gesamte Faktorenkreis der äußeren Bedingungen darbietet? Weshalb geht die Ausdifferenzierung der Raumanschauung einher mit der Ausbildung einer hochgradig geschichteten Gesellschaft, komplexer Technologie, Administration, mit der Erfindung der Schrift, der Entwicklung von Mathematik und Wissenschaft? Die von der Forschung bisher vorgelegten Analysen der frühen Organisationsformen wissen nur den äußeren Genesisprozeß zu beschreiben, seine Anlässe, nicht aber seine Ursachen. Weshalb werden – und was genauer berücksichtigt werden muß: in Parallele zur Raumbewußtwerdung – auf einmal äußere Voraussetzungen aufgegriffen und als kulturelle Möglichkeiten erkannt, ausgeschöpft und weiterentwickelt, während sie im Dunkel der Vorzeit brach liegen blieben?
Vielleicht ist die genannte Parallele zwischen der Entstehung komplexer Organisationsformen und der Ausdifferenzierung der Raumanschauung, wie sie im Neolithikum bis zu den frühen Organisationsformen verfolgt werden kann, signifikant, um Kultur als ein endogenes Phänomen zu begreifen. Die strukturalistische Raumtheorie bietet hier insofern eine Erklärung an, als sie die generativen Prinzipien der Kulturentwicklung in einen Zusammenhang mit der Apperzeption des Raumes bringt: Hier eine Kausalität zu vermuten, die sprunghafte Selbstorganisation des menschlichen Geistes aus der Apperzeption des Raumes gespiesen zu sehen, liegt nicht fern. Denn die Ausbildung eines differenzierten Raumbewußtseins bringt das Denken mit dem mathematischen Raum und seinen geometrischen Konstruktionsverhältnissen in Berührung. Dem mathematischen Raum eignet wie dem Anschauungsraum eine innere Gesetzmäßigkeit, deren Beziehungsmöglichkeiten dem archaischen Bewußtsein als Inspirationsquelle für hochdifferenzierte Organisationsmuster gedient haben könnten.

ABBILDUNGSNACHWEIS

1   Machteld J. Melling und Jan Filip: Frühe Stufen der Kunst, Berlin 1974 [Propyläen Kunstgeschichte, Bd. 13],
     Abb. 257 a.
2   Machteld J. Melling und Jan Filip: Frühe Stufen der Kunst, Berlin 1974 [Propyläen Kunstgeschichte, Bd. 13],
     Abb. 243.
3   Ernst Heinrich: Die Tempel und Heiligtümer im Alten Mesopotamien. Typologie, Morphologie und Geschich-
     te, Bd. 2, Berlin 1982, Abb. 114.
4   André Parrot: Sumer, Paris 1981, S. 210.
5   Staatliche Museen zu Berlin (ed.): Das Vorderasiatische Museum, Mainz 1992, Abb. 3.
6   Winfried Orthmann: Der Alte Orient, Berlin 1975 [Propyläen Kunstgeschichte, Bd. 14], Abb. 376.
7   Winfried Orthmann: Der Alte Orient, Berlin 1975 [Propyläen Kunstgeschichte, Bd. 14], Abb. 125 b.
8   Ernest de Sarzec: Découvertes en Chaldée, Bd. 2, Paris 1884–1912, pl. 32 b.
9   Samuel M. Paley, Richard P. Sobolewski: The reconstruction of the relief representations and their positions in
     the northwest-palace at Kalḫu (Nimrūd) II, Mainz 1987, pl. 4.
10   Jutta Börker-Klähn: Altvorderasiatische Bildstelen und vergleichbare Felsreliefs, Tafeln, Mainz 1982, 132 a–b.
11   Winfried Orthmann: Der Alte Orient, Berlin 1975 [Propyläen Kunstgeschichte, Bd. 14], Abb. 235.
12   Morris Jastrow jr: Bildermappe zur Religion Babyloniens und Assyriens, Giessen 1912, Abb. 35.
13   Morris Jastrow jr: Bildermappe zur Religion Babyloniens und Assyriens, Giessen 1912, Abb. 37.
14   Winfried Orthmann: Der Alte Orient, Berlin 1975 [Propyläen Kunstgeschichte, Bd. 14], Abb. 234 a.
15   Arne Eggebrecht: Das Alte Ägypten. 3000 Jahre Geschichte und Kultur des Pharaonenreiches, München
     1984, S. 377.
16   Arne Eggebrecht: Das Alte Ägypten. 3000 Jahre Geschichte und Kultur des Pharaonenreiches, München
     1984, S. 371.
17   Regine Schulz: Die Entwicklung und Bedeutung des kuboiden Statuentypus. Eine Untersuchung zu den soge-
     nannten Würfelhockern, Bd. 2, Hildesheim 1992, Tf. 72 a–b.
18   Max Raphael: Prehistoric pottery and civilisation in Egypt, New York 1947, pl. 22, 5 und 6.
19   William. M. Flinders Petrie: Dendereh 1898, London 1900, pl. 21 a.
20 a Pierre Demargne: Die Geburt der griechischen Kunst. Die Kunst im ägäischen Raum von vorgeschichtlicher Zeit
     bis zum Anfang des 6. vorchristlichen Jahrhunderts, aus dem Französischen übertragen von Franz Graf von
     Otting, München 1965, Abb. 128.
   b Pierre Demargne: Die Geburt der griechischen Kunst. Die Kunst im ägäischen Raum von vorgeschichtlicher Zeit
     bis zum Anfang des 6. vorchristlichen Jahrhunderts, aus dem Französischen übertragen von Franz Graf von
     Otting, München 1965, Abb. 202.
21   Jean Charbonneaux, Roland Martin, François Villard: Das klassische Griechenland. 480–330 v. Chr., aus
     dem Französischen übertragen von Werner Gebühr und Franz Graf von Otting, München 1971, Abb. 149.
22   P. de la Coste-Messelière: Au Musée de Delphe, Paris 1936 [Bibliothèque des Écoles Françaises d'Athènes
     et de Rome, Fasc. 138], Fig. 19. A.W. Lawrence: Greek Architecture, Harmondsworth 1957 [The Pelican
     History of Art ZII], Fig. 79.
23 a Winfried Orthmann: Der Alte Orient, Berlin 1975 [Propyläen Kunstgeschichte, Bd. 14], Abb. 11 b.
   b Winfried Orthmann: Der Alte Orient, Berlin 1975 [Propyläen Kunstgeschichte, Bd. 14], Abb. 342.
   c Winfried Orthmann: Der Alte Orient, Berlin 1975 [Propyläen Kunstgeschichte, Bd. 14], Abb. 172.
24   Winfried Orthmann: Der Alte Orient, Berlin 1975 [Propyläen Kunstgeschichte, Bd. 14], Abb. 409.
25 a Friedrich Matz: Die frühkretischen Siegel. Eine Untersuchung über das Werden des minoischen Stils, Berlin,
     Leipzig 1928, Abb. 30.
26 a Winfried Orthmann: Der Alte Orient, Berlin 1975 [Propyläen Kunstgeschichte, Bd. 14], Abb. 120.
27 a Winfried Orthmann: Der Alte Orient, Berlin 1975 [Propyläen Kunstgeschichte, Bd. 14], Abb. 178 a.
28 a Winfried Orthmann: Der Alte Orient, Berlin 1975 [Propyläen Kunstgeschichte, Bd. 14], Abb. 215.
29 a Winfried Orthmann: Der Alte Orient, Berlin 1975 [Propyläen Kunstgeschichte, Bd. 14], Abb. 62 b.
30 a Ernst Heinrich: Die Tempel und Heiligtümer im alten Mesopotamien. Typologie, Morphologie und Geschichte,
     Bd. 2, Berlin 1982, Abb. 75.
31 a Friedrich Matz: Die frühkretischen Siegel. Eine Untersuchung über das Werden des minoischen Stils, Berlin,
     Leipzig 1928, Abb. 32.
31 b Ernest de Sarzec: Découvertes en Chaldée, Bd. 2, Paris 1884–1912, pl. 32 b.
   c Winfried Orthmann: Der Alte Orient, Berlin 1975 [Propyläen Kunstgeschichte, Bd. 14], Abb. 86 b.
   d Winfried Orthmann: Der Alte Orient, Berlin 1975 [Propyläen Kunstgeschichte, Bd. 14], Abb. 124 e.
32 a Winfried Orthmann: Der Alte Orient, Berlin 1975 [Propyläen Kunstgeschichte, Bd. 14], Abb. 223.
33 a Winfried Orthmann: Der Alte Orient, Berlin 1975 [Propyläen Kunstgeschichte, Bd. 14], Abb. 62 a.
33 c Winfried Orthmann: Der Alte Orient, Berlin 1975 [Propyläen Kunstgeschichte, Bd. 14], Abb. 62 b.
34   Winfried Orthmann: Der Alte Orient, Berlin 1975 [Propyläen Kunstgeschichte, Bd. 14], Abb. 104.

Bibliographien

THEMATISCHES LITERATURVERZEICHNIS

STRUKTURALISTISCHE UND VOM STRUKTURALISMUS BEEINFLUSSTE UNTERSUCHUNGEN

HIMMELMANN-WILDSCHÜTZ, NIKOLAUS
Bemerkungen zur geometrischen Plastik, Berlin 1964

KASCHNITZ VON WEINBERG, GUIDO
Die Grundlagen der antiken Kunst, Bd. 1: Die mittelmeerischen Grundlagen der antiken Kunst, Frankfurt 1944, Bd. 2: Die eurasischen Grundlagen der antiken Kunst, Frankfurt 1961

Italien mit Sardinien, Sizilien und Malta, in: Reinhard Herbig (ed.): Handbuch der Archäologie, im Rahmen des Handbuchs der Altertumswissenschaft. Die Denkmäler. Jüngere Steinzeit und Bronzezeit in Europa und einigen angrenzenden Gebieten bis um 1000 v. Chr., München 1950, S. 311–397

Kleine Schriften zur Struktur, hrsg. von Helga von Heintze, Berlin 1965 [Ausgewählte Schriften Bd. 1]

Mittelmeerische Kunst. Eine Darstellung ihrer Strukturen, hrsg. von Peter H. von Blanckenhagen und Helga von Heintze, Berlin 1965 [Ausgewählte Schriften Bd. 3]

Rezension zu Alois Riegl, Spätrömische Kunstindustrie, in: Gnomon, Bd. 5 (1929), S. 195–213

Ricerca di struttura, in: Ranuccio Bianchi Bandinelli (ed.): Enciclopedia dell'arte antica classica e orientale, Bd. 8, Rom 1966, S. 519–521

KRAHMER, GERHARD
Figur und Raum in der ägyptischen und griechisch-archaischen Kunst, in: 28. Hallesches Winckelmannsprogramm, Halle 1931

Hellenistische Köpfe, vorgelegt von H. Tiersch, in: Nachrichten von der Gesellschaft der Wissenschaften zu Göttingen, Göttingen 1936 [Altertumswissenschaft NF, Bd. 1, Nr. 10], S. 217–255

LANGLOTZ, ERNST
Frühgriechische Bildhauerschulen, Nürnberg 1927

MATZ, FRIEDRICH
Bemerkungen zur römischen Komposition, in: Akademie der Wissenschaften und Literatur in Mainz, Abhandlungen der Geistes- und Sozialwissenschaftlichen Klasse, Jg. 1952, Nr. 8, S. 625–647

Die Ägäis, in: Reinhard Herbig (ed.): Handbuch der Archäologie, im Rahmen des Handbuchs der Altertumswissenschaft. Die Denkmäler. Jüngere Steinzeit und Bronzezeit in Europa und einigen angrenzenden Gebieten bis um 1000 v. Chr., München 1950, S. 179–308

Die frühkretischen Siegel. Eine Untersuchung über das Werden des minoischen Stils, Berlin, Leipzig 1928

Geschichte der griechischen Kunst, Bd. 1: Die geometrische und die früharchaische Form, Frankfurt 1950

Kreta und frühes Griechenland. Prolegomena zur griechischen Kunstgeschichte, Baden-Baden 1962, 2. Aufl. 1964

Strukturforschung und Archäologie, in: Studium Generale, 17. Jg. (1964), S. 203–219

Torsion. Eine formenkundliche Untersuchung zur aigäischen Vorgeschichte, in: Akademie der Wissenschaften und Literatur in Mainz, Abhandlungen der Geistes- und Sozialwissenschaftlichen Klasse, Jg. 1951, Nr. 12, S. 991–1015

MÜLLER, VALENTIN
Die monumentale Architektur der Chatti von Bogazköi, in: Mitteilungen des Deutschen Archäologischen Instituts, Athenische Abteilung, Bd. 42 (1917), S. 99–203

Die Raumdarstellung der altorientalischen Kunst, in: Archiv für Orientforschung, Bd. 5 (1928), S. 199–206

Frühe Plastik in Griechenland und Vorderasien. Ihre Typenbildung von der neolithischen bis in die griechisch-archaische Zeit (rund 3000 bis 600 v. Chr.), Augsburg 1929

PANOFSKY, ERWIN
Die Perspektive als symbolische Form, in: Vorträge der Bibliothek Warburg 1924/25, Leipzig, Berlin 1927, S. 258–330

SCHWEITZER, BERNHARD
Das Problem der Form in der Kunst des Altertums, in: Walter Otto (ed.): Handbuch der Archäologie, im Rahmen des Handbuchs der Altertumswissenschaft, München 1939, S. 363–399. Verändert wiederabgedruckt in:

72

Ulrich Hausmann (ed.): Handbuch der Archäologie. Allgemeine Grundlagen der Archäologie. Begriff und Methode, Geschichte, Problem der Form, Schriftzeugnisse, München 1969, S. 163–203

Die Begriffe des Plastischen und Malerischen als Grundformen der Anschauung, in: Zeitschrift für Ästhetik und allgemeine Kunstwissenschaft, Bd. 13 (1918), S. 259–269

Untersuchungen zur Chronologie und Geschichte der geometrischen Stile in Griechenland II, in: Mitteilungen des Deutschen Archäologischen Instituts, Athenische Abteilung, Bd. 43 (1918), S. 1–152

Vom Sinn der Perspektive, Tübingen 1953 [Die Gestalt. Abhandlungen zu einer allgemeinen Morphologie, Heft 24]

SEDLMAYR, HANS
Kunst und Wahrheit. Zur Theorie und Methode der Kunstgeschichte, Hamburg 1955

Verlust der Mitte. Die bildende Kunst des 19. und 20. Jahrhunderts als Symptom und Symbol der Zeit, Salzburg 1948, 10. Aufl. 1983

SPENGLER, OSWALD
Der Untergang des Abendlandes. Umrisse einer Morphologie der Weltgeschichte, München 1927–31, ungekürzte Sonderausg. in 1 Bd., München 1979

DER STRUKTURALISMUS IM SPIEGEL DER WISSENSCHAFTSGESCHICHTE

BORBEIN, ADOLF H.
Die Klassik-Diskussion in der Klassischen Archäologie, in: Helmut Flashar (ed.): Altertumswissenschaft in den 20er Jahren. Neue Fragen und Impulse, Stuttgart 1995, S. 205–245

BRENDEL, OTTO J.
Was ist römische Kunst?, mit einem Vorwort von Eberhard Thomas, aus dem Amerikanischen von Helga Willinghöfer, Köln 1990

BUSCHOR, ERNST
Vom Sinn der griechischen Standbilder, Berlin 1942 [Veröffentlichung des archäologischen Instituts des Deutschen Reiches], 2., um ein Nachwort erweiterte Aufl. Berlin 1977

FLASHAR, HELMUT (ED.)
Altertumswissenschaft in den 20er Jahren. Neue Fragen und Impulse, Stuttgart 1995

GOETHE, JOHANN WOLFGANG
Werke, Weimarer Ausgabe, 143 Bde., Weimar 1887–1919

HAUSMANN, ULRICH (ED.)
Handbuch der Archäologie. Allgemeine Grundlagen der Archäologie. Begriff und Methode, Geschichte, Problem der Form, Schriftzeugnisse, München 1969

HOFTER, MATHIAS RENÉ
Die Entdeckung des Unklassischen: Guido Kaschnitz von Weinberg, in: Helmut Flashar (ed.): Altertumswissenschaft in den 20er Jahren. Neue Fragen und Impulse, Stuttgart 1995, S. 247–257

HROUDA, BARTHEL
Vorderasien I. Mesopotamien, Babylonien, Iran und Anatolien, München 1971

KRAIKER, WILHELM
Struktur und Form, in: Wilhelm Kraiker (ed.): Archaische Plastik der Griechen, Darmstadt 1976, S. 261–266

Theorien zur archaischen Plastik, in: Wilhelm Kraiker (ed.): Archaische Plastik der Griechen, Darmstadt 1976, S. 235–260

RODENWALDT, GERHART
Goethes Besuch im Museum Maffeianum zu Verona, in: Winckelmannsprogramm der Archäologischen Gesellschaft zu Berlin, Bd. 102 (1942), S. 5–37

Zur begrifflichen und geschichtlichen Bedeutung des Klassischen in der bildenden Kunst. Eine kunstgeschichtsphilosophische Studie, in: Zeitschrift für Ästhetik und allgemeine Kunstwissenschaft, Bd. 11 (1916), S. 113–131

SCHEFOLD, KARL
Neue Wege der Klassischen Archäologie nach dem ersten Weltkrieg, in: Helmut Flashar (ed.): Altertumswissenschaft in den 20er Jahren. Neue Fragen und Impulse, Stuttgart 1995, S. 183–203

WEGNER, MAX
Geschichte der Archäologie unter dem Gesichtspunkt der Methode, in: Studium Generale, 17. Jg. (1964), S. 191–201

WÜNSCHE, RAIMUND
"Perikles" sucht "Pheidias". Ludwig I. und Thorvaldsen, in: Germanisches Nationalmuseum Nürnberg (ed.): Künstlerleben in Rom. Bertel Thorvaldsen (1770–1844). Der dänische Bildhauer und seine deutschen Freunde, Nürnberg 1991, S. 307–326

KUNSTWISSENSCHAFTLICHE VORLÄUFERTHEORIEN

BRINCKMANN, ALBERT E.
Plastik und Raum als Grundformen künstlerischer Gestaltung, München 1922

HILDEBRAND, ADOLF
Das Problem der Form in der bildenden Kunst, Straßburg 1893

JANTZEN, HANS
Über den kunstgeschichtlichen Raumbegriff, in: Sitzungsberichte der Bayerischen Akademie der Wissenschaften. Philosophisch-historische Abteilung, Jg. 1938, Heft 5

RIEGL, ALOIS
Die spätrömische Kunstindustrie nach den Funden in Österreich-Ungarn, 1. Teil, Wien 1901, Neudruck Wien 1927

SCHMID, HEINRICH A.
Ueber objektive Kriterien der Kunstgeschichte. Zugleich eine Recension, in: Repertorium für Kunstwissenschaft, Bd. 19 (1896), Sonderabdruck 1896, S. 269–284

SEMPER, GOTTFRIED
Der Stil in den technischen und tektonischen Künsten. Praktische Ästhetik. Ein Handbuch für Techniker, Künstler und Kunstfreunde, Bd. 1: Textile Kunst, Bd. 2: Keramik, Tektonik, Stereotomie, Metallotechnik, München 2. Aufl. 1878/79

TROSS, ERNST
Studien zur Raumentwicklung in Plastik und Malerei, Diss. Giessen 1913

WÖLFFLIN, HEINRICH
Kunstgeschichtliche Grundbegriffe. Das Problem der Stilentwicklung in der neueren Kunst, München 1915, 18. Aufl. Basel, Stuttgart 1991

NEUESTE LITERATUR ZUR THEORIE DER ARCHÄOLOGIE

BAPTY, IAN UND YATES, TIM (ED.)
Archaeology after structuralism. Post-structuralism and the practice of archaeology, London 1990

CARR, CHRISTOPHER UND NEITZEL, JILL E. (ED.)
Style, society, and person. Archaeological and ethnological perspectives, New York, London 1995

CONKEY, MARGARET W. UND HASTORF, CHRISTINE A. (ED.)
The uses of style in archaeology, Cambridge 1990

DARK, KENNETH R.
Theoretical archaeology, London 1995

EMBREE, LESTER (ED.)
Metaarchaeology. Reflections by archaeologists and philosophers, Dordrecht etc.1992

HACHMANN, ROLF (ED.)
Studien zum Kulturbegriff in der Vor- und Frühgeschichtsforschung, Bonn 1987

KLEJN, LEO S.
Archaeological typology, übersetzt aus dem Russischen von Penelope Dole, Oxford 1982

MACKENZIE, IAIN M. (ED.)
Archaeological theory: Progress or posture?, Aldershot etc. 1994

Rossi, Ino (ed.)
   The Logic of culture. Advances in structural theory and methods, London 1982

Salmon, Merrilee H.
   Philosophy and archaeology, New York etc. 1982

Sherratt, Andrew (ed.)
   Die Cambridge Enzyklopädie der Archäologie, übersetzt von Claus Bruder u. a., München 1980

Trigger, Bruce G.
   A history of archaeological thought, Cambridge 1989

Ucko, Peter J. (ed.)
   Theory in archaeology. A world perspective, London, New York 1995

Voorrips, Albertus (ed.)
   Mathematics and information science in archaeology. A flexible framework, Bonn 1990

Washburn, Dorothy K.
   Style, perception and geometry, in: Christopher Carr und Jill E. Neitzel (ed.): Style, society, and person. Archaeological and ethnological perspectives, New York, London 1995, S. 101–122

Wendowski, Marlies
   Archäologische Kultur und Ethnische Einheit. Möglichkeiten und Grenzen der Identifikation, Diss. Hamburg 1994, Frankfurt 1995

ALLGEMEINE THEORETISCHE GRUNDLAGEN

Hager, Werner
   Über Raumbildung in der Architektur und in den darstellenden Künsten, in: Studium Generale, 10. Jg. (1957), S. 630–645

Hegel, Georg Wilhelm Friedrich
   Enzyklopädie der philosophischen Wissenschaften im Grundrisse (1830), hrsg. von Friedhelm Nicolin und Otto Pöggeler, 7. Aufl. Hamburg 1969, Nachdruck Hamburg 1975

Kant, Immanuel
   Gesammelte Schriften, Akademie-Ausgabe, 25 Bde., Berlin 1902–1968

Weisgerber, Leo
   Die Sprache unter den Kräften des menschlichen Daseins, Düsseldorf 1949

Alphabetisches Literaturverzeichnis

Bapty, Ian und Yates, Tim (ed.)
Archaeology after structuralism. Post-structuralism and the practice of archaeology, London 1990

Bianchi Bandinelli, Ranuccio (ed.)
Enciclopedia dell'arte antica classica e orientale, 7 Bde., Rom 1958–1966

Blanckenhagen, Peter H. von und Heintze, Helga von (ed.)
Guido Kaschnitz von Weinberg: Mittelmeerische Kunst. Eine Darstellung ihrer Strukturen, Berlin 1965 [Ausgewählte Schriften Bd. 3]

Borbein, Adolf Heinrich
Die Klassik-Diskussion in der Klassischen Archäologie, in: Helmut Flashar (ed.): Altertumswissenschaft in den 20er Jahren. Neue Fragen und Impulse, Stuttgart 1995, S. 205–245

Börker-Klähn, Jutta
Altvorderasiatische Bildstelen und vergleichbare Felsreliefs, 2 Bde., Mainz 1982

Brendel, Otto J.
Was ist römische Kunst?, mit einem Vorwort von Eberhard Thomas, aus dem Amerikanischen von Helga Willinghöfer, Köln 1990

Brinckmann, Albert E.
Plastik und Raum als Grundformen künstlerischer Gestaltung, München 1922

Buschor, Ernst
Vom Sinn der griechischen Standbilder, Berlin 1942 [Veröffentlichung des archäologischen Instituts des Deutschen Reiches], 2., um ein Nachwort erweiterte Aufl. Berlin 1977

Carr, Christopher und Neitzel, Jill E. (ed.)
Style, society, and person. Archaeological and ethnological perspectives, New York, London 1995

Charbonneaux, Jean, Martin, Roland, Villard, Francois
Das archaische Griechenland. 620–480 v. Chr., aus dem Französischen übertragen von Nina Brotze und Franz Graf von Otting, München 1969

Das klassische Griechenland. 480–330 v. Chr., aus dem Französischen übertragen von Werner Gebühr und Franz Graf von Otting, München 1971

Conkey, Margaret W. und Hastorf, Christine A. (ed.)
The uses of style in archaeology, Cambridge 1990

Dark, Kenneth R.
Theoretical archaeology, London 1995

Demargne, Pierre
Die Geburt der griechischen Kunst. Die Kunst im ägäischen Raum von vorgeschichtlicher Zeit bis zum Anfang des 6. vorchristlichen Jahrhunderts, aus dem Französischen übertragen von Franz Graf von Otting, München 1965

Eggebrecht, Arne
Das Alte Ägypten. 3000 Jahre Geschichte und Kultur des Pharaonenreiches, München 1984

Embree, Lester (ed.)
Metaarchaeology. Reflections by archaeologists and philosophers, Dordrecht etc. 1992

Flashar, Helmut (ed.)
Altertumswissenschaft in den 20er Jahren. Neue Fragen und Impulse, Stuttgart 1995

Germanisches Nationalmuseum Nürnberg (ed.)
Künstlerleben in Rom. Bertel Thorvaldsen (1770–1844). Der dänische Bildhauer und seine deutschen Freunde, Nürnberg 1991

Goethe, Johann Wolfgang
Werke, Weimarer Ausgabe, 143 Bde., Weimar 1887–1919

Hachmann, Rolf (ed.)
Studien zum Kulturbegriff in der Vor- und Frühgeschichtsforschung, Bonn 1987

Hager, Werner
Über Raumbildung in der Architektur und in den darstellenden Künsten, in: Studium Generale, 10. Jg. (1957), S. 630–645

HAUSMANN, ULRICH (ED.)
Handbuch der Archäologie: Allgemeine Grundlagen der Archäologie. Begriff und Methode, Geschichte, Problem der Form, Schriftzeugnisse, München 1969

HEGEL, GEORG WILHELM FRIEDRICH
Enzyklopädie der philosophischen Wissenschaften im Grundrisse (1830), hrsg. von Friedhelm Nicolin und Otto Pöggeler, 7. Aufl. Hamburg 1969, Nachdruck Hamburg 1975

HEINRICH, ERNST
Die Tempel und Heiligtümer im Alten Mesopotamien. Typologie, Morphologie und Geschichte, 2 Bde., Berlin 1982

HEINTZE, HELGA VON (ED.)
Guido Kaschnitz von Weinberg: Kleine Schriften zur Struktur, Berlin 1965 [Ausgewählte Schriften Bd. 1]

HERBIG, REINHARD (ED.)
Handbuch der Archäologie, im Rahmen des Handbuchs der Altertumswissenschaft. Die Denkmäler, jüngere Steinzeit und Bronzezeit in Europa und einigen angrenzenden Gebieten bis um 1000 v. Chr., München 1950

HILDEBRAND, ADOLF
Das Problem der Form in der bildenden Kunst, Straßburg 1893

HIMMELMANN-WILDSCHÜTZ, NIKOLAUS
Bemerkungen zur geometrischen Plastik, Berlin 1964

HOFTER, MATHIAS RENÉ
Die Entdeckung des Unklassischen: Guido Kaschnitz von Weinberg, in: Helmut Flashar (ed.): Altertumswissenschaft in den 20er Jahren. Neue Fragen und Impulse, Stuttgart 1995, S. 247–257

HROUDA, BARTHEL
Vorderasien I. Mesopotamien, Babylonien, Iran und Anatolien, München 1971

JANTZEN, HANS
Über den kunstgeschichtlichen Raumbegriff, in: Sitzungsberichte der Bayerischen Akademie der Wissenschaften. Philosophisch-historische Abteilung, Jg. 1938, Heft 5

JASTROW, MORRIS JR
Bildermappe zur Religion Babyloniens und Assyriens, Giessen 1912

KANT, IMMANUEL
Gesammelte Schriften, Akademie-Ausgabe, 25 Bde., Berlin 1902–1968

KASCHNITZ VON WEINBERG, GUIDO
Die Grundlagen der antiken Kunst, Bd. 1: Die mittelmeerischen Grundlagen der antiken Kunst, Frankfurt 1944, Bd. 2: Die eurasischen Grundlagen der antiken Kunst, Frankfurt 1961

Italien mit Sardinien, Sizilien und Malta, in: Reinhard Herbig (ed.): Handbuch der Archäologie, im Rahmen des Handbuchs der Altertumswissenschaft. Die Denkmäler. Jüngere Steinzeit und Bronzezeit in Europa und einigen angrenzenden Gebieten bis um 1000 v. Chr., München 1950, S. 311–397

Kleine Schriften zur Struktur, hrsg. von Helga von Heintze, Berlin 1965 [Ausgewählte Schriften Bd. 1]

Mittelmeerische Kunst. Eine Darstellung ihrer Strukturen, hrsg. von Peter H. von Blanckenhagen und Helga von Heintze, Berlin 1965 [Ausgewählte Schriften Bd. 3]

Rezension zu Alois Riegl, Spätrömische Kunstindustrie, in: Gnomon, Bd. 5 (1929), S. 195–213

Ricerca di struttura, in: Ranuccio Bianchi Bandinelli (ed.): Enciclopedia dell'arte antica classica e orientale, Bd. 8, Rom 1966, S. 519–521

KLEIN, LEO S.
Archaeological typology, übersetzt aus dem Russischen von Penelope Dole, Oxford 1982

KRAHMER, GERHARD
Figur und Raum in der ägyptischen und griechisch-archaischen Kunst, in: 28. Hallesches Winckelmannsprogramm, Halle 1931

Hellenistische Köpfe, vorgelegt von H. Tiersch, in: Nachrichten von der Gesellschaft der Wissenschaften zu Göttingen, Göttingen 1936 [Altertumswissenschaft NF, Bd. 1, Nr. 10], S. 217–255

KRAIKER, WILHELM (ED.)
Archaische Plastik der Griechen, Darmstadt 1976

KRAIKER, WILHELM
Struktur und Form, in: Wilhelm Kraiker (ed.): Archaische Plastik der Griechen, Darmstadt 1976, S. 261–266
Theorien zur archaischen Plastik, in: Wilhelm Kraiker (ed.): Archaische Plastik der Griechen, Darmstadt 1976, S. 235–260

LANGLOTZ, ERNST
Frühgriechische Bildhauerschulen, Nürnberg 1927

MACKENZIE, IAIN M. (ED.)
Archaeological theory: Progress or posture?, Aldershot etc. 1994

MATZ, FRIEDRICH
Bemerkungen zur römischen Komposition, in: Akademie der Wissenschaften und Literatur in Mainz, Abhandlungen der Geistes- und Sozialwissenschaftlichen Klasse, Jg. 1952, Nr. 8, S. 625–647
Die Ägäis, in: Reinhard Herbig (ed.): Handbuch der Archäologie, im Rahmen des Handbuchs der Altertumswissenschaft. Die Denkmäler. Jüngere Steinzeit und Bronzezeit in Europa und einigen angrenzenden Gebieten bis um 1000 v. Chr., München 1950, S. 179–308
Die frühkretischen Siegel. Eine Untersuchung über das Werden des minoischen Stils, Berlin, Leipzig 1928
Geschichte der griechischen Kunst, Bd. 1: Die geometrische und die früharchaische Form, Frankfurt 1950
Kreta und frühes Griechenland. Prolegomena zur griechischen Kunstgeschichte, Baden-Baden 1962, 2. Aufl. 1964
Strukturforschung und Archäologie, in: Studium Generale, 17. Jg. (1964), S. 203–219
Torsion. Eine formenkundliche Untersuchung zur aigäischen Vorgeschichte, in: Akademie der Wissenschaften und Literatur in Mainz, Abhandlungen der Geistes- und Sozialwissenschaftlichen Klasse, Jg. 1951, Nr. 12, S. 991–1015

MELLING, MACHTELD J. UND FILIP, JAN
Frühe Stufen der Kunst, Berlin 1974 [Propyläen Kunstgeschichte, Bd. 13]

MÜLLER, VALENTIN
Die monumentale Architektur der Chatti von Bogazköi, in: Mitteilungen des Deutschen Archäologischen Instituts, Athenische Abteilung, Bd. 42 (1917), S. 99–203
Die Raumdarstellung der altorientalischen Kunst, in: Archiv für Orientforschung, Bd. 5 (1928), S. 199–206
Frühe Plastik in Griechenland und Vorderasien. Ihre Typenbildung von der neolithischen bis in die griechisch-archaische Zeit (rund 3000 bis 600 v. Chr.), Augsburg 1929

NICOLIN, FRIEDHELM UND PÖGGELER OTTO (ED.)
Georg Wilhelm Friedrich Hegel: Enzyklopädie der philosophischen Wissenschaften im Grundrisse (1830), 7. Aufl. Hamburg 1969, Nachdruck Hamburg 1975

ORTHMANN, WINFRIED
Der Alte Orient, Berlin 1975 [Propyläen Kunstgeschichte, Bd. 14]

OTTO, WALTER (ED.)
Handbuch der Archäologie, im Rahmen des Handbuchs der Altertumswissenschaft, München 1939

PALEY, SAMUEL M., SOBOLEWSKI, RICHARD P.
The reconstruction of the relief representations and their positions in the northwest-palace at Kalḫu (Nimrūd) II, Mainz 1987

PANOFSKY, ERWIN
Die Perspektive als symbolische Form, in: Vorträge der Bibliothek Warburg 1924/25, Leipzig, Berlin 1927, S. 258–330

PARROT, ANDRÉ
Sumer, Paris 1981

PETRIE, WILLIAM M. FLINDERS
Dendereh 1898, London 1900

RAPHAEL, MAX
Prehistoric pottery and civilisation in Egypt, New York 1947

RIEGL, ALOIS
Die spätrömische Kunstindustrie nach den Funden in Österreich-Ungarn, 1. Teil, Wien 1901, Neudruck Wien 1927

RODENWALDT, GERHART
Goethes Besuch im Museum Maffeianum zu Verona, in: Winckelmannsprogramm der Archäologischen Gesellschaft zu Berlin, Bd. 102 (1942), S. 5–37

Zur begrifflichen und geschichtlichen Bedeutung des Klassischen in der bildenden Kunst. Eine kunstgeschichtsphilosophische Studie, in: Zeitschrift für Ästhetik und allgemeine Kunstwissenschaft, Bd. 11 (1916), S. 113–131

ROSSI, INO (ED.)
The Logic of culture. Advances in structural theory and methods, London 1982

SALMON, MERRILEE H.
Philosophy and archaeology, New York etc. 1982

SARZEC, ERNEST DE
Découvertes en Chaldée, 2 Bde., Paris 1884–1912

SCHEFOLD, KARL
Neue Wege der Klassischen Archäologie nach dem ersten Weltkrieg, in: Helmut Flashar (ed.): Altertumswissenschaft in den 20er Jahren. Neue Fragen und Impulse, Stuttgart 1995, S. 183–203

SCHMID, HEINRICH A.
Ueber objektive Kriterien der Kunstgeschichte. Zugleich eine Recension, in: Repertorium für Kunstwissenschaft, Bd. 19 (1896), Sonderabdruck 1896, S. 269–284

SCHULZ, REGINE
Die Entwicklung und Bedeutung des kuboiden Statuentypus. Eine Untersuchung zu den sogenannten Würfelhockern, 2 Bde., Hildesheim 1992

SCHWEITZER, BERNHARD
Das Problem der Form in der Kunst des Altertums, in: Walter Otto (ed.): Handbuch der Archäologie, im Rahmen des Handbuchs der Altertumswissenschaft, München 1939, S. 363–399. Verändert wiederabgedruckt in: Ulrich Hausmann (ed.): Handbuch der Archäologie. Allgemeine Grundlagen der Archäologie. Begriff und Methode, Geschichte, Problem der Form, Schriftzeugnisse, München 1969, S. 163–203

Die Begriffe des Plastischen und Malerischen als Grundformen der Anschauung, in: Zeitschrift für Ästhetik und allgemeine Kunstwissenschaft, Bd. 13 (1918), S. 259–269

Untersuchungen zur Chronologie und Geschichte der geometrischen Stile in Griechenland II, in: Mitteilungen des Deutschen Archäologischen Instituts, Athenische Abteilung, Bd. 43 (1918), S. 1–152

Vom Sinn der Perspektive, Tübingen 1953 [Die Gestalt. Abhandlungen zu einer allgemeinen Morphologie, Heft 24]

SEDLMAYR, HANS
Kunst und Wahrheit. Zur Theorie und Methode der Kunstgeschichte, Hamburg 1955

Verlust der Mitte. Die bildende Kunst des 19. und 20. Jahrhunderts als Symptom und Symbol der Zeit, Salzburg 1948, 10. Aufl. 1983

SEMPER, GOTTFRIED
Der Stil in den technischen und tektonischen Künsten. Praktische Ästhetik. Ein Handbuch für Techniker, Künstler und Kunstfreunde, Bd. 1: Textile Kunst, Bd. 2: Keramik, Tektonik, Stereotomie, Metallotechnik, München 2. Aufl. 1878/79

SHERRATT, ANDREW (ED.)
Die Cambridge Enzyklopädie der Archäologie, übersetzt von Claus Bruder u. a., München 1980

SPENGLER, OSWALD
Der Untergang des Abendlandes. Umrisse einer Morphologie der Weltgeschichte, München 1927–31, ungekürzte Sonderausg. in 1 Bd., München 1979

STAATLICHE MUSEEN ZU BERLIN (ED.)
Das Vorderasiatische Museum, Mainz 1992

TRIGGER, BRUCE G.
A history of archaeological thought, Cambridge 1989

TROSS, ERNST
Studien zur Raumentwicklung in Plastik und Malerei, Diss. Giessen 1913

UCKO, PETER J. (ED.)
Theory in archaeology. A world perspective, London, New York 1995

VOORRIPS, ALBERTUS (ED.)
Mathematics and information science in archaeology. A flexible framework, Bonn 1990

WASHBURN, DOROTHY, K.
Style, perception and geometry, in: Christopher Carr und Jill E. Neitzel (ed.): Style, society, and person. Archaeological and ethnological perspectives, New York, London 1995, S. 101–122

WEGNER, MAX
Geschichte der Archäologie unter dem Gesichtspunkt der Methode, in: Studium Generale, 17. Jg. (1964), S. 191–201

WEISGERBER, LEO
Die Sprache unter den Kräften des menschlichen Daseins, Düsseldorf 1949

WENDOWSKI, MARLIES
Archäologische Kultur und Ethnische Einheit. Möglichkeiten und Grenzen der Identifikation, Diss. Hamburg 1994, Frankfurt 1995

WÖLFFLIN, HEINRICH
Kunstgeschichtliche Grundbegriffe. Das Problem der Stilentwicklung in der neueren Kunst, München 1915, 18. Aufl. Basel, Stuttgart 1991

WÜNSCHE, RAIMUND
"Perikles" sucht "Pheidias". Ludwig I. und Thorvaldsen, in: Germanisches Nationalmuseum Nürnberg (ed.): Künstlerleben in Rom. Bertel Thorvaldsen (1770–1844). Der dänische Bildhauer und seine deutschen Freunde, Nürnberg 1991, S. 307–326

Bd. 102   BENJAMIN SASS: *Studia Alphabetica*. On the Origin and Early History of the Northwest Semitic, South Semitic and Greek Alphabets. X–120 pages. 16 pages with illustrations. 2 tables. 1991.

Bd. 103   ADRIAN SCHENKER: *Text und Sinn im Alten Testament*. Textgeschichtliche und bibeltheologische Studien. VIII–312 pages. 1991.

Bd. 104   DANIEL BODI: *The Book of Ezekiel and the Poem of Erra*. IV–332 pages. 1991.

Bd. 105   YUICHI OSUMI: *Die Kompositionsgeschichte des Bundesbuches Exodus 20,22b–23,33*. XII–284 Seiten. 1991.

Bd. 106   RUDOLF WERNER: *Kleine Einführung ins Hieroglyphen-Luwische*. XII–112 Seiten. 1991.

Bd. 107   THOMAS STAUBLI: *Das Image der Nomaden im Alten Israel und in der Ikonographie seiner sesshaften Nachbarn*. XII–408 Seiten. 145 Abb. und 3 Falttafeln. 1991.

Bd. 108   MOSHÉ ANBAR: *Les tribus amurrites de Mari*. VIII–256 pages. 1991.

Bd. 109   GÉRARD J. NORTON/STEPHEN PISANO (eds.): *Tradition of the Text*. Studies offered to Dominique Barthélemy in Celebration of his 70th Birthday. 336 pages. 1991.

Bd. 110   HILDI KEEL-LEU: *Vorderasiatische Stempelsiegel*. Die Sammlung des Biblischen Instituts der Universität Freiburg Schweiz. 180 Seiten. 24 Tafeln. 1991.

Bd. 111   NORBERT LOHFINK: *Die Väter Israels im Deuteronomium*. Mit einer Stellungnahme von Thomas Römer. 152 Seiten. 1991.

Bd. 113   CHARLES MAYSTRE: *Les grands prêtres de Ptah de Memphis*. XIV–474 pages, 2 planches. 1992.

Bd. 114   THOMAS SCHNEIDER: *Asiatische Personennamen in ägyptischen Quellen des Neuen Reiches*. 480 Seiten. 1992.

Bd. 115   ECKHARD VON NORDHEIM: *Die Selbstbehauptung Israels in der Welt des Alten Orients*. Religionsgeschichtlicher Vergleich anhand von Gen 15/22/28, dem Aufenthalt Israels in Ägypten, 2 Sam 7, 1 Kön 19 und Psalm 104. 240 Seiten. 1992.

Bd. 116   DONALD M. MATTHEWS: *The Kassite Glyptic of Nippur*. 208 pages. 210 figures. 1992.

Bd. 117   FIONA V. RICHARDS: *Scarab Seals from a Middle to Late Bronze Age Tomb at Pella in Jordan*. XII–152 pages, 16 plates. 1992.

Bd. 118   YOHANAN GOLDMAN: *Prophétie et royauté au retour de l'exil*. Les origines littéraires de la forme massorétique du livre de Jérémie. XIV–270 pages. 1992.

Bd. 119   THOMAS M. KRAPF: *Die Priesterschrift und die vorexilische Zeit*. Yehezkel Kaufmanns vernachlässigter Beitrag zur Geschichte der biblischen Religion. XX-364 Seiten. 1992.

Bd. 120   MIRIAM LICHTHEIM: *Maat in Egyptian Autobiographies and Related Studies*. 236 pages, 8 plates. 1992.

Bd. 121   ULRICH HÜBNER: *Spiele und Spielzeug im antiken Palästina*. 256 Seiten. 58 Abbildungen. 1992.

Bd. 122   OTHMAR KEEL: *Das Recht der Bilder, gesehen zu werden*. Drei Fallstudien zur Methode der Interpretation altorientalischer Bilder. 332 Seiten, 286 Abbildungen. 1992.

Bd. 144 CHRISTL MAIER: *Die «fremde Frau» in Proverbien 1-9*. Eine exegetische und sozialgeschichtliche Studie. XII–304 Seiten. 1995.

Bd. 145 HANS ULRICH STEYMANS: *Deuteronomium 28 und die* adê *zur Thronfolgeregelung Asarhaddons*. Segen und Fluch im Alten Orient und in Israel. XII–436 Seiten. 1995.

Bd. 146 FRIEDRICH ABITZ: *Pharao als Gott in den Unterweltsbüchern des Neuen Reiches.* VIII–228 Seiten. 1995.

Bd. 147 GILLES ROULIN: *Le Livre de la Nuit. Une composition égyptienne de l'au-delà.* Iʳᵉ partie: Traduction et commentaire. XX-420 pages. IIᵉ partie: Copie synoptique. X-169 pages, 21 cartes. 1996.

Bd. 148 MANUEL BACHMANN: *Die strukturalistische Artefakt- und Kunstanalyse.* Exposition der Grundlagen anhand der vorderorientalischen, ägyptischen und griechischen Kunst. 88 Seiten mit 40 Abbildungen. 1996.

ORBIS BIBLICUS ET ORIENTALIS, SERIES ARCHAEOLOGICA

Bd. 1 JACQUES BRIEND / JEAN-BAPTISTE HUMBERT (Ed.), Tell Keisan (1971–1976), une cité phénicienne en Galilée. 392 pages, 142 planches. 1980.

Bd. 2 BERTRAND JAEGER, Essai de classification et datation des scarabées Menkhéperré. 455 pages avec 1007 illustrations, 26 planches avec 443 figures. 1982.

Bd. 3 RAPHAEL GIVEON, Egyptian Scarabs from Western Asia from the Collections of the British Museum. 202 pages, 457 figures. 1985.

Bd. 4 SEYYARE EICHLER / MARKUS WÄFLER, Tall al-Ḥamīdīya 1, Vorbericht 1984. 360 Seiten, 104 Tafeln, 4 Seiten Illustrationen, 4 Faltpläne, 1 vierfarbige Tafel. 1985.

Bd. 5 CLAUDIA MÜLLER-WINKLER, Die ägyptischen Objekt-Amulette. Mit Publikation der Sammlung des Biblischen Instituts der Universität Freiburg Schweiz, ehemals Sammlung Fouad S. Matouk. 590 Seiten, 40 Tafeln. 1987.

Bd. 6 SEYYARE EICHLER / MARKUS WÄFLER / DAVID WARBURTON, Tall al-Ḥamīdīya 2, Symposium Recent Excavations in the Upper Khabur Region, 492 Seiten, 20 Seiten Illustrationen, 2 Falttafeln, 1 vierfarbige Tafel. 1990.

Bd. 7 HERMANN A. SCHLÖGL / ANDREAS BRODBECK, Ägyptische Totenfiguren aus öffentlichen und privaten Sammlungen der Schweiz, 356 Seiten mit 1041 Photos. 1990.

Bd. 8 DONALD M. MATTHEWS, Principles of composition in Near Eastern glyptic of the later second millennium B.C., 176 pages, 39 pages with drawings, 14 plates. 1990.

Bd. 9 CLAUDE DOUMET, Sceaux et cylindres orientaux: la collection Chiha. Préface de Pierre Amiet. 220 pages, 24 pages d'illustrations. 1992.

Bd. 10 OTHMAR KEEL, Corpus der Stempelsiegel-Amulette aus Palästina/Israel. Von den Anfängen bis zur Perserzeit. Einleitung. 376 Seiten mit 603 Abildungen im Text. 1995.

Bd. 11 BEATRICE TEISSIER, Egyptian Iconography on Syro-Palestinian Cylinder Seals of the Middle Bronze Age. XII–224 pages with numerous illustrations, 5 plates. 1996.

UNIVERSITÄTSVERLAG FREIBURG SCHWEIZ

Zu diesem Buch

Das Buch bietet die Darstellung einer exakten Methode der Kunstbetrachtung und Artefaktanalyse des von den Archäologen Friedrich Matz, Guido Kaschnitz von Weinberg und Bernhard Schweitzer begründeten Strukturalismus. Wenngleich der strukturalistische Ansatz über Erwin Panofsky und Hans Sedlmayr in der Kunstgeschichte Fuss fasste und über Oswald Spengler bis in die Philosophie ausstrahlte, ist er Episode geblieben. Dass er dem Vergessen anheimfiel, steht allerdings in krassem Gegensatz zu der wissenschaftlichen Fundierung seiner Methode, ihren Resultaten und den noch unausgeschöpften Möglichkeiten weitergehender Anwendung. Die vorliegende Exposition behandelt Wissenschaftsgeschichte und theoretische Grundlagen. Sie diskutiert die strukturalistische Theorie insbesondere hinsichtlich der Suspendierung des Stilbegriffs durch den Begriff der Raumstruktur sowie deren Verbindung mit dem Begriff kultureller Identität. In diesem Rahmen werden die Strukturen der Kunst des Vorderen Orients, Ägyptens und Griechenlands untersucht.